More Critical Praise for Danny Goldberg

for *Serving the Servant: Remembering Kurt Cobain*

"Goldberg provides a fresh, eyewitness account of otherwise familiar tales . . . *Serving the Servant,* in its own understated, overprotective way, effectively conveys the frustration, the to-the-bone grief, that comes from losing a loved one who was fundamentally unknowable in the first place. It's the closest thing we have to a survivor's account . . ." —*Washington Post*

"A poignant memoir that spans the three and a half years that Goldberg knew the late musician." —*Rolling Stone*

"[This is] Goldberg's soulful account of Cobain as a close friend, gone way too soon, yet vividly alive on every page of this remarkable book." —Cameron Crowe

for *In Search of the Lost Chord: 1967 and the Hippie Idea*

"[A] legendary steward of the hip musical world . . . Goldberg plunges into a thorough, panoramic account of the culture, politics, media, music and mores of [1967] to demolish the idea that it was trivial. He has researched and interviewed widely—his section on underground newspapers is impressively detailed—and he's *been* there with many of the principals through all these years . . . Goldberg's deep purchase on his subject and his storytelling ease make it fresh . . . Personal asides give the account intimacy . . . [The book proves] that so much activism and passion can be crowded into barely more than a single year. When Goldberg was writing his book, that might have been a useful message. Today, in Trump's America, with a fueled and gathering resistance, it is a potentially mirroring one."
—Sheila Weller, *New York Times Book Review*

"Goldberg's book is what one might call a survey of the period. His narrative skillfully weaves the music, the drugs, the politics, and the spiritual searching of the hippie counterculture into a tale that moves quickly and smoothly . . . What Goldberg has achieved in *In Search of the Lost Chord* is laudable. Not only has he provided his contemporaries with a very readable and fairly wide-ranging look at an important time in their youth, he has also given today's younger readers a useful and well-told historical survey of a subculture and time they hear about quite often."
—*CounterPunch*

"Danny Goldberg is a relentless tracker of people. However elusive this Lost Chord may be, Danny G. searches it out and nails it to the tree flesh. Eternity now! 1967 forever!" —Wavy Gravy

"This extraordinary book transports us back to a 'moment' when, as Goldberg writes, the phrase "'peace and love" was not meant or taken ironically.' Beginning at sixteen, Goldberg was a participant in the rise and cresting of the hippie movement, the hippie ideal, which has been trivialized and disparaged in later decades. He cuts through the obfuscation and recreates the sense of magic, wonder, intimacy, and community that was in the air and you could breathe it in. If you want to know, or remember, what it was like to be alive and part of that historic wave, I can think of no better guide than *In Search of the Lost Chord.*"

—Sara Davidson, author of *Loose Change: Three Women of the Sixties*

for *Bumping into Geniuses: My Life Inside the Rock and Roll Business*

"Goldberg reminds us that the recording industry was remade in the late sixties and seventies by businessman-hippies seeking not just profit but proximity to artists they admired and a role in the countercultural ferment. It is one of many insights in this surprisingly excellent book, an engaging, droll, and . . . largely demystifying look at the evolution of the rock trade from Woodstock to grunge."

—*New York Times Book Review*

"[An] insightful behind-the-scenes view of the music industry from 1969 through 2004 . . . like having a laminated backstage pass to the music business, intertwined with a juicy slice of countercultural history."   —Paul Krassner, *Los Angeles Times*

"Danny Goldberg chronicles the phases of his career—rock journalist, record-company president, manager to musicians ranging from Kurt Cobain to Warren Zevon—with the sort of candor few record-biz execs would attempt . . . Admirably blunt, but also spiked with tart humor."   —*Entertainment Weekly*

for *How the Left Lost Teen Spirit*

"Danny Goldberg's new book is a stirring, brilliant, last-chance plea to Democrats that if they are unwilling to do their job—be a voice for working people, young people, women, the elderly, the poor, and people of color (in other words, for the MAJORITY of the country)—then their days as a party are numbered. Years from now, if the Democrats have long faded from American memory, anthropologists and historians will ask, 'Didn't any of them read this book by Danny Goldberg?'"

—Michael Moore

"An affecting memoir of Goldberg's experiences within the clash of popular culture and politics . . . The great value of his book is as an insider's tour of American cultural life from the sixties to the present."   —*Library Journal*

"Danny Goldberg's searing insights and straightforward recommendations for the future of the left should be required reading for anyone concerned with the state of democratic politics in this country. This book exemplifies the notion that the pen truly is mightier than the sword."   —Reverend Jesse L. Jackson Sr.

"Danny Goldberg's memoir contains the powerful reflections of the most progressive activist in the recording industry. His candor, vision, and sense of humor are infectious."

—Cornel West

BLOODY CROSSROADS 2020

BLOODY CROSSROADS 2020

ART, ENTERTAINMENT, AND RESISTANCE TO TRUMP

DANNY GOLDBERG

DRAWINGS BY KAY KASPARHAUSER

AKASHIC BOOKS

BROOKLYN, NEW YORK

Published by Akashic Books
©2021 Danny Goldberg

ISBN: 978-1-61775-979-6
Library of Congress Control Number: 2021935254
First printing

Drawings by Kay Kasparhauser
Lyrics from the song "Mother of Muses" by Bob Dylan
    are used courtesy of Universal Music

Akashic Books
Brooklyn, New York
Instagram: @AkashicBooks
Twitter: @AkashicBooks
Facebook: AkashicBooks
E-mail: info@akashicbooks.com
Website: www.akashicbooks.com

For Marge Tabankin,
who always walks the walk

TABLE OF CONTENTS

INTRODUCTION

Sing of the mountains and the deep dark sea
Sing of the lakes and the nymphs in the forest
Sing your hearts out, all you women of the chorus
Sing of honor and fame and glory be
Mother of Muses, sing for me
—Bob Dylan, "Mother of Muses"

THE DREAM LIFE OF A NATION

In August 2019, following a massacre at a Walmart in El Paso, Texas, the *Washington Post* published an article with the headline, "Rihanna, Cardi B, John Oliver and more lash out at Trump after deadly mass shootings." The story, about the political thoughts of singers and comedians on the issue of gun violence, did not appear in the *Post*'s Style section, but on its news pages. It was a placement that would have been unthinkable just a few years earlier but which seemed perfectly normal with a former reality television show host occupying the White House.

This is a book about the role of artists and entertainers in the resistance to Donald Trump and the forces he represented. The primary focus is on 2020, the year of Trump's unsuccessful reelection campaign, but the cosmic debates at the core of modern politics have been a part of the struggle to define America for more than a century, and they will continue long after the headlines of 2020 are forgotten. As Bruce Springsteen mused in 2019, "There are two sides of the American character. One is transient, restless, solitary. But the other is collective and communal, in search of family, deep roots, and a home for the heart to reside. These two sides rub up against one another, always and forever, in everyday American life."

Six decades earlier, in an article published in *Esquire* that anticipated John F. Kennedy's election, Norman Mailer pointed out another dichotomy: "Since the First World War Americans have been leading a double life, and our history has moved on two rivers, one visible, the other underground; there has been the history of politics which is concrete, factual, practical and unbelievably dull . . . and there is a subterranean river of untapped, ferocious, lonely, and romantic desires, that concentration of ecstasy and violence which is the dream life of the nation." I assume that Mailer specified "since the First World War" because it was during the decade after the war that mass entertainment became fully embedded in American culture, when radio became ubiquitous and silent movies gave way to talkies, creating a newly powerful connector between art and the nation's collective unconscious.

It also seems to me that Mailer must have meant "subterranean *rivers*"—plural. He was more than familiar with America's darkest impulses, such as racism, fear of immigrants, and conspiracy theories that dehumanized political opponents, forces that historian Richard Hofstadter would write about a few years later in *The Paranoid Style in American Politics* when describing the angry passions that animated Barry Goldwater's 1964 campaign. Updated versions of Goldwater's right-wing tropes energized Trump's most rabid supporters in 2016 and fueled their invasion of the Capitol building on January 6, 2021, a vain attempt to keep their hero in power.

Despite Mailer's fascination with America's dark side, he was also entranced with the utopian river that animated the most idealistic aspects of Kennedy's legacy, aspirational visions that would nourish social change movements in the ensuing decades, many of which were at the moral core of the resistance to Trump, a project in which artists and performers played a significant role.

This is not to suggest that all art is inherently progressive. The nihilism that animated Trump and his supporters owes a great deal to Ayn Rand, whose novels *The Fountainhead* (1943) and *Atlas Shrugged* (1957) presented selfishness as a virtue. As Lisa Duggan writes in *Mean Girl: Ayn Rand and the Culture of Greed*, "The lessons for the student/reader are: reason is superior to mysticism/religion, egoism is a truer morality than altruism, and individualism leads upward and forward via capitalism, while collectivism leads down and back to socialist barbarism."

Among Rand's acolytes was future chairman of the Federal Reserve Alan Greenspan. In 1974, Rand attended Greenspan's swearing in as Nixon's chairman of the Council of Economic Advisers; in 1982, Greenspan attended Rand's funeral, at which a floral wreath was shaped like a dollar sign. Decades later, Trump's secretary of state Mike Pompeo acknowledged that *Atlas Shrugged* "really had an impact on me," and the *Guardian* reported that Trump himself, not known as much of a reader, enthusiastically stated, "*The Fountainhead* relates to business, beauty, life, and inner emotions."

In the libertarian cosmology of Rand and Trump, the most important thing in life is to avoid being a loser. A contrasting philosophy can be found in a scene in *Casablanca* where Humphrey Bogart tells Ingrid Bergman, "It doesn't take much to see that the problems of three little people don't amount to a hill of beans in this crazy world," or in Springsteen's oft-repeated exhortation to concert audiences, "Nobody wins unless everybody wins."

Over the years, politicians have periodically acknowledged the unique role of art in transmitting political morality. As far back as the seventeenth century, Scottish politician Andrew Fletcher wrote, "If a man were permitted to make all the ballads, he need not care who should make the laws of a nation." The idea was that once public opinion reached a critical mass, political leaders would feel compelled to follow. President Kennedy once said, "If more politicians knew poetry and more poets knew politics, I am convinced the world would be a little better place to live."

During the last years of Pete Seeger's life, he often told audiences, "If there is still such a thing as the human race a hundred years from now, music will be one of the reasons why." To be clear, Seeger indicated that music would be *one* of the reasons mankind might survive. Art and entertainment are not in competition with politics, philosophy, or theology. They are intertwined.

Shortly after the 2020 election, Barack Obama was interviewed in the *Atlantic* and he discussed the ideal of American manhood by juxtaposing his successor's values to the personae of iconic movie stars. Obama compared Trump to a comic book character: "I thought that the model [for conservatives] wouldn't be Richie Rich. The complaining, lying, doesn't-take-responsibility-for-anything type of figure." Obama contrasted that lame character with the virtues of characters played by "the John Waynes, the Gary Coopers, the Jimmy Stewarts, the Clint Eastwoods . . . There was a code. The code of masculinity that I grew up with that harkens back to the thirties and forties and before that. There's a notion that a man is true to his word, that he takes responsibility, that he doesn't complain, that he isn't a bully—in fact he defends the vulnerable against bullies."

Although many entertainers were primarily concerned with the quality of their work and the commercial market for it, there were some for whom their vocation included a higher moral calling. After the successes of *Star Wars* and *Indiana Jones*, George Lucas affirmed that part of his agenda was to "tell the kids, 'Hey this is right and this is wrong.'" Judd Apatow, the preeminent comedy auteur of the Obama and Trump eras, told MSNBC's Ari Melber, "I hope when people watch the work that they think: it's better to be a nice person than an asshole."

Such impulses drove many artists to a related conviction—that society as a whole should not behave like an asshole. In a 2019 podcast with Michael Moore, Robert De Niro explained his antipathy to Trump, declaiming, "There's right and there's wrong."

I am well aware that there are cynics, hypocrites, sexists, thieves, liars, con artists, racists, predators, and scumbags in show business, and that even the most sincere and decent artists have big egos. Moral leadership, however, flows through flawed human beings from many backgrounds and disciplines. In a society where rich people put their names on buildings and professorships, politicians are influenced by polls and donors, news producers obsess over ratings and advertising revenue, and religious leaders are as likely as movie stars to have personal improprieties, it is my contention that poets, novelists, essayists, singers, screenwriters, comedians, actors, and directors have as much to usefully express about public morality as others with access to a mass audience.

Not everyone agrees. Some Democratic leaders and advisors have cautioned against taking politically active artists too seriously. For one thing, among the most destructive aspects of Trump's political success was a catastrophic disregard for expertise. In a 1984 TV commercial, Chris Robinson, who played Dr. Rick Webber on *General Hospital*, famously said, "I'm not a doctor but I play one on TV," before extolling the virtues of Vicks Formula 44. Obviously, it was one thing to wink at the difference between fiction and reality when it came to hawking cough syrup but something quite different when it came to crafting and executing government policy. However, one area of expertise that entertainers do possess is mass communication, a realm in which Democrats and progressives, in and out of government, often struggled during the Trump era.

Some liberal pundits worried that a public connection to celebrities was counterproductive for Democrats because artists represented the sensibilities of "coastal elites" who were out of touch with the rest of America. In 2019 Chris Matthews fretted on MSNBC that many Trump voters felt that there had been "a great party going on with the liberal elite and their Hollywood buddies and they were left out of it." De Niro prefaced his "right and wrong" comment with the apologetic qualifier, "I know that I'm from New York." However, most stars came from lower- or middle-class backgrounds, and from disparate parts of the country. While some art forms measured success based on the reception of a primarily cosmopolitan audience, such as theater or classical music, mass entertainment, by definition, was popular in all fifty states, as were celebrity-laden tabloids.

Even among those politicos who admired popular culture, the question was often raised about whether political art or celebrity activism actually makes a difference. There was certainly such a thing as "preaching to the choir," where one repeated feel-good bromides to an audience that already agreed with the speaker. However, in America's increasingly polarized political atmosphere, the primary agenda of twenty-first-century political campaigns was to motivate maximum participation from these very audiences— what pundits called "turning out the base." It was arguable that performers with tribal fan bases could help raise animal spirits and inspire those on the fence about casting a ballot. Such reluctant voters were often the very people who made the difference in close elections.

One thing was for sure: The collective efforts of political experts, Democratic campaign operatives armed with the biggest budgets in campaign history, Obama administration allies, Never-Trump Republicans, and most of the mainstream media had failed to stop Trump in 2016. Something had to change.

The primary political thought leaders in the resistance to Trump were politicians, historians, religious leaders, journalists, academics, and activist groups like the ACLU, Planned Parenthood, and Public Citizen, as well as movements led by Black Lives Matter, Me Too, and the Parkland students. Yet entertainers also became an increasingly formidable part of the resistance. Drama, comedy, rhythm, and poetry reached parts of the mind that linear political messaging rarely touched. In the 1920s, political philosopher Walter Lippmann referred to the tension between "the world outside and the pictures in our heads." At their best, ideologically minded artists created pictures that supported a more compassionate view of the world.

Although some Democrats continued to be ambivalent about the political relevance of entertainment, Republicans needed no convincing. The two Republican presidents with show business backgrounds, Trump and Ronald Reagan, were not anomalies but products of a political mindset that saw entertainment as one of the levers that generated populist political power. Lee Atwater, George H.W. Bush's campaign manager and a mentor to many modern Republican strategists, ostentatiously played guitar with Sam Moore of the R&B duo Sam and Dave, at Bush's 1989 inaugural party. Atwater later told Ron Brownstein, "I became very infatuated with the notion of American culture and how it is connected to politics."

On a parallel political track, other conservatives brooded over movies that they thought encouraged progressive views. In 1999, future vice president Mike Pence (then a talk radio show host who was about to embark on his first congressional campaign), wrote an op-ed that criticized *Mulan*, a popular animated feature about a woman who became a warrior in ancient China: "Despite her delicate features and voice, Disney expects us to believe that Mulan's ingenuity and courage were enough to carry her to military success on an equal basis with her cloddish cohorts . . . this is Walt Disney's attempt to add childhood expectation to the cultural debate over the role of women in the military." In 2015, Wisconsin senator Ron Johnson, who would soon become one of Trump's staunchest congressional allies, complained that *The LEGO Movie* was "insidious . . . antibusiness propaganda [that] taught children that government is good and business is bad."

Conservative media innovator Andrew Breitbart famously said that "politics flows downstream from culture." The publication he created was, for years, run by Steve Bannon, who would later serve as Trump's campaign manager in 2016. In 2020, *Breitbart News* had three writers assigned to a daily entertainment section that attacked show business progressives. When Joy Behar was asked if she was planning on retiring from *The View*, she quipped that she couldn't because "I'm a job creator over at *Breitbart*."

Show business was a bastard child of art and commerce. Over the last century, power relationships between artists (writers, directors, actors, musicians, and singers) and capitalists (bankers, marketers, and distributors) had gone through many twists and turns. By the time Trump was inaugurated in 2017, the creative community responsible for popular entertainment derived most of its power from its fans. The era when talent agents, studio moguls, and record company executives could routinely "deliver" talent to politicians or place political limits on the activity of auteurs had vanished.

One advantage entertainers had over politicians was that they didn't require the support of half of the population to be successful. A singer who appealed to even one percent of the American population had several million fans, made lots of money, and had the freedom to piss off the other 99 percent of the population with impunity. This was one of the reasons that mass entertainers felt comfortable shining a light on issues and opinions before they became viable political subjects on the campaign trail. Stories and songs, and the people who created them, were periodically able to add saliency to issues that were otherwise ignored or marginalized in the mainstream news media.

The most vivid recent example of artists shifting political reality was when gay marriage was legalized. The underlying change in mores was significantly enhanced by television shows like *Glee*, *Will & Grace*, *Modern Family*, and *Ellen*; plays like *Angels in America*; and films like *Brokeback Mountain* and *Milk*. Public statements made by performers such as Elton John and Melissa Etheridge added political momentum to the LGTBQ movement.

In 2020, in the wake of the police killing of George Floyd, the substantial increase in white support for counteracting systemic racism and reforming the criminal justice system had long been fertilized by hip-hop lyrics that spelled out these problems to a mass audience, years before most white politicians felt safe discussing the subject.

The creation of emotional support for political values via art was different than activism, but they were interrelated. Ever since Ronald Reagan became president in 1981 it was clear that performers could make a considerable impact on the "practical" political world. Reagan's path to power had been facilitated by the election of former song-and-dance man George Murphy, who in 1964 was elected as a Republican to the United States Senate. Murphy candidly explained that "people remember me from all those old movies, and I never played a bad guy. I was always the good guy. It sounds corny, but don't knock it." The most effective actor-activists brought a residue from the parts they played to their political personae.

Although the blacklisting period of the 1950s divided the creative community, the image of a "liberal Hollywood" took hold in the 1960s and largely continued despite a few notable exceptions such as Clint Eastwood. Warren Beatty spoke for many when, in 2008, he accepted an American Film Institute award before a star-studded audience that also included his politician friends John McCain, Gary Hart, George McGovern, Bill Clinton, and Jerry Brown: "I am still an old-time, unrepentant, unreconstructed, tax-and-spend, bleeding-heart, die-hard liberal Democrat."

Beatty was the auteur of the radical Hollywood films *Reds* and *Bulworth*, and was also a political thought leader in the creative community in the decades before 2016, one of a handful whose enthusiasm for a candidate or cause helped attract Hollywood dollars. Donald Trump's ascension to the presidency, however, triggered a reaction from artists and entertainers that dwarfed the levels of political engagement of previous eras. Even during the 1960s, when many performers embraced the civil rights and antiwar movements, activist artists like John Lennon and Eartha Kitt were the exception. In the Trump era, they became the rule.

A world-class self-promoter, Trump had played himself in films such as *Home Alone 2, Zoolander,* and *Two Weeks Notice,* as well as TV episodes of *Sex and the City, Suddenly Susan,* and *The Fresh Prince of Bel-Air* (in which the character Hillary Banks, played by Karyn Parsons, gushed, "You know, you look much richer in person"). His rise to political power was fueled by the image of Trump as a successful businessman when he starred in the reality television show *The Apprentice,* which was broadcast in prime time on NBC for fourteen years.

One of the dilemmas that the resistance to Trump encountered was that, to millions of people, "reality TV host" was not an insult but a badge of credibility. People in show business knew that reality shows had little resemblance to actual reality. Programs like *The Apprentice* were heavily scripted and story lines were created in the editing room. Similar to Democratic officeholders and progressive pundits, many artist-activists saw themselves as custodians of American values and thus felt that they shared the blame for Trump's political ascendance. If show business gimmicks were going to affect American politics, artists in the resistance knew that they could not live with themselves if they idly stood by.

I am using the word "resistance" as a catchall for forces that temporarily united in order to defeat Trump. Although I often use terms like "mainstream Democrats" to identify those who represent the policies of Bill Clinton and Barack Obama, I recognize that a number of Republicans were also part of the coalition that ultimately defeated Trump. Notwithstanding Beatty's embrace of the word "liberal," the word has come to have so much baggage that I mostly use "progressive" as a reference to the Bernie Sanders, Elizabeth Warren, and Alexandria Ocasio-Cortez wing of the Democratic Party. I am aware that "progressive" has meant something different at various points of the twentieth century, but in the context of the Trump era it was often used as a catchall for those who felt that the economic policies of the Clinton and Obama administrations were overly influenced by bankers and thus insufficient to slow down or reverse the disparity of wealth between the super-rich and everybody else.

This middle-of-the-road economic philosophy was often referred to as "neoliberalism" by pundits on the left. However, I refrain from using the word neoliberal for the same reason I avoid using the term "Bernie Bros," which is a slogan mainstream Democrats deployed to trivialize progressives. Far too often, such words were weaponized by tribes on the left and center to dehumanize each other, a syndrome that neither side could afford in 2020.

Although the underlying arguments among Democrats (and Democratic Socialists) were serious and of great concern to many artists, they were largely sublimated during Trump's reelection campaign. Whether or not the American health care system should be delivered through "Medicare for All" or be incrementally broadened via the Affordable Care Act was an important debate, but it was subordinated to defeating libertarian arguments against the government having *any* role in facilitating health care. Much of the infighting that the American left was known for temporarily dissipated in 2020 because the vast majority of anti-Trump activists, in and out of show business, came to believe that all other arguments were less urgent than the struggle between democracy and fascism.

Billy Ray, who wrote the screenplay for *The Hunger Games* and wrote and directed the miniseries *The Comey Rule*, told me he was motivated to intensify his focus on politics because "the 2016 election destroyed me. It triggered anxiety like that of a ten-year-old who has lost track of his parents." Several weeks after Biden won the 2020 election, Ray had lost none of his intensity: "I don't believe that I'll ever be able to write anything that ignores politics ever again. For the rest of our lives we'll be trying to figure out how we got Trump." (In March 2021, Showtime announced that Ray would write and direct a miniseries about the January 6 insurrection at the Capitol by Trump supporters.)

When Jon Stewart began hosting *The Daily Show* in 1999, it was the only daily late-night program in which the comedy revolved around politics. After Trump become president, it was every one of those shows, every night. In the decades before Trump, two of the biggest pop divas—Mariah Carey and Whitney Houston—rarely alluded to political issues and almost never to political elections. (Katy Perry was a rare exception when she campaigned with Hillary Clinton in 2016.) In the Trump era, Cardi B, Demi Lovato, Taylor Swift, and Billie Eilish were among dozens of pop stars who were outspoken about the political landscape. Before Trump, the realm of the artist–activist was populated by a few dozen "usual suspects" who weighed in on progressive issues and showed up for fundraisers. After Trump, entertainers like De Niro, Jim Carrey, and Bette Midler, who had often kept their political views to themselves, became obsessively engaged.

Trump's racism triggered the sizable portion of the creative community that had come to view civil rights as a profound and overarching American issue as far back as the early 1960s when Harry Belafonte organized stars like Marlon Brando to support Dr. Martin Luther King Jr. (The entertainment business had its own problems over the years when it came to appropriately empowering and respecting people of color, flaws which would be reexamined in 2020 after the murder of George Floyd.)

The president's attitude toward women was also a significant motivator for this newfound political engagement. Not only had he defeated a female candidate who got three million more popular votes than he did, Trump had secured the nomination despite the release of the *Access Hollywood* tape, which displayed the future president boasting about grabbing women "by the pussy" without consequence because "when you're a star, they let you do it. You can do anything."

Rosanne Cash told me that after the 2016 election was called, her daughter phoned her and "was so devastated that she was crying and said, 'I feel like I don't matter.' I felt the same way. A sexual predator had been elected to the highest office and people didn't care." Like many mothers, Cash was later horrified by Trump's policy of separating children from their parents at the Mexican border and was determined to be part of the opposition. "To be silent was to be complicit."

There was another large demographic that was more important to artists than most politicians: young people, whose tastes determined what was fashionable but who were often ignored by political players. The zeitgeist that created hit songs, blockbuster movies, and viral music videos was usually driven by people in their teens and twenties who, in the Trump era, were far more progressive than their elders, especially on issues of climate change, economic inequality, and gun safety.

The sudden emergence of COVID-19 led many Americans to reassess the role of the federal government. Ronald Reagan's stump speech famously included the line, "The nine most terrifying words in the English language are 'I'm from the government and I want to help.'" Reagan was tapping into the libertarian dream river, the idea of the lonely independent hero who didn't need anything from anyone. Trump took modern conservatism's contempt for federal government agencies to the next level and delivered his message in the crude patois of a New York gangster instead of conveying it with Ronald Reagan's syrupy charm.

In the spring of 2020, as the COVID-19 quarantine became the norm, much of show business shifted from scripted dramas to improvised transmissions delivered from the homes of those who could perform without conventional production values. Many of these performances were impacted by the same age-old moral arguments that Springsteen had alluded to: Should citizens be responsible for each other or is everyone on their own? Is every community a sovereign state that exists on its own terms? What is the trade-off between money and health?

Entertainment's heightened role in politics was recognized by several mainstream political pundits. On his MSNBC show, Ari Melber often quoted song lyrics (mostly hip-hop) and moderated panels that combined political commentators like William Kristol with artists like Fat Joe. The *New York Times* launched a regular column that documented political jokes made by late-night TV hosts. However, most political media still tended to treat art and entertainment as a sideshow rather than a meaningful current of ideological energy.

This narrative is framed by my biases. I am a straight white male (he/him) baby boomer, and English is the only language I understand. Martin Luther King Jr. is my favorite figure in American history. I identify with the Bernie Sanders/Elizabeth Warren/ AOC wing of the Democratic Party but I had no hesitation in voting for Hillary Clinton and Joe Biden against Trump and I have close friends in both the center and the left. I was opposed to the war in Iraq and supported Medicare for All and wish that so many Democrats were not on the other side. I recognize that progressive change invariably begins with activists who are disrespected by mainstream politicians and their allies in the media. However, I also know that on every issue I have cared about in recent decades, the worst Democratic leader has been better than the best Republican, and that few activists understand the pressures that politicians face on a daily basis.

As a Vietnam War–obsessed teenager in the 1960s, my attitude about the Cold War was emotionally crystallized by songs like Buffy Sainte-Marie's "Universal Soldier," Bob Dylan's "With God on Our Side," Phil Ochs's "I Ain't Marching Any More," and Marvin Gaye's "What's Going On," and movies like *Seven Days in May*, *Fail Safe*, and *Dr. Strangelove*. My ideas about race were influenced by plays like James Baldwin's *Blues for Mister Charlie*, LeRoi Jones's *Dutchman*, and Lorraine Hansberry's *A Raisin in the Sun;* Dick Gregory's comedy; and Big Bill Broonzy's blues.

I am the parent of two millennials and am grateful that their generation is far more progressive than my own. I believe that young people have a unique moral authority on political matters because policy decisions affect their lives more than those of their elders.

For most of my life I have made my living working with musicians, including politically active artists such as Bonnie Raitt, Kurt Cobain, and Steve Earle, and I tend to romanticize them. I am a longtime ACLU board member with a broad view of the value of artistic free speech. When I lived in Los Angeles in the 1980s and early 1990s, I was part of a loosely knit progressive Hollywood community and I was inspired by the role that people like Warren Beatty, Ed Asner, Richard Dreyfuss, Mike Farrell, Barbra Streisand, Danny Glover, Jane Fonda, Jackson Browne, Morgan Fairchild, Alfre Woodard, Sarah Jessica Parker, and dozens of others played in championing progressive ideologies during the Reagan and George H.W. Bush presidencies.

I have hijacked the phrase "bloody crossroads" as a metaphor for the effect of art on political culture from two anticommunist intellectuals who would undoubtedly be appalled. Lionel Trilling first used it in an essay in the late 1940s that opined that fiction should be judged by its aesthetic quality, not by its political subtext. I have virtually no memory of my high school reading of works by Henry James and John Dos Passos (the writers Trilling analyzed), but I agree with his general point: bad art is not redeemed by good politics, and good art does not require them. I can appreciate Jon Voight's brilliant acting in *Ray Donovan* even though I am nauseated by the actor's pro-Trump videos.

In 1986, Norman Podhoretz repurposed "bloody crossroads" as a title for his anthology about literature and politics, explaining that his use of the word "blood" referred to victims of the Soviet Union's dictator Joseph Stalin who, in Podhoretz's view, was enabled by left-wing intellectuals. Podhoretz was a leading neo-conservative intellectual who supported Ronald Reagan and who would later champion both Iraq wars. I detest neoconservatism, but I share Podhoretz's conviction that art is vitally important to the politics of any society.

Some political art is overt agitprop, some has a clear ideological subtext, and some is merely informed by a progressive point of view. My focus here is limited to mass entertainment, movies, television, and music that reached millions of fans. I do not attempt to document the avant-garde nor do I focus on fashion, literature, theater, video games, and the new generation of YouTube auteurs, nor do I analyze the remarkable political role that professional athletes played in 2020, other than when they intersected with show business. Even within this limited field of vision, the examples I give are but a small fraction of the thousands of speeches, statements, jokes, songs, dramas, and tweets that the creative community produced in 2020.

The mosaic that follows is my subjective notion of which artists had the greatest impact on the resistance, which includes the fact that there are often contradictory opinions, even among people with similar political views, about the impact of art. To give an example from the Trump era, when the live-action version of *The Lion King* was released in 2019, a writer for the *Washington Post* complained that the story reinforced antidemocratic aristocracy because of the film's premise that Mufasa's son Simba was destined to rule the Pride Land. However, when I saw the film and heard Mufasa (voiced by James Earl Jones) tell his young cub, "While others search for what they can take, a true king searches for what he can give," it struck me as a timely dig at Trump's selfishness and greed. To others, *The Lion King* seemed devoid of any political subtext.

Despite the wide aesthetic range of political art, and the varying effectiveness of performers who act as ideological megaphones, I am convinced that American political culture is more progressive as a result of the involvement of artists. Manifestos are sometimes necessary but are never sufficient. Actual transformation requires a deep connection to the subjective world of mythology, which, as Joseph Campbell declared, is "the homeland of the muses, the inspirers of art, the inspirers of poetry." These are my flawed protagonists.

The tradition of artists who confront those in power dates back to the plays of Aristophanes after the Periclean age of ancient Greece. Yet the particular turn in the subterranean river that inspired and empowered show business activists in 2020 first gathered momentum in the first half of the twentieth century, during the Golden Age of Hollywood.

CHAPTER 1
TRIBUTARIES
1940-2002

THE GREAT DICTATOR

Many conflicts in the Trump era—such as racism and sexism versus equality, or democracy versus authoritarianism—had deep roots in American history. In 2020, the ghosts of past struggles were ubiquitous.

There are those who date the beginning of the "Hollywood left" to the 1930s, when a number of artists were drawn into the fight against fascism in the Spanish Civil War, or got involved in Upton Sinclair's unsuccessful socialist campaign for governor of California in 1934. However, both of these battles were limited to discrete political subcultures. Hollywood's first political expression that captured the entire nation's attention was Charlie Chaplin's film *The Great Dictator*.

A devastating satire of Adolf Hitler and Nazi Germany, the film was released in 1940, more than a year before the United States entered World War II, when there was still a fierce domestic debate about whether or not the European conflict was any of America's business. A quarter century earlier, Chaplin became the country's first cinematic superstar. His most famous persona, "the Tramp," spoke to working people around the world, but the brilliance of his comedy also led to wide acceptance among the cultural elite. He knew both Winston Churchill and his Indian antagonist, Mahatma Gandhi, and Chaplin was befriended by progressive literary elders like George Bernard Shaw and H.G. Wells.

The perceived global impact of a Chaplin satire was such that when the script for *The Great Dictator* first circulated, Nazi Germany's government pressured distributors in Hollywood to reject the film while, at the same time, Franklin D. Roosevelt personally urged Jack Warner to make the project as quickly as possible. (The president later screened it at the White House.)

In addition to writing and directing *The Great Dictator*, Chaplin stars as the film's two look-alike characters: a poor Jewish barber and Hynkel, the dictator of the fictitious country of Tomania, an unmistakable parody of Hitler replete with a mustache, anti-Semitism, murderous rage, and sycophantic populist salutes of "Heil Hynkel." After a convoluted plot twist, the barber is mistaken for the dictator and asked to broadcast a speech to the world. In the final scene, he confounds expectations with an extended inspirational speech intended as a commentary on the looming horror of World War II, which resonates eighty years later:

> *I don't want to rule or conquer anyone. I should like to help everyone, if possible: Jew, Gentile, Black man, white . . . Greed has poisoned men's souls, has barricaded the world with hate, has goose-stepped us into misery and bloodshed . . . In the seventeenth chapter of Saint Luke it is written: "The Kingdom of God is within man"—not one man, nor a group of men, but in all men! In you! You, the people, have the power . . . Let us fight for a new world, a decent world that will give men a chance to work, that will give you a future and old age and security. By the promise of these things, brutes have risen to power. But they lie! They do not fulfill their promise. They never will! Dictators free themselves but they enslave the people. Now let us fight to fulfill that promise. Let us fight to free the world, to do away with national barriers, to do away with greed, with hate and intolerance. Let us fight for a world of reason, a world where science and progress will lead to all men's happiness.*

When the film was first announced, the British government banned it out of deference to the Nazi government. However, by the time it was ready for release, the UK was at war with Germany and the film became Britain's second-highest-grossing film that year. It was also a huge commercial and critical success in the US. Several months after *The Great Dictator*'s premiere, Chaplin gave his character's final speech at a celebration of Franklin D. Roosevelt's third inauguration, upon the president's request.

FDR's enthusiasm for the power of the Hollywood left was mirrored by hostility from those who wanted to keep the US from fighting Hitler. Shortly after *The Great Dictator* was released, Congressman Martin Dies Jr. wrote an article for *Liberty* magazine titled "Reds in Hollywood," where he accused filmmakers of "warmongering." In response, Dorothy Parker argued that "people want . . . real democracy, Mr. Dies, and they look toward Hollywood to give it to them because they don't get it anymore in their newspapers . . . that's why you want to destroy the Hollywood progressive organizations, because you've got to control this medium if you want to bring fascism to this country."

After Roosevelt died in 1945, the power of the left quickly diminished both in Washington and in Hollywood. In 1946, as producer Hal Wallis developed a film about the dropping of nuclear bombs on Hiroshima and Nagasaki, he hired Ayn Rand to write the script. As Greg Mitchell describes in *The Beginning or the End*, Rand cautioned the producer, "If the movie advances statism, we will have blood on our hands." In Rand's view, making FDR a hero would be "committing a moral crime." The film was never made.

As I searched for the dots that connected *The Great Dictator* to the anti-Trump resistance, it became clear that progressive entertainers had their greatest impact during times of conservative power in Washington, filling the void created when Democratic leaders were diminished in influence and leftist activists were under siege. To indicate the trajectory of ideals that motivated the resistance to Trump, I focus on four pivotal years during periods of right-wing political power: 1947, 1970, 1987, and 2002.

1947: REPUBLICAN RESURGENCE AND THE HOLLYWOOD BLACKLIST

In 1947, Republicans took control of the Congress for the first time in sixteen years. Newly elected Republican members included Senator Joseph McCarthy of Wisconsin and Congressman Richard Nixon of California, and the Democrats elected a young congressman from Massachusetts, John F. Kennedy. The Cold War between the United States and Soviet Union began its gravitational pull on American politics with the creation of the American national security state and the founding of the CIA.

An embattled president Truman signed a "Loyalty Order" that was designed to root out supposed communist influence in the government. This led to the creation of the Attorney General's List of Subversive Organizations, which included many noncommunist progressive groups that had no relationship with the Soviet Union. Although the investigative power was intended to scrutinize government agencies, its methods were soon used to intimidate the entertainment business.

In March 1947, conservatives in the Screen Actors Guild (SAG) purged several liberal board members including Harpo Marx and James Cagney. Soon-to-be conservative hero Ronald Reagan was elected president of the union. Director Leo McCarey announced that he would not cast Katharine Hepburn because she spoke at a rally with FDR's former vice president and Cold War critic Henry Wallace. Hepburn responded, "Silence the artist and you have silenced the most articulate voice the people have."

At a 1947 California conference of left-leaning artists who were attempting to combat the repressive threats coming from Washington, one of the speakers was screenwriter Albert Maltz, who had written *The House I Live In*, an Oscar-winning musical short starring Frank Sinatra on the subject of racial and religious tolerance. Maltz called art "the conscience of the people" and spoke of former literary role models who paid a political price, such as Émile Zola, who was attacked for his exposure of French anti-Semitism; Victor Hugo, who spent seventeen years in exile from royalist France for simply criticizing antidemocratic policies of Napoleon; and Fyodor

Dostoyevsky, who served four years in a Siberian labor camp for circulating books banned by Tsar Nicholas I.

In phrases that could have applied to some of Trump's supporters seventy years later, the journalist Carey McWilliams described the newly empowered right to be "shot through and through with the self-hatred, the blind mole-like fear of change, the deep-seated social envy and sense of personal inadequacy, the cheap cynicism, and the pseudo-hard-boiled know-nothingism of those who cannot imagine the existence of values really worth defending and who traduce, by their every act and statement, the basic American ideals."

Similarly, Howard Koch, the screenwriter for *Casablanca*, attacked "words that tell half truths or no truths, words that half explain or don't explain at all, brash words out of the vocabulary of a Goebbels, high-sounding words that have been distorted into caricatures of their once precious meanings, words cunningly contrived to confuse, words fashioned out of malice, fear, and self-interest, words that have lost all connection with the real world—the world of fact."

The resistance of 1947 failed. In October of that year, the House Un-American Activities Committee (HUAC) held hearings about the supposed communist influence in Hollywood and eventually subpoenaed ten screenwriters and directors including Maltz, Ring Lardner Jr., and Dalton Trumbo. These witnesses, who came to be known as the "Hollywood Ten," refused to answer the committee's questions.

Ayn Rand also testified. Aided by the FBI, she wrote a pamphlet called *Screen Guide for Americans*, which claimed, "The purpose [of the communists] is to corrupt non-political movies by introducing small, casual bits of propaganda into innocent stories, thus making people absorb the basic principles of Collectivism by indirection and implication." Further, she exhorted producers not to smear the free enterprise system, wealth, the profit motive, success, or "the independent man."

One film singled out for opprobrium was *It's a Wonderful Life*, which stars Jimmy Stewart as a saintly savings and loan proprietor. In recent decades, the film has become a Christmas classic beloved by movie fans of all political persuasions. However, in her pamphlet, Rand condemned the film for "attempting to instigate class warfare . . . this picture deliberately maligned the upper class . . . [and attempts] to discredit bankers by casting Lionel Barrymore as a 'scrooge-type' so that he would be the most hated man in the picture."

Anyone who thought that the Trump era was uniquely challenging for dissenters should consider that in the late 1940s, the brilliant African American singer and actor Paul Robeson was banned from several speaking engagements because of his supposedly subversive political views; he was even deprived of his passport, which took him ten years of litigation to get back. Chaplin, who had retained his British citizenship, was forced to leave the United States in 1952. The Hollywood Ten were ultimately convicted of contempt of Congress and given sentences ranging from six months to one year in prison.

After that, witnesses who did not want to cooperate with the FBI invoked the Fifth Amendment. However, because the studios caved to HUAC demands, those who did not identify colleagues with left-wing views were barred from working in Hollywood or on network television for more than a decade. Under Reagan's leadership, the Screen Actors Guild became an instrument that helped enforce the blacklist.

1970: RESISTING NIXON

The blacklist lasted until 1960, when Kirk Douglas hired Dalton Trumbo to write the screenplay for *Spartacus*. When the film premiered at the end of the year, the American Legion picketed to protest the legitimization of Trumbo, who was one of the Hollywood Ten. Yet president-elect John F. Kennedy walked past the right-wing protesters and into the theater, putting the final nail in the blacklist's coffin.

The next time Republicans held executive power was 1969, when Richard Nixon began his presidency after a campaign characterized by a "Southern strategy" to attract white voters who detested Kennedy and Lyndon B. Johnson's support for civil rights legislation. Although many were horrified that Donald Trump's racist campaign was able to secure 47 percent of the popular vote in 2016 and 48 percent in 2020, it is worth remembering that in 1968, the total votes for Nixon and George Wallace—the Alabama governor and segregationist, running on a third-party ticket—added up to more than 57 percent of the popular vote. As Martin Luther King Jr. said shortly before his death, "White backlash . . . is a new name for an old phenomenon."

Despite the 1968 election results, the entertainment business's creative community was far stronger in 1970 than it was during the blacklisting period. Changes in technology and demographics gave artists more power to influence the culture, regardless of what was happening in Washington, where Nixon was escalating the war in Vietnam.

Edwin Starr's "War" was the fifth-best-selling single of 1970. The song's first line clarifies its message in crystal clear terms: "War, huh, yeah / What is it good for? / Absolutely nothing!" Later, Starr laments that the Vietnam War had "caused unrest within the younger generation / Induction, then destruction."

Equally significant was Crosby, Stills, Nash & Young's "Ohio," which was written by Neil Young in response to the killing of four unarmed students by National Guard troops at Kent State University on May 4, 1970. Its haunting opening lines are: "Tin soldiers and Nixon's coming / We're finally on our own / This summer I hear the drumming / Four dead in Ohio." At the time of the song's release, Crosby, Stills, Nash & Young's *Déjà Vu* was the best-selling album in America.

Movie and TV culture also moved left in 1970. *The Mary Tyler Moore Show* premiered on CBS, the first network sitcom to revolve around a single workingwoman. *The Flip Wilson Show*, a rare network show hosted by an African American, became the second-most-watched series in the country, seen weekly in more than fifty million households. Among other achievements, Wilson introduced the politically subversive George Carlin to a prime-time audience. On Johnny Cash's weekly ABC show, the singer gave a network platform to the previously blacklisted Pete Seeger.

The music business changed rapidly in the mid-sixties. Musicians and songwriters quickly internalized a counterculture that was intertwined with the civil rights and antiwar movements, and with the increasing popularity of psychedelics. Because of the time it took to write, finance, produce, and distribute films, Hollywood needed until the end of the decade to catch up. In 1968, the Academy Award for Best Picture was given to *Oliver*, a sanitized old-school musical comedy. In 1969, the Best Picture award was given to *Midnight Cowboy*, an X-rated film whose protagonist is a male hustler. Hollywood films released in 1970 included *M*A*S*H*, ostensibly about the Korean War but widely viewed as an antiwar satire about Vietnam; *The Strawberry Statement*, whose main character is an antiwar protester; *Zabriskie Point*, whose protagonists are radicals; *Myra Breckinridge*, which stars Raquel Welch as a man who has a sex-reassignment surgery to become a woman; and *Woodstock*, which documents the 1969 rock festival and is replete with joyous profanity and antiwar messages. At the time, *Woodstock* was the highest-grossing documentary film in history.

The 1970 movie that most vividly anticipated the cultural divide of the Trump era was *Joe*, starring Peter Boyle as the title character, a white working-class hater of sixties counterculture. Joe meets a guy in a bar whose daughter (played by Susan Sarandon in her film debut) has just landed in the hospital from a drug overdose. The two of them proceed to go on a rampage and kill hippies at a commune. In a famous monologue, Joe says, "The n****** are getting all the money. So why work? Welfare! They even give them free rubbers. You think they use them? Hell no—they sell them and use the money for booze." Nobody who watched this film could mistake the subtext. Joe was the bad guy.

Jane Fonda, then thirty-two years old, emerged as a political activist in 1970, making frequent public comments in opposition to the Vietnam War. Despite bitter attacks from supporters of the war, Fonda won the 1971 Academy Award for Best Actress for her performance as a prostitute in *Klute*.

Nevertheless, conservative energy of the macho underground river still flourished in corners of Hollywood. In *Patton*, George S.

Scott played the controversial army general; President Nixon repeatedly screened the movie in the White House. (Trump has also cited *Patton* as one of his favorites.) The film would win the Best Picture Oscar in 1970. In his memoir *Chasing the Light*, Oliver Stone writes, "The horrible truth was Americans loved this Patton, the movie and the man, a sick man who'd gone too far. We loved killers."

1987: REAGAN STUMBLES

After Nixon imploded with the Watergate scandal in 1974, Jimmy Carter was elected in 1976 but was defeated in his reelection attempt in 1980 by Ronald Reagan, whose popularity was based on many of the reactionary emotions that Donald Trump would exploit forty years later.

Like Trump, Reagan's connection to the public was rooted in his history as a TV star. He served as governor of California before running for president, but his real "training" for presidential politics wasn't his time as governor—it was as an actor. As the popular host of *General Electric Theater*, Reagan became the darling of the Republican Party after giving a televised speech in support of Barry Goldwater's 1964 presidential bid.

Mike Farrell, who played B.J. Hunnicutt on the popular TV series spin-off of M*A*S*H, told *Los Angeles Times* reporter Ron Brownstein, "What we were seeing was Frankenstein's monster . . . we were seeing this media product . . . and we knew! We knew who this guy really was." Robert Foxworth, star of *Falcon Crest*, wondered, "Why did the public buy an act we could see through so easily?"

Like Trump, Reagan was not personally religious, yet nonetheless cultivated a relationship with the leaders of the Christian right who liked his opposition to abortion. Reagan's most visible evangelical supporter was Jerry Falwell; Trump's was Jerry Falwell Jr.

As part of his 1980 presidential campaign, Reagan gave a speech at the Nebosha County Fair, just a few miles from Philadelphia, Mississippi, a small town where three civil rights workers had been murdered in 1964. In his speech Reagan said, "I believe in states' rights" and "the South shall rise again." During the campaign, Reagan claimed that the Voting Rights Act humiliated Southern states. He repeatedly made references to an African American "welfare queen," who supposedly abused the system. Reagan fancifully speculated about "a strapping young buck using food stamps to buy T-bone steaks at the grocery store." Like Trump, Reagan appeared indifferent to the police killing of unarmed African Americans. Public Enemy's debut album, *Yo! Bum Rush the Show*, was partially inspired by the 1983 police killing of twenty-five-year-old artist Michael Stewart, who was arrested for spraying graffiti on a New York City subway platform. He was beaten in a police van and died thirteen days later. In 1989, Spike Lee dedicated his film *Do the Right Thing* to six Black families, five of whom had lost loved ones at the hands of the police, including the Stewart family.

Bill Stephney, who produced *Yo! Bum Rush the Show*, reflects that it is "hard to explain to young people how much of a political amateur Donald Trump is compared to Ronald Reagan." While Trump would lose in his reelection effort, Reagan was reelected in 1984 with 60 percent of the popular vote.

Besides race, the most divisive issues that motivated show business activists in the Reagan era were related to the perpetuation of the Cold War. For the 1984 production of John Milius's *Red Dawn*, MGM/UA recruited Reagan's first secretary of state, Alexander Haig, to consult with the writer and director. Studio executive Peter Bart wrote, "[Haig] took Milius under his wing. Suddenly Milius found himself welcomed into right-wing think tanks."

Red Dawn's absurd plot portrays a Soviet–Cuban invasion of America's Southwest in which communists take over several American towns. A group of high school kids retreat to the mountains and form a guerrilla army called "the Wolverines" and, somehow, successfully fight back.

Another government-approved movie, *Top Gun*, the country's top-grossing film of 1986, starred Tom Cruise as a naval pilot. The film glamorizes military service to the stylized level of a fashion layout. The US Navy even permitted the filming of F-14 aircrafts for fight scenes. In his book *Back to Our Future: How the 1980s Explain the World We Live in Now*, David Sirota recalls, "Recruitment spiked 400 percent in the months after *Top Gun* was released, leading the navy to set up tables at theaters upon realizing the movie's effect."

Even so, those successes were overwhelmed by the response of the Hollywood left. Vietnam vet Oliver Stone burst the revisionist bubble with *Platoon*, which depicts the war as morally bankrupt. Stone chose Charlie Sheen—who had starred as one of the teenage anticommunists in *Red Dawn*—to play army volunteer Chris Taylor. In the film, Taylor is assigned to an infantry platoon near the Cambodian border; he ultimately kills his human rights–abusing sergeant. Jackie Kennedy wrote to Stone after seeing *Platoon* that his film had "changed the direction of the country's thinking. It will always stand there as a landmark—like Rachel Carson's *Silent Spring*, like Thomas Paine's *Common Sense*." *Platoon* won four Academy Awards in 1986, including Best Picture and Best Director.

The policy issues that galvanized many activists in the creative community at the time revolved around Central America, where progressives feared that Reagan would get the US into a Vietnam-type conflict. In 1981, Ed Asner, star of the TV series *Lou Grant*, was elected as the president of the Screen Actors Guild, the post Reagan had held decades earlier. Shortly after assuming his new position, Asner gave a SAG check to the Air Traffic Controllers Union to support them in their vain fight against Reagan. The following year, accompanied by fellow actors Howard Hesseman and Lee Grant, Asner held a press conference outside of the State Department, where they presented a $25,000 SAG check to the human rights group Medical Aid for El Salvador.

Reagan's cold warriors freaked out when, in 1984, Daniel Ortega, the candidate of the left-wing Sandinista Party, was elected president of Nicaragua. The administration began a program of aid to the Contras, a paramilitary group of Nicaraguans who wanted to restore right-wing leadership to the country. While progressives saw the Contras as brutal criminals intent on overthrowing an elected government, Reagan referred to them as "the moral equivalent of our Founding Fathers." M*A*S*H star Mike Farrell and *LA Weekly* editor Jay Levin created the Committee of Concern to organize a Hollywood opposition to Reagan's Central American policy.

Despite over a decade of vitriol from the right, Jane Fonda was more successful than ever. The movie business website The Numbers listed Fonda as the number one box office attraction of the 1980s, which was based on the grosses from thirteen films, including explicitly political ones she produced such as *Coming Home*, *The China Syndrome*, and *9 to 5*.

In 1984, Fonda's longtime business colleague Paula Weinstein, songwriter Marilyn Bergman, producer Anthea Sylbert, CBS Entertainment executive Barbara Corday, and attorney Susan Grode formed the Hollywood Women's Political Committee (HWPC), which raised two million dollars for congressional candidates in the 1986 midterms. In 1987, Margery Tabankin, who ran the AmeriCorps VISTA program during the Carter administration, was hired to run the HWPC.

The ideological clash between the HWPC and the corporate film establishment came to a head in February 1987, when two of the most powerful Hollywood moguls—Disney president Michael Eisner and CAA head Michael Ovitz—announced a fundraiser for Senator Bill Bradley, a New Jersey Democrat who, the previous year, had voted to provide federal aid to the Contras. The HWPC took out a full-page advertisement in *Variety* that read, "When a senator from the East Coast comes to California to raise money from our community, then this becomes a community issue, and one we feel we must speak out about. We hope Senator Bradley will change his position."

In the rock and roll world, Bruce Springsteen released a live concert version of "War." He made it clear that the release was a commentary on Reagan's Central American aspirations. Around the same time, Jackson Browne released the album *Lives in the Balance*, a devastating critique of American interventionism, and Kris Kristofferson released his first solo album in five years, *Repossessed*, which also attacked Reagan's policies.

The other foreign policy issue that inspired Hollywood progressives was the struggle to end apartheid in South Africa. Quincy Jones, Alfre Woodard, Harry Belafonte, Danny Glover, and many others worked with Randall Robinson on the Free South Africa movement to release Nelson Mandela from prison, an effort Mandela frequently acknowledged after he was finally released in 1990.

Oliver Stone followed up *Platoon* with another massive hit, *Wall Street*, a frontal attack of the byproducts of Reagan's libertarian economic philosophy. Michael Douglas plays Gordon Gekko, a corrupt corporate raider who makes a cynical speech to shareholders where he memorably asserts, "Greed is good." Douglas won the Academy Award for Best Actor.

The Simpsons also premiered in 1987, beginning what would be the longest-running entertainment series in the history of television. Among its most memorable characters is the immoral business tycoon Mr. Burns, whose venality makes Gordon Gekko look like a Boy Scout.

The most-watched television show in America in 1987 was *The Cosby Show*, which had debuted three years earlier. Unlike previous shows with African American characters, the lead characters, Cliff and Claire Huxtable, were college-educated and financially successful, happily raising five children. Through a modern lens, it's difficult to imagine Bill Cosby, a convicted rapist, of being an important cultural role model. But in 1987, the persistent image of a Black family achieving the American dream was a significant step in the painfully long evolution of white America's reckoning with racism.

In March 1987, Los Angeles rapper Eazy-E released his first single, "Boyz-n-the-Hood," which graphically conveys life in the Los Angeles ghetto. He was also a member of N.W.A ("Niggaz Wit Attitudes"), whose first studio album, *Straight Outta Compton*, included the song "Fuck tha Police," which was released several years before the infamous beating of Rodney King by members of the Los Angeles Police Department was caught on videotape.

As had been the case in previous eras, there were also conservative strains in show business. In *Family Ties*, Michael J. Fox played Alex P. Keaton, the materialistic, Reagan-loving son of former sixties activists who are depicted as ineffectual anachronisms. In one episode, Keaton made fun of his parents' old friends: "Every time one of these ex-hippies come prancing in from yesteryear, we gotta get out the love beads and pretend we care about people."

The World Wrestling Federation (WWF) thrived during the Reagan years. The fake wrestling universe polarized by cartoonish good guys and bad guys reached an apex on March 29, 1987, when 93,173 fans headed to the Pontiac Silverdome for WrestleMania III, which featured a "battle" between Hulk Hogan and André the Giant.

The phenomenon was not lost on Donald Trump, who arranged for the next WrestleMania to take place at the Atlantic City Convention Hall. Trump made an appearance in the ring, pretending to fight the organization's CEO, Vince McMahon. In 2017, the newly elected president appointed McMahon's wife and partner, Linda McMahon, to be the head of the Small Business Administration.

In August 1987, there was a change in federal policy, little noticed by political elites at the time, that would resonate powerfully in 2020. The Reagan administration's Federal Communications Commission ended the "fairness doctrine," which required broadcasters to balance political opinions with opposing views. One immediate beneficiary was Rush Limbaugh, then the host of a Sacramento talk radio show. Freed of political restrictions, he transformed his broadcast to one of shrill right-wing demagoguery. He demonized liberals and referred to those who fought for women's rights as "feminazis," as if the notion of equal pay for equal work was the moral equivalent of Hitler's death camps for German Jews. In subsequent decades, high ratings not only made Limbaugh a national radio star but a primary influence on right-wing talk radio and Fox News.

On the left, the most influential person in Hollywood in 1987 was producer Norman Lear, who had extraordinary success with *All in the Family, Maude, The Jeffersons,* and *Sanford and Son,* each of which attracted tens of millions of weekly television viewers. Lear's shows combined comic story lines with a wide array of political commentary framed from a progressive point of view. In 1980, Lear created People For the American Way (PFAW) in an effort to express a different concept of patriotism and morality than Reagan's retro model.

PFAW made its biggest mark in 1987, after Reagan announced the Supreme Court appointment of Robert Bork, whose extreme views represented a threat to many of the progressive accomplishments of the preceding decades. PFAW produced a TV commercial that showed a family on the steps of the Supreme Court, while Gregory Peck's voice intoned, "Robert Bork wants to be a Supreme Court justice. But the record shows he has a strange idea of what justice is. He defended poll taxes and literacy tests, which kept many Americans from voting. He opposed the civil rights law that ended *Whites Only* signs at lunch counters. He doesn't believe the Constitution protects your privacy. Please urge your senators to vote against the Bork nomination. Because if Robert Bork wins a seat on the Supreme Court, it will be for life. His life . . . and yours."

Not all Democrats were thrilled. Joe Biden, then the chairman of the Senate Judiciary Committee, which ultimately rejected Bork, said it "demeaned" the committee to suggest that it was swayed by the PFAW campaign rather than by Bork's own testimony. Jackie Blumenthal, who was on the PFAW communications team at the time, explained to me the Washington perspective: "No one had ever run a public campaign against a Supreme Court nominee before. Nearly everyone in DC but us thought that if you politicize the selection of justices, you risk politicizing the court." Those were the days.

One politician who welcomed Hollywood support was Senator Gary Hart, who developed such a close relationship with Warren Beatty that he affectionately referred to Beatty as "the pro." In 1986, most of the creative community was on board with Hart's campaign for the 1988 Democratic nomination for president, including Barbra Streisand, who was at the height of her Hollywood power. The following year, however, Hart was forced to drop out of the race due to an allegedly scandalous relationship he had with Donna Rice, an aspiring actress best known for a small role in an episode of *Miami Vice*. They had met at a New Year's Eve party hosted by Don Henley of the Eagles.

2001–2002: 9/11 AND THE IRAQ WAR

After twelve years of Reagan and Bush, Bill Clinton served two terms as president from 1993–2000. In 2000, despite receiving half a million fewer popular votes, George W. Bush was elected president after defeating Clinton's vice president, Al Gore. Bush's Electoral College victory came about as the result of a 5-4 Supreme Court decision to certify Bush's Florida "win," which he claimed by only a few hundred votes. After several months of postelection partisan bitterness, the lethal terrorist attacks on the World Trade Center and the Pentagon on September 11, 2001, created a brief period of national unity

Bruce Springsteen wrote and recorded "The Rising," a song about the resilience of Americans. Neil Young released "Let's Roll," a tribute to the passengers who lost their lives after overpowering terrorists on Flight 93. There were two post-9/11 televised extravaganzas: *The Concert for New York City* and *America: A Tribute to Heroes*, which featured musical performances by Springsteen, Tom Petty, Willie Nelson, Billy Joel, The Who, John Mellencamp, Melissa Ethridge, Sheryl Crow, Destiny's Child, Paul McCartney, Stevie Wonder, Faith Hill, Alicia Keys, and the Backstreet Boys, as well as speeches by Muhammad Ali, Tom Hanks, Robert De Niro, Will Smith, George Clooney, and Cameron Diaz.

Saturday Night Live's first post-9/11 show aired on September 29, 2001. New York City mayor Rudy Giuliani, surrounded by first responders, lamented the lives tragically lost and the heroes who fought to save them. *SNL* executive producer Lorne Michaels joined Giuliani onstage, asking, "Can we be funny?" to which Giuliani replied, "Why start now?" The bit got a big laugh, but the post-9/11 ideological cease-fire didn't last long. A few months later, cast member Will Ferrell resumed his impersonation of George W. Bush with increasing satiric intensity.

The West Wing was set to premiere its third season on September 11, 2001. In the show's first two seasons it had won the Emmy Award for Outstanding Drama Series (and would win for the next two as well). *The West Wing* portrayed an aspirational notion of the American political system in which liberals and conservatives argued sincerely about how to achieve the same general goals.

The West Wing's creator and principal writer, Aaron Sorkin, built the template for the hit series in his 1995 feature film *The Ameri-*

can President, starring Michael Douglas as president Andrew Shepherd and Martin Sheen as Chief of Staff A.J. MacInerney. (Sheen would eventually play the fictitious President Josiah Bartlet in *The West Wing*.) In *The American President's* denouement, President Shepherd describes his creepy right-wing rival Bob Rumson, played by Richard Dreyfuss: "He is interested in two things, and two things only—making you afraid and telling you who's to blame for it." Shepherd then proposes legislation to combat the effects of global warming and another to ban assault rifles and handguns, policies that progressives still yearned for a quarter of a century later.

The West Wing's third-season premiere, "Isaac and Ishmael," follows the secret service as they suspect a young Muslim White House aide of being a terrorist. After an intimidating round of questioning, he is released because authorities discover that his name is merely similar to the suspected terrorist.

The feeling of post-9/11 national unity dissipated after Bush and Vice President Dick Cheney harnessed American anger and fear to launch a war against Iraq, a country that had nothing to do with the World Trade Center attack. Although a few Democrats, such as Senator Ted Kennedy, opposed the war, top Democrats like Hillary Clinton, John Kerry, and Tom Daschle voted to authorize the war. Artist-activists filled the antiwar vacuum, playing a leading public role in articulating opposition to the Bush–Cheney vendetta against Iraq.

A group formed under the name Artists United to Win Without War included stars like Martin Sheen, Kim Basinger, Matt Damon, Laurence Fishburne, Ethan Hawke, Uma Thurman, Samuel L. Jackson, and Jessica Lange. Dustin Hoffman commented, "This war is about what most wars are about: hegemony, money, power, and oil." Richard Gere urged, "We have to say 'stop.' There's no reason for a war. At the moment, [Saddam] Hussein is not threatening anybody." Sean Penn traveled to Iraq and criticized the Bush administration's tenuous rationale for the war: "I cannot conceive of any reason why the American people and the world would not have shared with the Iraqis the evidence of the claim to have weapons of mass destruction."

After the war began, a censorious wrath from Bush's allies was directed at the Dixie Chicks, the country trio whose lead singer, Natalie Maines, proclaimed during a London concert that, as a fellow Texan, she was "ashamed" of Bush. After this comment, most country music radio stations stopped broadcasting the Dixie Chicks. Maines remained undaunted in her criticism of the Iraq War.

The highest-profile Hollywood antiwar protest took place in March 2003, after Michael Moore's *Bowling for Columbine* won the Academy Award for Best Documentary. The film surpassed *Woodstock* as the most successful documentary in history, grossing $58 million in the United States. (Moore would eclipse that number with his next documentary film, *Fahrenheit 9/11*, a devastating indictment of the Bush–Cheney administration.) In his Oscar acceptance speech, Moore said, "We live in a time where we have a man sending us to war for fictitious reasons . . . Shame on you, Mr. Bush, shame on you. And anytime you've got the pope and the Dixie Chicks against you, your time is up."

While HUAC, Nixon, Reagan, Bush, and Cheney were all daunting adversaries and exquisite foils for progressive artists, Donald Trump's White House occupation starting in 2017 presented a new peril to democracy and triggered a renewed determination by the creative community to resist it.

CHAPTER 2
PRESIDENT TRUMP
2017-2019

CROWD ENVY

The shock of Trump's electoral college victory in 2016 was magnified by the fact that he succeeded Barack Obama. Trump had cynically embraced the "birther" theory that America's first African American president had not been born in the country, and it was likely that a twenty-first-century white backlash was a contributing factor to the 2016 result. But there was also the unsettling fact that several million people who had previously voted for Obama chose Trump in 2016.

There were various theories about why this occurred, including sexism, Russian interference, and anti–Hillary Clinton public statements by FBI director James Comey. Another significant factor was that Clinton's 2016 campaign failed to unite the left and center because of a lingering disappointment with the limited economic progress for large swaths of the middle class during the previous eight years.

Despite Obama's many virtues, some of his voters were unhappy with the administration's handling of the aftermath of the 2008 financial crisis. Their feelings were summarized by the chants of Occupy Wall Street protesters, such as, "Banks got bailed out, we

got sold out!" and in progressive critiques of "neoliberal" econom-
ics by writers like Naomi Klein and Joseph Stiglitz. This was the
issue that animated Bernie Sanders's unsuccessful effort to win
the nomination from Clinton in 2016 (Sanders won 43 percent of
the votes in the Democratic primaries).

In the 2016 general election, more than six million people voted
for candidates of small parties, mostly for the Green Party's Jill
Stein and the Libertarians' Gary Johnson. Those voters accounted
for 5.7 percent of the total in 2016, far greater than the 1.7 percent that voted "third party" in 2012. If that four-point increase
in third-party votes had gone instead to Clinton, she would have
easily won the swing states and an electoral vote majority.

After the 2016 election, Democrats and progressives, and the
artists who identified with them, were suddenly united in a grim
determination to resist as much of Trump's agenda as possible, a
resistance that temporarily merged Mailer's practical river of politics and the subterranean one of ideals.

Although political tradition restrained most Democratic officials from immediately criticizing a newly elected president, entertainers were not bound by such conventions. Younger artists
were connected to youthful fan bases that overwhelmingly rejected
Trump's racist and sexist qualities. Older ones did not want to
wait, as they had when they let Ronald Reagan and George W. Bush
have their postelection honeymoons.

A week before the 2017 inauguration, Meryl Streep, upon receiving a lifetime achievement award at the Golden Globes, criticized the president-elect's anti-immigration positions. Trump
promptly tweeted that the three-time Academy Award winner was
"overrated."

Barbra Streisand wrote in the *Huffington Post* that the president-
elect was "clueless, reckless, graceless, mindless, and heartless . . .
He doesn't just bring economic policies I happen to disagree with,
or an approach to health-care funding that could hurt millions of
people . . . This is a man who, on record and often on video, disparaged or outright ridiculed women, immigrants, the disabled,
and others." Streisand had been supporting Democrats for most

of her career, but the cultural playing field in which artists would make their views known was significantly different in 2017 than it had been in the past. Trump's reality-show savvy, his effective use of Twitter, and his blithe disregard for the truth when it interfered with his daily agenda overwhelmed the ability of Democrats, public interest groups, and conventional media to compete for the attention of a significant percentage of the American public. Steve Bannon had been clear about Trump's strategy: "The real opposition is the media. And the way to deal with them is to flood the zone with shit."

In this new context, in which pop celebrities had exponentially more Twitter followers than even the most popular Democrats in Congress, artist-activists went from being part of the background of America's daily political conversation to part of an increasingly cacophonous foreground, and Trump knew it.

When Trump married his third wife, Melania, in 2005, he booked Billy Joel and Elton John to perform at his wedding. Shortly after he won the election in 2016, Trump told the *New York Times* that there would be "plenty of movie and entertainment stars" at his inaugural festivities. While it would not have been reasonable to expect any Republican to attract Bruce Springsteen, Beyoncé, Aretha Franklin, and Bono to perform at their inauguration, as Barack Obama had, even George W. Bush's inaugural committee had booked pop stars Jessica Simpson, 98 Degrees, Destiny's Child, Ricky Martin, and Texans such as Lyle Lovett and ZZ Top.

By contrast, Trump struck out with the vast majority of performers, including those who had appeared at his wedding. Among others who declined were Charlotte Church and Rebecca Ferguson, who wrote an open letter stating she'd only attend if she could sing "Strange Fruit," a song about the lynching of African Americans that had been popularized by Billie Holliday. (The inaugural committee declined.) A Springsteen tribute group, The B Street Band, initially agreed to perform at the inauguration but later pulled out.

Even some members of authoritarian ensembles balked at identifying with the president. As *USA Today* reported, "A member of the Mormon Tabernacle Choir resigned from the group rather than perform, and MSG Entertainment, the organization that owns the Rockettes, said it was each dancer's choice to perform after a dancer expressed concern on social media." (Thirteen of the eighty dancers opted out.)

For most of his illustrious career, Robert De Niro had rarely expressed political opinions, but he labeled Trump "a con, a bullshit artist, a mutt who doesn't know what he's talking about." De Niro encouraged performers to reject inauguration requests lest they appear to endorse Trump's behavior: "We have to be on our guard."

Bette Midler, who like De Niro had little previous history of partisanship, sarcastically tweeted, "This just in: Trump Inauguration invitations have been declined by several Bibles that would rather he not touch them." Ultimately, the best-known names who showed up for the new president were conservative country singers Toby Keith and Lee Greenwood, as well as rock band 3 Doors Down, whose brief period of popularity had come more than a decade earlier.

In the past, celebrity appearances at inaugurations were not that big of a deal one way or the other, but Trump's was different. Show business energy that had been part of framing previous celebration was largely absent. There was a consensus within the resistance that it was morally critical not to normalize the unprecedented level of racism and misogyny that had characterized Trump's rise to political power.

The day after the inauguration, over four million people across the world marched in honor of the Women's March. In Washington, DC, half a million people attended to express their support for women's rights and to indicate a different vision of America from that of the president. In addition to political speakers, several entertainers appeared at the march, including Janelle Monáe, Madonna, Alicia Keys, Scarlett Johansson, and *Ugly Betty* star America Ferrara, who called for unity among the anti-Trump forces: "If we—the millions of Americans who believe in common decency, in the greater good, in justice for all—if we fall into the trap by separating ourselves by our causes and our labels, then we will weaken our fight and we will lose. But if we commit to what aligns us, if we stand together steadfast and determined, then we stand a chance of saving the soul of our country."

At the same time the Women's March was taking place, Sean Spicer, the White House press secretary, told the Washington press corps that the inaugural crowd for Trump the day before had been "the largest audience ever to witness an inauguration—period." When several TV and print outlets displayed photographs that proved that Obama had drawn a much bigger inaugural audience, Spicer accused the media of lying to "lessen the enthusiasm of the inauguration."

Two weeks later, on *Saturday Night Live*, Melissa McCarthy did a devastating impersonation of Spicer manically sucking up to his boss: "The crowd greeted [Trump] with a standing ovation which lasted a full fifteen minutes . . . Everyone was smiling. Everyone was happy. The men all had erections, and every single one of the women was ovulating left and right." Within days, the clip got more than thirty-five million views on YouTube.

The following Sunday, on *Meet the Press*, Trump aide Kellyanne Conway told Chuck Todd that Spicer had merely presented "alternative facts" about the inauguration. In the weeks that followed, SNL cast member Kate McKinnon performed several brutal impressions that focused on Conway's apparent disregard for truth and her need for constant media attention.

Trump had hosted SNL in 2004 during the first year of *The Apprentice*. In his days as a mere real estate celebrity he had been impersonated on the show by several cast members, most memorably Darrell Hammond, who did Trump twenty-seven times between 1999 and 2016. Trump hosted SNL again in November 2015, after he had announced his candidacy for president, an appearance which was widely criticized by show business progressives who bristled at offering the man a platform to normalize his views. Perhaps to compensate, SNL's executive producer, Lorne Michaels, asked Alec Baldwin to impersonate Trump. Over the course of the next several years, Baldwin repeatedly depicted the president as a crude idiot. On March 2, 2018, Trump tweeted, "Alex Baldwin [*sic*], whose dieing [*sic*] mediocre career was saved by his impersonation of me on

SNL, now says playing DJT was agony for him. Alex, it was agony for those who were forced to watch. You were terrible. Bring back Darrell Hammond, much funnier and a far greater talent!"

ENEMY OF THE PEOPLE

In a presidency that thrived on conflict, Trump and his minions demonized the mainstream news media. Soon after taking office, Trump tweeted, "The FAKE NEWS media (failing @nytimes, @CNN, @NBCNews and many more) is not my enemy, it is the enemy of the American people. SICK!" This was one of many times that Trump appropriated language previously associated with totalitarian regimes, thus reinforcing an antimedia meme that was a feature of his campaign rallies. In an article in the *Guardian* about Trump's fondness for the words "enemy of the people," Emma Graham-Harrison explained how "the phrase was first deployed in a modern political sense during the French Revolution . . . a law was passed in 1794 explicitly targeting 'enemies of the people,' which made crimes including 'spreading false news' punishable by death. Over a century later, Hitler's propagandist Joseph Goebbels and other Nazis would describe Jews and other groups that his government targeted for detention and murder as 'enemies of the people.'" Communist dictators Joseph Stalin of the Soviet Union and Mao Zedong of China also adopted the phrase to delegitimize their critics in the press.

Dramatists had long romanticized the American press as a positive moral force in films such as *The Front Page, All the President's Men,* and, most recently, *Spotlight,* which won the 2016 Academy Award for Best Picture. In June 2019, upon receiving a Tony Award for his performance in the Broadway drama *Network,* Bryan Cranston declared, "I would like to dedicate this to all the real journalists around the world . . . who actually are in the line of fire with their pursuit of the truth. The media is not the enemy of the people. Demoguery is the enemy of the people."

Another artist alarmed by Trump's attacks on journalism was Steven Spielberg, whose oeuvre included several films that depicted an idealized notion of America, including *Lincoln* and *Sav-*

ing *Private Ryan*. A few months before the 2016 election, Spielberg was presented with a script about the *Washington Post's* successful fight against the Nixon administration to publish the Pentagon Papers. Although the director initially passed, Trump's victory and subsequent demonization of the news media caused Spielberg to reverse course and agree to direct *The Post*. He expedited production with a sense of mission that transcended commercial logic. As he explained to *USA Today's* Patrick Ryan, "[T]his wasn't something that could wait three years or two years—this was a story I felt we needed to tell today." Spielberg recruited Tom Hanks to play former *Washington Post* editor Ben Bradlee and Trump's nemesis, Meryl Streep, to play publisher Katharine Graham. In the film's climax, a *Post* staffer quotes from Supreme Court Justice Hugo Black's opinion that affirmed the newspaper's right to publish the Pentagon Papers: "The Founding Fathers gave the free press the protection it must have to fulfill its essential role in our democracy—the press was to serve the governed, not the governors."

For many artists, Trump's victory reflected a broad and sinister authoritarian agenda. David Simon, best known as the creator of the hit HBO show *The Wire*, experienced a similar reversal to Spielberg. During the Obama administration, Simon declined an opportunity to dramatize Philip Roth's novel *The Plot Against America*—which imagined Nazi sympathizer Charles Lindbergh defeating Franklin Roosevelt in 1940 for president—but after the 2016 election, Simon decided to produce a miniseries based on the book. "I only did it because Trump won," Simon told me in 2019. "It had been presented to me during Obama's second term and I passed." After the 2016 election, Simon reread the book "and was impressed by how startlingly prescient it was regarding populism and white nationalism, the sense in which a demagogue could use fear of the other and xenophobia to fashion a political moment. All you have to do is substitute Black and brown people and Muslims for American Jews. Just change the nature of the 'other' and watch a demagogue go to work."

Trump and his allies recognized show business as a populist threat to their worldview. After Trump took office, *Breitbart News* began publishing a daily rebuttal of celebrity activism. In October 2017, a post on the website 4chan commenced the public emergence of a group known as QAnon. Someone with the username "Q" claimed to have access to classified information about a planned coup d'état against Trump by Barack Obama, Hillary Clinton, and George Soros, all of whom Q accused of participating in an international child sex-trafficking ring that included Oprah Winfrey, Ellen DeGeneres, and Tom Hanks. QAnon also accused John Legend and Chrissy Teigen of being part of the evil cabal. As Legend told me, "If you can accuse someone of running a secret pedophile ring and believe that they are actually doing it, then you can justify all kinds of behavior toward them." Trumpists knew who their enemies were.

Although Spielberg worked at breakneck pace to finish *The Post*, the film was not ready for release until 2018. Similarly, *The Plot Against America* miniseries did not air on HBO until early 2020. In the immediate aftermath of Trump's inauguration, artists who were able to make their voices heard the fastest were those who told jokes. Just as music had been the soundtrack of the 1960s civil rights and antiwar movements, comedy became the soundtrack of the Trump era.

In Wanda Sykes's Netflix special, *Not Normal*, she began, "Let me just start by saying: if you voted for Trump and you came to see *me*—you fucked up again! This shit's not normal, y'all . . . The lying, the tweeting, the playdates with dictators . . . This shit is not normal!" (The following year, regarding on an op-ed by an anonymous Trump official that lambasted Trump's Oval Office behavior, Barack Obama indignantly commented, "This is not normal." He used the phrase again while campaigning for Joe Biden in 2020.)

At the 2016 Democratic National Convention, Michelle Obama famously proclaimed, "When they go low, we go high." From a spiritual point of view, it was sound guidance, but after Trump prevailed over Hillary Clinton, some performers understood that, tactically, before they could "go high" they had to stand up to the bully in kind, lest his insults take on a reality of their own.

In George Lopez's comedy special *We'll Do It for Half*, he mocked

Trump's campaign pledge to build a wall along the Mexican border: "Building a wall after eleven million people are in the country—that's like putting on a condom after you fuck." Regarding Trump, Lopez yells, "Fuck him today, fuck him tomorrow, and fuck him three and a half years from now! And if you voted for him, fuck you!"

KATHY GRIFFIN

No performer attracted the rage of the president the way Kathy Griffin did, perhaps because her reality show *My Life on the D-List* had won two Emmys. (Trump often complained that he never won one.) Griffin was fluent in the populist culture of the Kardashians and thus was able to infiltrate tabloid afficionados, a capability that still eluded other left-leaning artist-activists. Much of her humor was in the tradition of insult comics, but she made a distinction between her approach and Trump's: "I punch up. Trump punches down."

Griffin had frequently interacted with Trump over the years, including a guest appearance on *The Celebrity Apprentice*. "I saw him as an over-the-top, fame-hungry, harmless blowhard," Griffin told me. The comedian was horrified as Trump brought his reality show mentality into the White House. "The premise of *The Apprentice* is antithetical to what actually makes a good business. Trump advised the contestants to be as divisive among themselves as possible. That's not how you run an administration. I'm not a historian. I'm not Michael Beschloss—but I know *that!*"

Four months into Trump's presidency, Griffin posted a gag photo on Instagram in which she held up a rubber mask of Donald Trump's face smeared with ketchup—a fantasy of the president's head cut off. Trump's team felt they'd found a fight they could win: destroying the career of a show business critic while intimidating other entertainers in the process.

As Griffin ruefully recalled, "I thought the photo would have a shelf life of two days. I learned that there is such a thing as bad publicity." The photographer leaked the image to the celebrity gossip website TMZ, whose founder, Harvey Levin, subsequently told the *Daily Beast* that he kept in regular touch with Trump, boasting, "I consider myself to be his personal publicist."

The president tweeted: "Kathy Griffin should be ashamed of herself. My children, especially my 11 year old son Barron, are having a hard time with this. Sick!" Melania also chimed in: "As a mother, a wife, and a human being, that photo . . . makes you wonder about the mental health of the person who did it." On Fox News, Sean Hannity called Griffin an ISIS sympathizer, as if the stylized photo was in the same moral universe as actual beheadings.

These attacks were soon followed by a cascade of rejections from mainstream show business. Griffin had twenty-five stand-up performances scheduled in the coming months, but the offers were abruptly pulled because of the supposed risk of violent protest. Each cancellation was reported in real time on TMZ. CNN fired Griffin from her New Year's Eve correspondent gig and reported their decision as "breaking news." Anderson Cooper, who had cohosted the annual celebration with Griffin for years, cravenly tweeted: "I am appalled by the photo shoot Kathy Griffin took part in." Griffin's agency, WME, dropped her as a client.

Trump followers sent death threats to Griffin, her sister (who was in the hospital receiving cancer treatment), and their octogenarian mother. The Justice Department placed the comedian on the No Fly List for two months and formally investigated her for conspiracy to assassinate the president. On *Good Morning America*, Donald Trump Jr. said that "she deserved everything." Griffin complained that the *GMA* host, George Stephanopoulos, "didn't push back at all."

Amid the public onslaught, the embattled comedian earned emotional support from Jim Carrey, who reassured her that "you are going to put it through your Kathy Griffin comedy prism . . . make the story funny and you're gonna go tell it." Indeed, there was a certain amount of cognitive dissonance with Griffin. On the one hand, she was a victim, but on the other, she brilliantly exploited the predicament. By the fall of 2017, Griffin had booked an eighteen-country international tour, despite being on an Interpol notice. She was detained at every airport. "They'd scan my passport. I'd put on my

'I'm not in ISIS's face, but they'd send me into a locked room alone for an indeterminate amount of time. Eventually, I would get my stuff back and, thank God, I didn't have to miss any of my shows."

Yet Griffin's place in Trumpist demonology endured. In 2019, at a Miami event for the pro-Trump super PAC American Priority, a doctored video was shown in which the president's face was superimposed on a scene from the film *Kingsman: The Secret Service*. In it, Trump is depicted brutally murdering his political enemies, including Hillary Clinton, Maxine Waters, and Griffin.

Another performer who attracted Trump's ire was John Legend, whose musicianship and songwriting had made him the only singer to ever win all four major entertainment awards: Emmy, Grammy, Oscar, and Tony. Legend had long seen himself as a socially conscious artist. When he was a fifteen-year-old growing up in Springfield, Ohio, McDonald's launched a contest in which applicants wrote an essay responding to the question, "How do you plan to make Black history?" Legend told me that his essay "basically said I was going to become a successful recording artist and use my success to help make my community better and fight for justice and equality. I've been thinking that I was going to do that since I was a teenager. I was influenced by Stevie Wonder, Marvin Gaye, Aretha Franklin, Nina Simone, Paul Robeson, Harry Belafonte, and all the artists that spoke out against the war. I read about Dr. King, a lot. I read about so many others who struggled for equality and for justice. They were my superheroes. I didn't read comic books; I read books about history makers."

Legend was an early supporter of Obama in 2008 and, in 2014, he and Common wrote and performed the song "Glory" for *Selma*, Ava DuVernay's film about one of Dr. King's most famous civil rights campaigns. Legend and his wife, model and TV star Chrissy Teigen, were appalled when Trump was elected. "Trump literally is the worst person we could imagine being president," Legend said. "We felt even more urgency because he came from the celebrity world. We would see him at events. Chrissy and I always thought he was a joke, always thought he was an idiot, always thought he was full of shit."

In September 2019, Legend appeared in *Justice for All*, a television special hosted by NBC's Lester Holt about mass incarceration. During the special, there was a brief mention about a reform bill Trump had signed that initiated incremental progress but fell far short of remedying America's mass incarceration crisis (the US had more people in prison than any other nation, disproportionately people of color). Legend recalled Trump's reaction: "[He] felt he didn't get enough credit in the conversation. He wanted us to kiss his ass. He thought he had done all that was needed. We didn't acknowledge him much and he was pissed about it. He clearly watched it with one lens, which was, 'How much do they talk about me and how awesome am I?'"

Afterward, Trump tweeted that John Legend was "a boring musician" and referred to Teigen as his "filthy mouthed wife." The next night, James Corden quipped, "Trump has done a lot of work to support criminal justice. He's had half his campaign staff thrown in jail." Stephen Colbert told his audience that Teigen's nickname for Trump, #PresidentPussyAssBitch, was trending. According to Colbert, "[Teigen] just beat Trump at Twitter and nicknames."

THE JIMMY KIMMEL TEST

It was a rare weeknight in 2017 when Jimmy Fallon, Conan O'Brien, Stephen Colbert, James Corden, Seth Meyers, or Trevor Noah did not make fun of the president, but no one actually influenced policy the way Jimmy Kimmel did. Kathy Griffin survived Trump, but Kimmel helped beat him on an issue that mattered to millions of Americans.

When ABC began airing *Jimmy Kimmel Live* in 2003, the show was virtually apolitical. When Kimmel performed at the 2012 White House Correspondents' Association dinner, most of the routine was politically tame, though it did have one prophetic moment: "Last year at this time—in fact, on this very weekend—we finally delivered justice to one of the world's most notorious individuals." It seemed as if he was alluding to the killing of Osama Bin Laden, but the gag paid off when a photo of Trump was projected behind Kimmel. The jab was a reference to Barack Obama's dis at the previous correspondents' dinner, when Trump was peddling the "birther" theory that Obama wasn't born in the United States and, thus, didn't qualify to be president.

In 2013, Kimmel broadcast a bit in which he asked people on the street whether they preferred "Obamacare" or "the Affordable Care Act." The point was that even though these were two different names for the same law, if people liked Obama they said they preferred Obamacare and if they didn't they said the Affordable Care Act. By satirizing this issue, Kimmel suggested that both parties cared more about tribal identity than actual policy. (Jay Leno had broadcast a similar bit when the ACA first passed.)

Yet it was only when Trump emerged as the frontrunner for the Republican presidential nomination that Kimmel truly showed his political leanings. One night, Kimmel's guests Nathan Lane and Matthew Broderick reprised their roles as Max Bialystock and Leo Bloom in *The Producers*. Instead of playing Broadway impresarios, however, the pair pretended to be political consultants who chose to back a candidate guaranteed to lose: Donald Trump. Lane called Trump "a real train wreck, a schmuck, a putz, a grade-A, world-class, gold-plated nincompoop." As was the case in the original musical, the supposedly sure loser turned out to be a winner.

However, nothing could have prepared Kimmel's audience for the comedian's monologue on May 1, 2017. Normally lighthearted and jovial, Kimmel choked back tears as he described his son Billy's emergency open-heart surgery, which had been successfully performed right after his birth the previous week. At the time, congressional Republicans continued to call for the repeal of the Affordable Care Act. With Trump in the White House, a united Republican Party could eliminate the law. But in the years since its passage, Obamacare had become very popular. As Kimmel explained, "Before 2014, if you were born with a congenital heart disease, like my son was, there was a good chance you'd never be able to get health insurance because you had a preexisting condition . . . If your baby is going to die . . . it shouldn't matter how much money you make. I think that's something that whether you're a Republican or a Democrat, or something else, we all agree on that, right? . . . We need to make sure that the people who are supposed to represent us, the people who are meeting about this right now in Washington, understand that very clearly. Let's stop with the nonsense—this isn't football. There are no teams. We are the team, it's the United States. Don't let their partisan squabbles divide us on something every decent person wants." Over the next several days, more than ten million people viewed Kimmel's monologue on YouTube, far more than had viewed any newscast.

Republican senator Bill Cassidy announced that he would only vote for a bill that would pass the "Jimmy Kimmel test." A week later, Cassidy was a guest on the show and Kimmel said to him, "Since I *am* Jimmy Kimmel, I would like to make a suggestion as to what the Jimmy Kimmel test should be. I'll keep it simple. The Jimmy Kimmel test, I think, should be: No family should be denied medical care, emergency or otherwise, because they can't afford it." Under the glare of the TV lights, the senator agreed.

Yet several months later, a Senate bill to repeal Obamacare, co-authored by Cassidy and Lindsay Graham, failed to protect those with conditions like Kimmel's son. The comedian angrily complained that Cassidy had "lied right to my face" and joked that the Republican bill would pass a different Jimmy Kimmel test: "With this one, your child with a preexisting condition will get the care he needs—if, and only if, his father is Jimmy Kimmel. Otherwise, you might be screwed." He earnestly concluded that "health care is complicated. It's boring. I don't want to talk about it, the details are confusing and that's what these guys are relying on." Kimmel posted the Senate switchboard number on screen and urged his audience to call Washington and tell members of Congress to reject this "scam" of a bill. "Let them know that this bill doesn't pass *your* test."

A *New York Times* article labeled Kimmel "the unlikely face of opposition." On the NPR show *All Things Considered*, host Michel Martin observed, "Kimmel is coming across as the honest broker because he doesn't really stand to directly benefit from this. He's picking a fight with legislators. He's not necessarily going to get anything out of it. It's an example of how a media figure with a certain constituency can make arguments with the persuasiveness that maybe like pundits who are, you know, perceived to be too liberally biased or whatever, they might not have the same impact."

In a Public Policy poll conducted in September 2017, voters said that they trusted Jimmy Kimmel over congressional Republicans by a margin of 42–34 percent. Ultimately, the Trump-supported bill was defeated when Senator John McCain cast the decisive vote against it, and the Affordable Care Act, with its protections for those with preexisting conditions, was preserved.

Days later, at a rally, Trump called Colbert, Fallon, and Kimmel "lowlifes," "lost souls," and "terrible." In response, Colbert and Fallon teamed up in a taped segment that opened both *The Late Show* and *The Tonight Show*. The bit began with Colbert seated behind a computer working on a monologue, when a video call from Fallon comes in. "Hey, lowlife," Fallon said, to which Colbert responded jovially, "Hey, lost soul. What are you up to?" Barely suppressing a grin, Fallon replied, "Mostly whimpering."

CHAPTER 3
BLACK TALENT MATTERS

The fact that America's first Black president was succeeded by a guy who courted white nationalist support was impossible for socially conscious artists to ignore. As Stephen Colbert told *Vanity Fair*, "Our own sense of the purpose of America [has gotten] lost." Bill Maher told his HBO audience, "It's certainly not true to say that all Republicans are racist." Brandishing his trademark smirk, Maher then added, "But if you're a racist, you're probably a Republican."

Trump was not the only celebrity to have migrated from entertainment to politics. Following a successful career as an actress, Whoopi Goldberg had been the moderator and cohost of the most widely watched American daytime television talk show, *The View*, since the fall of 2007. In addition to hosting a variety of celebrity guests, *The View* regularly featured political arguments among its panelists, whose ideologies ranged from Joy Behar's brand of sixties liberalism to Meghan McCain's traditional conservatism. Obama appeared on the show before and after becoming president. Trump was a guest on *The View* eighteen times prior to his presidency, including a notorious 2006 appearance with his daughter, when he told Goldberg, "You know if Ivanka weren't my daughter, perhaps I'd be dating her."

In a 2013 appearance, Trump trotted out the theory that Obama was not born in the US, to which Goldberg responded, "[That's] the biggest pile of dog mess I've heard in ages." Two years later, as Trump was test-driving the anti-immigrant rhetoric he would soon orient his presidential campaign around, Goldberg confronted him again: "I just want to be clear: not every Mexican American is a rapist or murderer." Yet there was often a weird camaraderie with the hosts, as if they were all just entertainers putting on a show. Trump even told Goldberg he loved her after one of these segments. In 2018, after playing a montage of the president's many earlier appearances on *The View*, Goldberg lamented, "The person he became once he was running . . . is not the person that I knew."

During the last years of the Obama administration, several African American auteurs developed films that helped provide a counternarrative to America's racist toxins. The resulting movies took on an even greater meaning when they were released after Trump occupied the White House.

Jordan Peele's *Get Out* premiered at festivals in early 2017. An independently produced feature film with a $4.5 million budget, *Get Out* was a phenomenal success, grossing more than $250 million. It received four Academy Award nominations, including Best Original Screenplay (which Peele won).

The film marked the thirty-eight-year-old Peele's directorial debut and transformed him from a popular sketch comic to a cultural thought leader. He had initially emerged as a public figure a dozen years earlier, as a *Mad TV* cast member. Later, he costarred in his own sketch comedy series, *Key & Peele*, on which he periodically impersonated President Obama. Peele also created gag videos with Obama's likeness saying funny things, in an early and benign use of deepfake technology.

Get Out is a hybrid of the horror and satire genres. The protagonist, Chris Washington (played by Daniel Kaluuya), is a Black photographer meeting his white girlfriend Rose's family for the first time. Driving to her parents' place, the couple is pulled over by a cop. Rose is outraged but Chris restrains her. (The message is clear: arguing with cops is a privilege reserved for white people.) The next day at Rose's parents' house, dozens of wealthy white people arrive for a party. Some of them patronizingly express admiration for Chris's physique and for Black celebrities like Tiger Woods. There is only one African American among these guests, a man named Logan King (LaKeith Stanfield), who is married to an older white woman. He has a haunted look on his face and when Chris tries to photograph him and the flash goes off, Logan becomes hysterical, shouting at Chris to "get out" in a tone of desperate warning. Unconvinced by assurances that Logan merely had an epileptic attack, Chris tries to leave. But Rose's mom, Missy (Catherine Keener), is a hypnotist and she renders Chris unconscious with a "trigger" word she implanted in him the night before.

Chris awakens strapped to a chair in the basement and is forced to watch a video that explains what's really going on: Rose's family transplants their brains into Black bodies, granting them preferred physical characteristics and a twisted form of immortality that destroys Black souls. Missy attempts hypnosis to prepare him for this dreadful surgery, but Chris is able to escape.

Another African American auteur, Boots Riley, made his directorial debut in 2018 with *Sorry to Bother You*, a hybrid of horror, satire, and magic realism. Riley's script also added a political subtext that balances observations about racism with a sharp focus on the perils of unrestrained capitalism. In the film, a young African American man named Cassius "Cash" Green (LaKeith Stanfield) obtains a job as a telemarketer for a fictitious company named RegalView. An older coworker, played by Danny Glover, teaches him to use his "white voice," a gimmick that Cash quickly masters. Promoted to work in the luxurious "Power Caller suite," Cash's new job is to sell labor from a corporate division known as WorryFree, whose ubiquitous TV ads offer desperate people room and board in return for a lifetime of work as indentured servants.

Cash is invited to a party hosted by WorryFree's intimidating CEO, Steve Lift (Armie Hammer). When Cash goes to a bathroom in the boss's mansion, he is accosted by a grotesque half-horse, half-human hybrid who begs for help.

Trying to calm the freaked-out Cash, Lift explains that Worry-

Free makes their workers stronger (i.e., more profitable) by transforming them into "equisapiens" via a gene-modifying powder. Cash refuses a $100 million offer to become an equisapien and instead accepts a position posing as a mock revolutionary to keep the employees in line.

Cash records the creature's plea on his cell phone and gets the video broadcast on a popular TV show. Yet the strategy backfires. The equisapiens are hailed as a groundbreaking scientific advancement, and WorryFree's stock skyrockets to an all-time high. After various plot twists, however, Cash frees several equisapiens and they attack Lift, eventually killing the demonic billionaire.

Spike Lee's *BlacKkKlansman* was also released in 2018. Based on the memoir by former cop Ron Stallworth (played by John David Washington), it is set in the 1970s in Colorado Springs. The plot follows Stallworth, the first African American detective in the city's police department, and his white partner (Adam Driver) as they infiltrate and expose the local Ku Klux Klan chapter. Topher Grace plays national Klan leader David Duke, who in real life enthusiastically supported Trump's runs for president. Having been nominated four times in the past for Academy Awards, Spike Lee finally won his first Oscar for Best Adapted Screenplay. At the end of his acceptance speech, Lee pointedly noted that the 2020 elections were "just around the corner." He then evoked the title of the film that had made him famous (and which Barack and Michelle Obama had seen on their first date): "Do the right thing."

Boots Riley posted a long critique of *BlacKkKlansman* on Twitter, in which he wrote that although Lee had been an inspiration to him in the past, he had issues with the new film because "attacks and terrorizing due to racism" were a problem "not just from White cops. From Black cops too. So for Spike to come out with a movie where story points are fabricated in order [to] make [a] Black cop and his counterparts look like allies in the fight against racism is really disappointing, to put it very mildly." Lee gave a measured response: "Look at my films: they've been very critical of the police, but on the other hand I'm never going to say all police are corrupt, that all police hate people of color. I'm not going to say that."

George Tillman Jr.'s film *The Hate U Give* (based on Angie Thomas's best-selling novel), also released in 2018, centers around an African American teenager, Starr Carter (Amandla Stenberg), who witnesses the police killing of her best friend from childhood and then organizes protests to combat the murder's cover-up.

The most impactful indictment of racism in the justice system during the Trump years was a four-part Netflix miniseries, *When They See Us*, directed by Ava DuVernay, whose previous credits included *Selma*, a historical drama about Dr. King's leadership during a pivotal moment of the Civil Rights Movement, and the documentary *13th*, about the pervasive racism in the prison-industrial complex.

When They See Us dramatizes the travails of the "Central Park Five," a group of African American and Latino teenagers who'd been coerced into giving false confessions that led to their wrongful convictions. In 1989, they were falsely accused of brutally raping and beating a young white woman who became known as the "Central Park jogger." Thirteen years later, the five young men were exonerated by DNA evidence that proved the crimes were committed by a man who then admitted he was the lone culprit. The "Five" were released by the New York Supreme Court, where they soon filed a civil lawsuit against New York City for malicious prosecution, racial discrimination, and emotional distress. The case was finally settled in 2014 for $41 million.

When They See Us touches on the news media's demonization of Black males, the tendency of corrupt prosecutors and police officers to bend the rules to achieve politically expedient results, and the way that some elected officials pander to the public mood du jour (Ed Koch, the mayor of New York City when the rape occurred, called it "the crime of the century").

Integral to the drama was the role of Donald Trump, who whipped up racist hysteria when he was a real estate developer in search of celebrity status. He bought full-page ads in New York newspapers headlined, "Bring Back the Death Penalty. Bring Back Our Police!" *When They See Us* uses actual footage of Trump embracing the idea of "hating" accused criminals and suggesting that it was an advantage, not a disadvantage, to be Black in America in the late eighties.

Critics of the resistance to Trump's presidency would sometimes refer to "Trump derangement syndrome." Trumpists accused liberal elites of condescension to people who were not cosmopolitan or highly educated. DuVernay's focus on Trump's behavior during the Central Park Five trial was a reminder that the soul of the resistance was rooted in a moral opposition to the substance of Trump's career, not his style. Even after the five young men were legally exonerated, Trump would not admit that he had been wrong to call for their executions.

The film with a racial subtext that reached the largest audience in the Trump years was the opposite of docudrama. *Black Panther* was the latest in a series of box office blockbusters based on Marvel Comics characters. The film was directed by the thirty-year-old Ryan Coogler, whose debut film *Fruitvale Station* was based on the 2009 police shooting of a young unarmed African American man at an Oakland train station. *Fruitvale Station* starred Michael B. Jordan, who was also a lead actor in *Black Panther*. Chadwick Boseman played T'Challa, who had been introduced to filmgoers in a previous Marvel blockbuster, *Captain America: Civil War*. *Black Panther* grossed $700 million in North America, making it the highest-grossing film of 2018 and the fourth highest all-time.

Although most of *Black Panther* occurs on a planet known as Wakanda, which is populated solely by Black people, there is a crucial subplot revolving around Oakland, California. The film's primary subtext operates on two levels. First, the mere existence of Black superheroes was a big deal. Comic book blockbusters carried a distinctive cultural power that gave *Black Panther* a unique resonance. The other level is the radical value system of the Wakandan leaders, who eschewed colonialism even though they possessed weapons that enabled them to conquer other countries. In a scene shown at the end of the film, T'Challa appears before the United Nations to reveal this aspect of Wakanda's nature.

There was another major film in the Trump years that dealt with race relations, *Green Book*, whose white director, Peter Farrelly, was previously known for commercial comedies such as *Dumb and Dumber* and *There's Something About Mary*. *Green Book* was based on the real-life relationship between the African American pianist Dr. Don Shirley (Mahershala Ali) and his driver (Viggo Mortensen). To its admirers, *Green Book* was an emotionally satisfying exploration of racism in the American South in the early 1960s. The film was none-theless criticized by members of Shirley's family, who felt that, among its many alleged inaccuracies, it exaggerated the role of the driver. Some critics felt that *Green Book* reinforced the liberal Hollywood cliché of Black characters who are reliant on white saviors. Among Academy Award voters, the film's admirers outnumbered its critics; *Green Book* won Best Picture in 2018.

There were also several series on cable and streaming services that dramatized African American life during Trump's presidency, including *The Chi*, *Dear White People*, and *Black-ish*. *Watchmen*, which premiered on HBO in 2019, was based on a DC Comics series of the same name, and its first episode depicted the real-life 1921 massacre of Tulsa's Black Wall Street. *Watchmen* would gain renewed relevance in 2020 in the wake of Trump's choice of Tulsa as the location for his first rally after the murder of George Floyd.

THE REAL SLIM SHADY

A number of white artists also addressed America's racial divisions during the Trump administration. Kathryn Bigelow directed *Detroit*, a film about the infamous 1967 riot (some called it a rebellion) that was triggered by the police killing of an African American man. Chelsea Handler, whose career had been defined by raunchy stand-up comedy, was so devastated by Trump's presidential victory that she shifted her efforts into the political realm, producing and starring in a Netflix documentary that explored white privilege.

In Trump's first year in office, America's most successful white rapper also felt a need to weigh in. Like Whoopi Goldberg, Eminem had previously associated himself with Trump. In 2004, Trump had appeared on an Eminem television special to "endorse" the artist for a fictional political run for office. Standing at a podium with a title card identifying him as "Chairman of the Joint Chiefs of Cash,"

Trump introduced the "candidate" during the fictitious Shady National Convention. "Slim Shady is a winner. He's got brains, he's got guts, and he's got Donald Trump's vote."

Thirteen years later, in October 2017, Eminem performed "The Storm" at the BET Hip Hop Awards. In it, he made clear that he no longer wanted any association with Trump. The song included the lines: "But better give Obama props / 'Cause what we got in office now is a kamikaze that'll probably cause a nuclear holocaust . . . And any fan of mine who's a supporter of his, I'm drawing in the sand a line / You're either for or against." Eminem also praised a frequent Trump target, Colin Kaepernick, who had been effectively barred from the NFL because of his practice of kneeling during the national anthem to protest police violence against unarmed African Americans. After the BET broadcast, Kaepernick tweeted, "I appreciate you @Eminem," and attached a fist emoji.

On his album *Revival*, which was released shortly after the broadcast, Eminem referred to Trump as a racist and a Nazi. On one track, he concocted a fantasy of being "framed" for murdering Ivanka Trump. TMZ, the celebrity website that played a pivotal role in Kathy Griffin's travails, sent the lyrics to the Secret Service, who investigated Eminem. *BuzzFeed* printed excerpts from Secret Service documents in which the agency characterized Eminem as "exhibiting inappropriate behavior" and claimed that he "threatens protectee."

On his subsequent album, *Kamikaze*, Eminem offered his version of events on the track "The Ringer": "Agent Orange just sent the Secret Service / To meet in person to see if I really think of hurtin' him / Or ask if I'm linked to terrorists / I said, 'Only when it comes to ink and lyricists.'"

RESISTANCE CONTRARIANS

No account of race relations in show business during this era would be complete without referencing Trump's two highest-profile celebrity supporters: Kanye West and Roseanne Barr.

West was one of the most talented and influential musical performers of his generation. The winner of twenty-one Grammy

Awards and one of the best-selling artists of the twenty-first century, his talent was admired by most of his peers in the pop, R&B, and hip-hop worlds. His fame transcended music due to his success in the fashion industry, his marriage to Kim Kardashian, his Christian faith, his open discussion of his bipolar disorder, and his propensity for political controversy.

West made headlines in 2005 when he harshly criticized George W. Bush for his response to Hurricane Katrina, saying on national TV, "George Bush doesn't care about Black people." Thus, it was a shock when West endorsed Trump for president in 2016. John Legend, who had worked closely with West on several records, texted him, "Hey it's JL. I hope you'll reconsider aligning yourself with Trump. You're way too powerful and influential to endorse who he is and what he stands for. As you know, what you say really means something to your fans. They are loyal to you and respect your opinion. So many people who love you feel so betrayed right now because they know the harm that Trump's policies cause, especially to people of color. Don't let this be part of your legacy. You're the greatest artist of our generation." West pointedly responded: "I love you John and I appreciate your thoughts. You bringing up my fans or my legacy is a tactic based on fear used to manipulate my free thought."

Legend told me, "I don't see Kanye as a political person at all. We never talked about politics. He had never voted before 2020." Legend speculated that West's endorsement of the president might have been because "he saw in Trump the kind of underdog narcissist that he sees in himself."

Shortly after the election, on December 13, 2016, West met with Trump. Afterward, he explained that he "wanted . . . to discuss multicultural issues . . . [including] bullying, supporting teachers, modernizing curriculums, and violence in Chicago. I feel it is important to have a direct line of communication with our future president if we truly want change." West subsequently posted a picture of himself wearing a red hat embroidered with Trump's campaign slogan, Make America Great Again (MAGA). He then published a series of tweets defending Trump, who promptly retweeted them.

In May 2018, West told radio host Charlamagne tha God that he had been asked by friends, "What makes George Bush any more racist than Trump?" to which West replied, "Racism isn't the deal breaker for me. If that was the case, I wouldn't live in America."

Not long thereafter, Kim Kardashian visited the White House to advocate for criminal sentencing reform. It was reported that she helped spur a presidential pardon for a sixty-three-year-old woman who was sentenced to life in prison in 1996 on charges related to cocaine possession and money laundering.

On October 11, 2018, West visited the White House wearing a MAGA hat, which he said made him feel "like Superman." He gave a ten-minute monologue in which he concluded, "Trump is on his hero's journey right now." As the *New York Times* observed, "All the while, Mr. Trump sat with his hands clasped on the Resolute Desk, nodding along as the musician continued." Although West was widely criticized for the visit, his music remained popular and widely respected.

Roseanne Barr's infatuation with Trump did her far more professional harm than West's did. Several decades earlier, ABC had created the sitcom *Roseanne*, in which Barr played Roseanne Connor, the mother of a working-class family struggling to get by on a limited household income. Roseanne, her husband Dan (John Goodman), and her sister Jackie (Laurie Metcalf) live in the drab fictional exurb of Lanford, Illinois. The show was one of the first sitcoms to realistically portray a blue-collar American family with both parents working outside the home. It was also a trailblazer in introducing a gay character in a network TV series (Roseanne's friend Nancy Bartlett, played by Sandra Bernhard). From 1988–1997, *Roseanne* was a huge hit; in 2002, *TV Guide* ranked the series thirty-fifth on its list of the "50 Greatest TV Shows of All Time."

In 2018, ABC revived *Roseanne* with most of the original cast. Roseanne Conner was now a Trump supporter (Roseanne Barr also supported Trump in 2016), while Jackie had voted for Green Party candidate Jill Stein. With the kind of clever writing that had made the show a hit the first time around, the new iteration of *Roseanne* had the potential to be a Trump-era comedy well-suited to explore

America's cultural divide, similar to how *All in the Family* did in the 1970s. The rebooted series premiered on March 27, 2018, to an audience of more than twenty-seven million people, making it the most popular network TV show in many years. Trump congratulated Barr on her great ratings.

The triumph was short lived. Two months later, Barr posted a message on Twitter reading, "Muslim brotherhood & planet of the apes had a baby=vj." The initials "vj" referred to Valerie Jarrett, who served as a high-profile assistant to President Obama during his eight years in office. *Planet of the Apes* was a cult movie in 1968 when Barr was a teenager and it spawned eight subsequent films and two TV series. Based on the 1963 satirical French novel *La planète des singes* by Pierre Boulle, all iterations of the *Planet of the Apes* franchise revolved around a race of intelligent apes who want to conquer humans. They are animals and they are the enemy. Barr's reference to the Muslim Brotherhood, a group that originated in Egypt, was evidently a stand-in for the right-wing libel that Obama and the people around him were somehow aligned with Islamic enemies of the United States. In a single tweet, Barr had smeared Obama's former aide as both an animal and a terrorist.

Within hours, Wanda Sykes, a consulting producer on the reboot of *Roseanne*, announced that she was quitting the show. The series' executive producer, Bruce Helford, said he was "personally horrified and saddened" by Barr's remarks. Sara Gilbert called her costar's remarks "abhorrent" and not reflective of the "beliefs of our cast and crew or anyone associated with our show." Channing Dungey, the president of ABC Entertainment Group at the time, had the last word, announcing, "Roseanne's Twitter statement is abhorrent, repugnant, and inconsistent with our values, and we have decided to cancel her show."

ABC was a division of the Walt Disney Company and, as *New York Times* media reporter John Koblin explained, "For Disney, there was more at stake than a hit show. The company has been widely praised in recent years as a leader in efforts to combat racial stereotypes through its movies and TV series, whether on *Doc McStuffins*, a Disney Channel cartoon about an African American girl who wants to be a doctor; *How to Get Away with Murder*, a vehicle for Viola Davis that led her to become the first Black woman to win a lead-actress Emmy; and *Black Panther*, which proved that movies rooted in Black culture and with predominantly Black casts could become global blockbusters."

Even big pharma didn't want to be associated with the infamous tweet. When Roseanne apologized, she said that she had written the tweet while addled on the sleeping pill Ambien. The pharmaceutical company issued a tart statement: "Racism is not a side effect [of Ambien]."

In 1947, while socialists were forced out of show business, racist and sexist powerbrokers were not hindered by their words or actions. In the Trump era, the dynamic was reversed. From a progressive point of view, this was a significant improvement, but attaining the right balance between freedom of speech and opposition to bigotry was still a work in progress. In a Netflix special, Dave Chappelle lamented that it was a "dangerous time to be a comedian."

CHAPTER 4
SORRY, NOT SORRY

ME TOO

After a campaign during which his misogyny was gleefully on vivid display, Trump won the White House by defeating the first woman nominated for president by a major party. Three months into Trump's term, in April 2017, Hulu launched a series based on Margaret Atwood's novel *The Handmaid's Tale*, which depicts a dystopian world where women are relegated to the role of breeders and servants by a totalitarian government. (The book was first published in 1985 at the peak of Reagan's popularity.) The presence of Elizabeth Moss as the star of the *The Handmaid's Tale*, combined with the book's cult status, guaranteed the series a significant level of media attention, but the fact that it premiered while Trump was in the White House gave the grim fantasy an unsettling relevance.

Powerful men taking sexual advantage of subordinate women was as pervasive an issue in American show business as racism. The issue belatedly boiled over in October 2017, when the *New York Times* and the *New Yorker* both reported that more than a dozen women had accused the legendary film producer and studio executive Harvey Weinstein of sexual harassment and rape. Rosanna Arquette was among the most vocal of Weinstein's victims, providing information to Ronan Farrow that would help flesh out his *New Yorker* piece and connect him with several other women. She accompanied Farrow to the luncheon at which he was awarded the 2018 Pulitzer Prize for Public Service.

Within weeks, Weinstein was fired from his production company. The Los Angeles Police Department opened a criminal investigation for alleged rape, and the police departments in New York and London began investigating similar allegations against him. It was an unprecedented fall from grace for an executive of that stature.

The following week, actress Alyssa Milano posted on Twitter: "If all the women who have been sexually harassed or assaulted wrote 'Me too' as a status, we might give people a sense of the magnitude of the problem." (The phrase was coined in 2006 by activist Tarana Burke.) Within twenty-four hours, "Me Too" appeared twelve million times on various social media platforms.

In the days after Milano's tweet, several high-profile actresses, including Gwyneth Paltrow, Uma Thurman, Rose McGowan, and Jennifer Lawrence, followed up on the suggestion and shared the powerful message: Me too. The two-word phrase soon became a ubiquitous feminist creed.

Born in Brooklyn in 1972, Milano appeared in a touring company of the musical *Annie* when she was seven years old. At the age of eleven, she was cast as Tony Danza's daughter in the sitcom *Who's the Boss?*, a part that she played for the next eight years. Subsequently, she starred in the fantasy drama series *Charmed* from 1998–2006.

Milano's activism began when she was fifteen and met Ryan White, a teenager who had contracted AIDS through a blood transfusion. Together they appeared on *The Phil Donahue Show* and Milano gave White an on-camera kiss to prove that the disease could not be spread that way. She later became a Goodwill Ambassador for UNICEF and, in 2016, endorsed Bernie Sanders in the presidential primaries and Hillary Clinton in the general election. By the beginning of 2017, Milano had 3.7 million Twitter followers. In April 2019, she started a podcast called *Sorry Not Sorry*. Joe Biden was one of the show's first guests.

Over the next several months, in the wake of Weinstein's disgrace, powerful men whose careers ended or were significantly curtailed via sexual misconduct allegations included *Today Show* host Matt Lauer, *60 Minutes* cohost Charlie Rose, CBS chairman Les Moonves, and performers Kevin Spacey and Louis C.K. In October 2018, Bill Cosby, who had been accused of rape by multiple women, was convicted of drugging and sexually assaulting Andrea Constand, a crime for which he would receive a three-to-ten-year prison sentence.

The Me Too movement was a response to decades during which many powerful men paid little or no price for sexual abuse, but it was no coincidence that the breakthrough occurred in the context of the outrage of millions of women that Hillary Clinton had been deprived of the presidency by a misogynist who got fewer popular votes than she did. In the 2020 premiere of *The Good Fight*'s third season, the show's liberal protagonist, Diane Lockhart (played by Christine Baranski), has a lifelike dream in which Hillary Clinton actually had won the 2016 election. In that imaginary universe, in which women didn't have the pain over Hillary's loss, the Me Too movement never happened and Weinstein remained a powerful mogul despite his predatory behavior.

Women had long struggled in Hollywood to obtain equal pay and access to positions of power, yet some progress was made during the Trump years. There were several TV series starring and produced by women, including Reese Witherspoon's *Big Little Lies*, Jane Fonda and Lily Tomlin's *Grace and Frankie*, Issa Rae's *Insecure*, and Phoebe Waller-Bridge's *Fleabag*.

In 2017, the blockbuster comic book saga *Wonder Woman* was released, starring Gal Gadot in the title role. It was directed by Patty Jenkins and grossed over $400 million in the United States, the highest-grossing film ever by a female director and the most successful film about a female superhero.

One non-superhero feminist also received the attention of filmmakers around this time. In 2018, Supreme Court Justice Ruth Bader Ginsburg was the subject of two films: the drama *On the Basis of Sex*, which starred Felicity Jones as a young Ginsburg, and the Oscar-nominated documentary *RBG*.

RUSSIA

In the 1960s, there were a few films that depicted Russians as classic bad guys, such as the James Bond film *From Russia with Love*. But Hollywood just as frequently satirized the Cold War in films like *The Russians Are Coming, the Russians Are Coming* and in the animated show *The Adventures of Rocky and Bullwinkle and Friends*, in which the hapless villains were Russian spies named Boris Badenov and Natasha Fatale. The most celebrated satire of the Cold War was *Dr. Strangelove*, which was released in 1964 and starred the British comedic genius Peter Sellers, who played three separate roles. Directed by Stanley Kubrick, the film's plot centers around a right-wing general played by Sterling Hayden, who, despite lacking legal authority, launches a preemptive nuclear attack on the Soviet Union.

I was not the only baby boomer for whom the film was a major touchstone. Al Franken recalled that he "grew up thinking there was a pretty good chance I'd die in a nuclear inferno. *Strangelove* came out in January 1964, when I was twelve, just fourteen months after the Cuban missile crisis. This is the movie that made me realize what satire is and how powerful and friggin' funny it could be and inspired me to write and perform satire. Peter Sellers . . . became my hero."

In June 2017, as many in the resistance were preoccupied with Trump's affinity for Vladimir Putin, Showtime aired a series of interviews that Oliver Stone conducted with the Russian leader, one of which revolved around a screening of *Dr. Strangelove* (Putin had not previously seen it). David Swanson described Putin's humorless reaction in the *Foreign Policy Journal:* "He says the problem depicted in the film, the risk of nuclear holocaust, is accurate but more dangerous now than when the movie was made."

To much of the resistance, Russia was now irrevocably tied to Trump. In October 2016, the British documentarian Adam Curtis released *HyperNormalisation*, a film about how propaganda affects political culture. The film focuses on how Russia fomented despair and cynicism as tools to maintain power. Curtis presciently singled out Trump as an American who had mastered the art of personal and corporate branding.

Several Hollywood creatives, including music producer T Bone Burnett and *The Big Short* director Adam McKay, became ardent admirers of Curtis after watching his 2002 documentary series *The Century of the Self*, which connected post-9/11 political propaganda with the methods used by Sigmund Freud's nephew, Edward Bernays, to create public support for World War I. Kanye West also voiced his enthusiasm for Curtis, tweeting a link to *The Century of the Self* with the note: "It's 4 hours long but you'll get the gist in the first twenty minutes." Curtis's dark view of how government could manufacture consent in a supposedly free society seemed, in retrospect, like a primer for Trump's political rise.

The FX drama series *The Americans*, which was conceived by former CIA officer Joseph Weisberg, aired its final two seasons during Trump's first eighteen months in office. The show takes place in Washington, DC, during the 1980s when Reagan was president. The plot revolves around two characters (played by Keri Russell and Matthew Rhys) who are sent by the Soviet Union to live in the United States and pose as an American couple in order to carry out espionage against the US. The real-life context of the Trump–Russia drama gave the fictional version of the eighties a weirdly contemporary echo. At the core of the drama is the conflict between personal morality and adherence to the dictates of an intimidating immoral government.

The comedy series *Veep*, starring Julia Louis-Dreyfus as Vice President Selina Meyer, began its run at the end of Obama's first term and ended during the first eighteen months of Trump's presidency. Billy Kimball, one of *Veep's* writers and producers, told me, "We were shooting a script I'd written about Selina inadvertently interfering in an election in the Republic of Georgia when Trump was elected. It was surreal, to put it mildly."

The final season of *Veep* depicts Selina's run for president, a campaign in which she is aided by the Chinese government. Although many fans considered this story line to be a commentary on how the Russians may have aided Trump, Kimball insists that the effect of the news media coverage of Trump's relationship with Russia actually restrained the *Veep* writers from mimicking it: "The more the Russia thing became known, the more we became worried that people would think that's what we were winking at."

After former FBI director Robert Mueller was named as special counsel to investigate Russian interference in the 2016 election, many Democrats, anti-Trump pundits, and progressive artists naively pinned their hopes on what would eventually be known as "the Mueller report." Yet when the report was finally released in 2019, it was densely written and confounded headline writers. Despite Mueller identifying multiple instances of obstruction of justice and not ruling out Trump's complicity in Russia's election interference, the report was preemptively distorted by Attorney General William Barr, who falsely implied that Mueller's findings exonerated Trump. House Democrats did their best to reposition the narrative in televised committee hearings, but they were unsophisticated when it came to dramatizing the report's nuances in a way that most Americans could readily understand.

To help spread the word about the Mueller report's actual findings, Rob Reiner directed a video that was narrated by Robert De Niro, who had recently impersonated Mueller on *SNL*. The video, which was distributed by the website NowThis, featured former prosecutors opining that the evidence justified an indictment of the president for obstruction of justice. In another effort to clarify the report's findings, playwright Robert Schenkkan livestreamed *The Investigation: A Search for the Truth in Ten Acts* at Manhattan's Riverside Church, a live reading of excerpts from the Mueller report. Annette Bening narrated the transitions, Kevin Kline played Mueller, Michael Shannon played Don McGahn, Alfre Woodard played Hope Hicks, Joel Grey played Jeff Sessions, Alyssa Milano played Trump's attorney Jay Sekulow, and Jason Alexander played Chris Christie. The performance opened with Trump (played by John Lithgow) meeting then-FBI director James Comey (Justin Long) over dinner. Trump tells Comey, "I need loyalty!" Comey carefully answers, "You will always get honesty from me," to which Trump responds, "That's what I want: honest loyalty," which got a big laugh from the live audience, one more laugh than the actual hearings had generated.

In the *New York Times* review of the show, James Poniewozik compared Jason Alexander's performance as Chris Christie to the character he played on *Seinfeld:* "In Mr. Alexander's mouth, Mr. Christie's prediction that the investigation of Michael Flynn would stick to the administration 'like gum on the bottom of your shoe' recalls George Costanza saying that the sea was angry, like an old man trying to send back a bowl of soup."

SUBTERRANEAN DREAMS OF THE MODERATES

Parallel to the twenty-four-hour news cycle, the slower-moving but subterranean river of art still occupied a sizable space in the minds of the public. The FX series *American Horror Story: Cult* melded art and politics when making an explicit reference to the Trump administration. In the 2017 season premiere, Trump wins the presidency and a group of clowns begins murdering people.

There was still a large network TV audience that embraced narratives of liberal orthodoxy. On December 8, 2019, the CBS series *Madam Secretary* aired its series finale, which, for the most part, the mainstream press either ignored or patronized. The political drama starred Téa Leoni as Secretary of State Elizabeth McCord and Keith Carradine as the president who appoints her. In the show's final season, McCord is elected America's first female president. In an affectionate farewell, Margaret Lyons of the *New York Times* called *Madam Secretary* "one of the least-hip of shows on TV."

In its ongoing mission to demonize Hollywood, *Breitbart* often linked to the "conservative" website MRC, whose slogan was "Exposing and Combating Liberal Media Bias." MRC published three separate attack pieces about *Madam Secretary* during its final season, beginning with the snarky exhortation, "Liberals rejoice! Your dream of a Hillary Clinton presidency is finally coming true."

Despite the increasingly fragmented television playing field, old-school networks remained a surprisingly big fragment. At its peak, *Madam Secretary* was seen by over fourteen million viewers a week, which was almost triple the number of people who watched the highest-rated cable news programs. Although a fictional series about Washington was not "news," in a country where a large percentage of voters made decisions based on emotions, a drama that directly addressed political issues was part of the mosaic that formed contemporary mythology. *Madam Secretary*'s creator, Barbara Hall, agreed with my assumption that a large part of the show's audience consisted of older, educated suburban females responsible for Nancy Pelosi regaining the position of speaker of the House in 2019. When creating *Madam Secretary*, Hall copied the formula made famous on *The West Wing*: intelligent idealistic characters who engage in witty banter (no antiheroes among them) and make earnest attempts to present political issues with humor and drama. Like *The West Wing*, *Madam Secretary* depicted a Washington in which conservatives and liberals had principled arguments, a portrayal which strained credulity even during the Obama administration and which seemed like a fairy tale in the Trump era.

Madam Secretary's concept of "the center" included a sentimental (some would say *too* sentimental) view of the national security establishment. Both McCord and her husband Henry (played by Tim Daly) are CIA alumni, and the 2018 season premiere included cameos by Madeleine Albright, Colin Powell, and Hillary Clinton.

The final season's story arc revolved around election interference by Iran, which was a favorite bogeyman of neoconservatives. Unlike Trump, McCord knows nothing of the foreign country's meddling and is outraged when she finds out. She cooperates unreservedly with congressional investigations. Yet there was an unsettling aftertaste of "both sides do it" in the convoluted formulation.

Madam Secretary also critiqued the military industrial complex on issues that rarely received attention from the mainstream media. In one episode, McCord pushes for the "de-alerting" of nuclear missiles to reduce the chance of an accidental war, persuading the Russians to reciprocate.

Near the end of the series, the drama depicts a deepfake video that makes it look like the president and her husband are insulting the Korean president, a deception that temporarily delays a trade deal. McCord delves into YourVid (a fictional version of YouTube) and recognizes that the website's algorithm leads viewers from the fake to a series of increasingly radical right-wing content. She despairingly tells her husband, "It all leads to white nationalism." When McCord confronts the CEO of YourVid, his response echoes the kind of disingenuous free speech arguments that Facebook executives had recently been making.

The Media Research Center objected that "*Madam Secretary* subscribes to the theory that fake videos not only spread lies but radicalize people into racists as well." (Like that didn't happen in real life!) The complaint obscured the actual reason why a painstakingly centrist drama became the source of libertarian ire. The show's real sin was that it portrayed an effective female president who oversaw an executive branch populated by earnest, hardworking policy wonks who strive to serve the greater good of the United States.

Madam Secretary costar Tim Daly was also an activist. In 2004, he campaigned for John Kerry and four years later became president of the Creative Coalition, which was formed in 1989 by Ron Silver and other actors who wanted a nonpartisan vehicle to interact with the political world. Robin Bronk was the organization's longtime executive director and in pre-COVID presidential election years, she brought groups of performers to both the Democratic and Republican conventions.

From the beginning, the Creative Coalition's biggest proactive effort was retaining governmental support of the arts via the National Endowment for the Arts (NEA). Bronk recalled that "in the eighties, when Reagan was gonna zero it out, Christopher Reeve, Susan Sarandon, Alec Baldwin, and Ron Silver successfully lobbied congresspeople from both parties to keep it alive. It was the same decade after decade." In 2019, Daly and *The Goldbergs* star Wendi McLendon-Covey "went through the same drill and managed to help keep the NEA alive, even in the Trump era."

Like Daly and Milano, *Will & Grace* star Debra Messing—who had been a UN global ambassador to advocate treatment for HIV/AIDS—increased her activism during the Trump years. After a fundraiser in LA for Trump, Messing called for a full disclosure of Trump's Hollywood supporters, arguing that the public should know who was donating to and fundraising for his reelection campaign.

In the fall of 2019, Messing tweeted a photo of a sign in front of an Alabama church that read, "A Black vote for Trump is mental illness." It is never a great idea for a white person, no matter how well-intentioned, to suggest how African Americans should vote. Messing apologized but not before Trump tweeted: "Bad 'actress' Debra The Mess Messing is in hot water. She wants to create a 'Blacklist' of Trump supporters, & is being accused of McCarthyism. Is also being accused of being a Racist because of the terrible things she said about black and mental illness . . . Will Fake News NBC allow a McCarthy style Racist to continue? ABC fired Roseanne. Watch the double standard!"

Messing's response reminded her followers of one of the most powerful issues that motivated the resistance: the Trump policy of separating children from their parents at the Mexican border. She tweeted, "It is surreal . . . Why can't you be talking about the kids who are in cages right now? . . . [or the] things that really mattered and I really wasn't one of them."

In 2020, Messing and Mandana Dayani started a podcast called *The Dissenters*, the title an homage to Ruth Bader Ginsburg. Among their early guests were Congressman Adam Schiff, Jane Fonda, and Black Lives Matter cofounder Patrisse Cullors.

THE GREEN AND OTHER NEW DEALS

The results of the 2018 midterm elections indicated that the resistance spoke for the majority of Americans. Democratic candidates for the House of Representatives received eight million more votes than Republicans, recaptured the majority they had lost eight years earlier, and Nancy Pelosi reclaimed her position as speaker of the House.

The seventy-eight-year-old speaker was a brilliant legislative tactician, and she stayed on favorable terms with all factions in the ideologically disparate Democratic House caucus. Several sophisticated Democratic legislators, such as Jerry Nadler, Adam Schiff, Elijah Cummings, and Maxine Waters, became committee chairpeople. Pelosi and her leadership team expressed themselves in the language of law and legislation, however, not in the poetic cadence of the subterranean river.

That limitation was not shared by the youngest member of the new Democratic House caucus, the twenty-nine-year-old Alexandria Ocasio-Cortez (usually referred to by her initials, AOC), who harnessed a once-in-a-generation set of political skills to promote an unapologetically progressive agenda. Within her first weeks in office, AOC became the first Democrat since Obama to obtain Hollywood-level star power due to her unpretentious glamour and her mastery of social media. Her primary defeat of Joe Crowley, a middle-of-the-road Democratic lifer who was reportedly Pelosi's choice to be her successor, was memorialized in the Netflix documentary *Knock Down the House*. On the day she took office, AOC had one and a half million Twitter followers, which was more than the sixty-two other incoming House freshmen combined. By the spring of 2021, AOC had over twelve and a half million Twitter followers and nine million Instagram followers.

Although AOC weighed in on many issues, she made her chief priority known within days of being elected when she expressed her support for a "Green New Deal," a vision that would dramatically increase the government's efforts to combat climate change by facilitating conversion from carbon-based energy sources through a set of programs that would provide millions of well-paying jobs to offset the decline of coal and oil. She frequently said that her inspiration to run for office came after her participation in the protests against building an oil pipeline through Native American lands on Standing Rock.

Issues regarding the environment, pollution, and climate change had long been prioritized by people in Hollywood. In 1989, Norman Lear formed the Environmental Media Association (EMA), which sought to educate producers, performers, and writers interested in the environment. EMA also gave awards to politicians and artists involved in environmental work.

In addition to advocacy, a number of filmmakers created stories that revolved around environmental issues. Paul Schrader's 2017 film *First Reformed* is the story of a Dutch Reformed pastor (Ethan Hawke) whose anguish about climate change brings him to the brink of personal destruction.

In November 2019, *Dark Waters* was released. Based on a true story and directed by Todd Haynes, the film starred Mark Ruffalo as Robert Bilott, a lawyer who sues chemical-manufacturing corporation DuPont after they contaminate a town with chemical waste that kills local livestock and dramatically raises the cancer rate of residents. Over the course of a decade, despite enormous pressure on his career and personal life, Bilott persevered, eventually securing a $671 million settlement for a class action lawsuit on behalf of the town's victims and their families. Anne Hathaway and Tim Robbins also star in *Dark Waters*, but the film would not have been financeable without Ruffalo, who had become a significant box office draw because of his role as Bruce Banner/the Hulk in seven Marvel Comics films. Ruffalo first emerged as a political activist in 2008 and soon became the antifracking movement's most famous advocate. In 2016, Ruffalo was one of the entertainment community's most prominent Bernie Sanders supporters.

Given the growing concern about the environment and the ominous shadow of Russian influence in the early Trump years, there was an uncanny synchronicity to the 2019 broadcast of *Chernobyl*, a five-part historical miniseries about the Chernobyl nuclear power plant accident of April 1986 and the cleanup efforts that followed in the wake of the Soviet government's denial of the extent of the disaster. The ensemble cast included Stellan Skarsgård and Emily Watson. *Chernobyl* won Emmy Awards for Limited Series, Directing, and Writing.

Another 2019 film that put a spotlight on an issue that the news media rarely covered was *The Report*, which details the Senate investigation around the American government's use of torture after 9/11. The film was written and directed by Scott Z. Burns, whose previous writing credits included *The Bourne Ultimatum*.

Burns told me that he "was interested to see how people came up with the conclusion that you could somehow torture the truth out of people. That seemed like a concept that the Nazis and other brutal regimes had employed." After a redacted version of the Senate Select Committee's report on torture was released, Senator Dianne Feinstein's office put Burns in touch with Daniel Jones, who had written the report despite resistance from the Obama administration, who wanted to "turn the page" from the Bush/Cheney years. Since Jones couldn't publicly reveal most of what he knew, Burns decided to make a film about the creation of the report itself, depicting "this one guy who sat in a windowless room for seven years piecing together the jigsaw puzzle of the torture program. He was a tracer bullet through our political system."

While growing up, Burns had been inspired by the film *All the President's Men* ("That's how I learned the story of Watergate"). He also loved the Clash because they wrote "powerful songs that still worked as songs. You don't get a pass as an artist because you are doing something ethical." Burns insisted that "all art is political. Making the decision *not* to do something is an endorsement of the status quo."

For *The Report*, Burns was limited to a $9 million budget, which was doable because his stars Adam Driver, who played Jones, Annette Bening, who played Feinstein, and Jon Hamm, who played Obama's chief of staff Denis McDonough, all worked for scale.

Burns eschewed the impressionistic style of Oliver Stone films: "My operating principal going in was that I didn't want to find the drama from invention or exaggeration." The truth was sufficiently dramatic. After learning of the treatment of Khalid Sheikh Mohammed, Feinstein's character asks a CIA official, "If waterboarding is effective, why did you have to do it 183 times?"

Former FBI special agent Ali Soufan, a passionate opponent of torture for both moral and practical reasons, was played by Fajer Kaisi. In Hulu's 2018 miniseries *The Looming Tower*, Soufan was played by the French actor Tahar Rahim. Soufan told me that he cooperated with both productions due to frustration around the false narratives about terrorist interrogations in TV shows like *24* and films like *Zero Dark Thirty*, both of which suggested that "if you beat someone up, the terrorist tells you everything about the plot and then you catch Bin Laden. The producers allowed themselves to be used for state propaganda. I thought good guys needed to use film also to explain the truth."

HOLLYWOOD VALUES

In the spirit of Ayn Rand, hard-core Trumpists defined "reality" solely by short-term gain. Trump's attorney general, William Barr, told a CBS interviewer that "everyone dies and . . . I don't believe in the Homeric idea that, you know, immortality comes by, you know, having odes sung about you over the centuries." In a similar vein, Trump's consigliere, Rudy Giuliani, told the *New Yorker* that he was unconcerned about what words would be on his gravestone. "What do I care? I'll be dead." His boss was on the same page. Trump's former communications director Anthony Scaramucci told CNN's Chris Cuomo that "the president wants to transact . . . He's told people privately, 'Why do I care about my legacy? I'll be dead. Why would I need or care about my legacy?'"

This cynical value system of these right-wingers was at the core of many of Trump's political positions. Why worry about global warming when its effects wouldn't transpire until some nebulous point in the future? Why worry about the minimum wage if you earned seven figures? Why worry about Black lives if you weren't Black? Why worry about COVID-19 if no one close to you contracted it?

One of the ways political subtext played out in drama was based on which kinds of people were depicted as heroes or villains. In early cinematic Westerns, the color of a character's cowboy hat—white equated good guy and black equated bad guy—marked who the audience should root for. In the Golden Age of Hollywood, heroic figures like Gregory Peck in *To Kill a Mockingbird* or Henry Fonda in *12 Angry Men* embodied a virtuous ideal of unselfishness and ethical behavior. Hollywood also celebrated Trumpian role models from time to time. In that same interview, Barr said that one of his favorite films was Clint Eastwood's *Dirty Harry*, a precursor to *24* in depicting brutality enacted by law enforcement as a necessity for stopping crime.

Ever since 1999, when *The Sopranos* expanded the creative scope of serial television shows, some of the best dramatic writing and acting was found in novelistic-style TV programs. Many shows in the Trump era explored political themes that seemed to cast a jaundiced eye at the most ruthless members of the financial elite. The reigning aesthetic of the genre required main characters who were morally flawed antiheroes but whose humanity periodically shone through their sins. There was often enough nuance that the question of political subtext was a subjective one. Were James Gandolfini's Tony Soprano, Bryan Cranston's Walter White (*Breaking Bad*), or Jon Hamm's Don Draper (*Mad Men*) role models or cautionary tales? To much of the audience they were merely great dramatic characters, but some of the Trump era's long-form dramas were more ideological.

In 2016, Showtime premiered *Billions*, a show that revolved around a battle of wills between a billionaire Wall Street investor, Bobby Axelrod (played by Damian Lewis) and a federal prosecutor, Chuck Rhoades (played by Paul Giamatti). Axelrod's character became like a Rorschach inkblot in which fans revealed their values based on whether they hated or loved him. Although the show clearly strived for balance, it seemed to me that, by exposing the grotesque behavior of Wall Street titans, the series confronted the morality of greed and materialism. In the third season of *Billions*, the show added a new character: US Attorney General Waylon Jeffcoat (played by Clancy Brown). Although the real-life president's name was not mentioned, the portrayal of Jeffcoat as an immoral authoritarian bully was an implicit commentary on Trump's Justice Department.

In HBO's *The Wizard of Lies*, Robert De Niro portrayed the fraudulent money manager Bernie Madoff in a performance filled with bravado and double-talk eerily reminiscent of Trump. The following year, 2018, HBO launched *Succession*, starring Brian Cox as Logan Roy, the patriarch of a media empire loosely based on Rupert Murdoch's Fox News. Like Murdoch, Roy has two sons and a daughter vying to take over leadership of the company. Like *Billions*, the series depicts its rich and powerful lead characters as power-hungry, amoral assholes. HBO also broadcast the BBC series *Years and Years*, which imagined a not-too-distant dystopia dominated by unregulated big tech, libertarian leaders like Trump (who is mentioned repeatedly), and a populist demagogue who becomes England's prime minister (played by Emma Thompson).

By the time Trump took office, Netflix was the most valuable media company in the world. Unlike US broadcast and cable networks, Netflix was a global company. While Trump withdrew the United States from global treaties, Netflix expanded the horizons of its American audience. The Norwegian series *Occupied* imagines a dystopia in which Russia occupies Norway to exploit its oil and gas production, a political fantasy that seemed eerily relevant in light of Trump's affection for Vladimir Putin. The German series *Babylon Berlin*, a drama that takes place in the Weimar Republic before the Nazis took power, depicts political and psychological similarities with Trump's America. Netflix also produced Alfonso Cuarón's *Roma*, which brought the lives of poor and middle-class Mexicans into many American minds in a sympathetic way, at a time when Trump was demonizing them. At the 2018 Academy Awards, *Roma* was nominated for Best Picture and Cuarón won Best Director.

The increasing comfort level that American filmgoers had reading subtitles helped the Korean-produced *Parasite* find an immediate audience when it was released in 2019. Cowritten and directed by Bong Joon-ho, the film was a combination of black comedy and thriller. It opens with the Kim family, who live in a ramshackle basement apartment, scheming to manipulate a wealthy family to employ them for jobs they are unqualified to work. The film focuses sharply on the disparity of income between wealthy and lower-class Koreans, a syndrome Americans are all too familiar with.

There were two series that debuted during the Trump administration that would not survive until the 2020 election, but which left unique political footprints. *I Love You, America*, which streamed on Hulu, combined talk show conversations with stand-up and sketch humor from Sarah Silverman, who found a unique balance between uncompromising progressive views (she was an enthusiastic Bernie Sanders supporter) and recognition of the humanity of people she disagreed with. In one segment, Silverman traveled to Louisiana to visit a family of rabid Donald Trump supporters with whom she found common ground by talking about family issues. Although the family had a low opinion of Barack Obama, they got health insurance via the Affordable Care Act (aka Obamacare), but

Silverman chose not to point out the apparent disconnect. She told the *Washington Post*'s Geoff Edgers, "I don't want to make people look dumb . . . I think people can be changed, but they're never going to be changed by feeling judged."

In the fall of 2018, Netflix debuted *Patriot Act with Hasan Minhaj*, which also presented a stylized twist on the traditional talk show. Minhaj, a Muslim Indian American, was a regular correspondent on Jon Stewart's iteration of *The Daily Show*. As Mano Sundaresan wrote in *New York Magazine*, "*Patriot Act* provided biting comedy and cultural analysis with an eye to the South Asian diaspora, a population that has historically suppressed such discourse . . . Inspired by *The Arsenio Hall Show*, which deployed frequent cutaways to a majority-Black live audience, Minhaj showcased and played off the mostly brown people in the studio with him." *Patriot Act* was the first national show to give extensive exposure to Andrew Yang's presidential campaign. Moreover, Minhaj was willing to take on wonky subjects avoided by mainstream political shows, such as when he devoted an entire episode to ranked-choice voting.

During the last week of 2019, Michael Moore launched a new podcast called *Rumble*. His first guest was Robert De Niro, whose contempt for Trump had continued to grow over the last three years. Moore complimented him on his "Fuck Trump trilogy," referring to the three times De Niro had uttered the phrase on national television. De Niro replied, "I'm more angry than ever that this guy is where he is."

In the past, it would have been reasonable to ask whether a movie star's profane opinion of the president had any political impact. But throughout Trump's presidency, the resistance struggled to not normalize the president's many departures from moral behavior. Talking points crafted by political consultants were necessary but insufficient. For millions of Americans, the language of conventional politics was too dry to counteract the vitriol and dishonesty coming from Trump supporters on YouTube, Facebook, Twitter, Instagram, Reddit, 4chan, 8chan, etc. In that context, a profane reaction to Trump coming from the star of *Goodfellas* seemed appropriate.

De Niro was mystified that congressional Republicans continued to be intimidated by Trump: "They're all stars in their own community, many from well-to-do families." De Niro felt that by enabling the president, "they've done something to their souls. They've made a deal with the devil to be with this guy . . . You're a public servant and you've . . . prostituted yourself to be with this fool who taints everybody . . . Nobody is gonna forget years down the line . . . I say shame on you." Moore chimed in that there had to be a "correction." De Niro agreed there had to be "consequences."

Moore and De Niro had different preferences for who should run against Trump in 2020. Moore liked Sanders and De Niro leaned toward Biden, who he said was like "the good uncle . . . A gaffe here and there, but he's well-intentioned . . . Trump is not." But the legendary actor cautioned against overconfidence: "It ain't over till it's over . . . He could win again, and then I think it would be a really, really, really bad situation in the country . . . He's joked about being president for life . . . He's not joking . . . He means it."

Trump's bid for reelection was at hand.

CHAPTER 5
PRIMARY AND AWARDS SEASONS
JANUARY 1–MARCH 3, 2020

On January 15, 2020, the first impeachment trial of Donald Trump began. In contrast to the Mueller hearing, the Democrats produced a TV star this time: Congressman Adam Schiff, the chairman of the House Intelligence Committee. Schiff gave eloquent orations about Trump's moral and political abuses of power, specifically citing how the president and his minions pressured Ukrainian president Volodymyr Zelensky to hurt Joe Biden and his son Hunter (Zelensky had been a popular TV comedian in Ukraine before he became the country's leader).

Alyssa Milano attended the Senate trial and, after the first day of hearings, told the *Washington Post*, "I think when we stop showing up to these events and we stop caring, when we stop physically putting our boots on the ground, that's when corruption creeps in . . . So I thought it was important to . . . give people some insight into what it was like in the room . . . I thought Schiff was really interesting, especially from a performer's perspective . . . It felt like you were watching a one-man show on Broadway."

Jay Sekulow, one of Trump's personal lawyers, attended the trial as well. Ironically, Milano had played him in a theatrical rendering of the Mueller report. "Sekulow . . . spotted me in the crowd," she said, "and half of the first day, he was giggling and looking up at me to see if I caught him laughing, which was so bizarre. Like, dude, you are defending the president of the United States!" Given the partisan polarization of the Trump era, and the necessity of a two-thirds majority to remove a president from office, it was a foregone conclusion that Trump would be acquitted. Progressive activists and entertainers were primarily focused on the contest among those who sought the Democratic nomination to run against Trump.

Most Democratic insiders viewed their success in the 2018 congressional midterms as an indication that a "mainstream" message was the way to win over moderates who often voted for Republicans but who couldn't stomach Trump's misogyny and racism. However, progressives pointed out that Trump's success in 2016 had been driven by despair among many in the middle class about stagnant wages coupled with higher health care and education costs, and that the Democrats' midterm victory was also due to their defense of the Affordable Care Act and a revulsion at Trump's tax cuts for the super-wealthy.

As Kurt Andersen documented in his book *Evil Geniuses: The Unmaking of America*, economic policy makers for both parties had been enacting changes since the 1970s that resulted in the US having the most extreme disparity of income of any developed country, far worse than had been the case in the decades immediately after World War II. One of the animating forces in Bernie Sanders's 2016 campaign was a desire to reverse the series of mechanisms that Congress and various agencies had employed since the Reagan years that had helped the rich get richer at the expense of everybody else.

Mainstream Democratic leaders and pundits felt that "Democratic Socialist" ideas were politically unrealistic and distracted from real-life options. Many Clinton supporters felt that Sanders stoked an impractical absolutism that contributed to her electoral college loss, and some of that lingering bitterness spilled into the entertainment community. Susan Sarandon, a passionate Sanders supporter who never endorsed Clinton in 2016, attracted particular ire.

In August 2019, actress Debra Messing tweeted: "Hey Susan Sarandon, how are you liking the revolution?" She was expressing the rage of Democrats who thought that third-party votes likely provided Trump with his margin of victory in swing states. Sarandon wasn't having it: "Happy so many ideas labeled impossible/radical in 2016 like Medicare 4 All, fighting climate change, $15 min wage & tuition free college are now mainstream & supported by majority. Racial, economic & social injustice must be addressed with systemic change. You're welcome to join."

As many Sanders supporters pointed out, although the Vermont senator endorsed Clinton, his followers were not ideological robots whose behavior could be controlled by any one leader. The solution was for the Democrats to run a more progressive campaign in 2020. Performers had long recognized that if they didn't get applause from the audience, the answer was not to blame the audience but to improve the show. Sarandon's succinct list of issues was not a bad place to start.

The underlying arguments between the left and center were serious and substantive and would surface again in the future, but as 2020 began, the overriding question for both the left and center among Democrats in general, as well as their advocates in the creative community, was: who had the best chance of beating Donald Trump?

In January, as the long list of Democratic presidential candidates vied for votes in Iowa, many progressive entertainers focused on the California primary. In previous election cycles, California's primary was not held until June, thus having little to no impact on deciding the nomination. But in 2017, in one of his last actions as governor, Jerry Brown signed a bill to move the California primary to Super Tuesday. Typically held in February or March, the states that voted on Super Tuesday amounted to almost one-third of the delegates needed to secure the nomination. Brown wanted to give the nation's largest state (and the epicenter for the country's entertainment industry) a more significant voice in selecting the presidential nominee.

Unlike in 1988, when a critical mass in mainstream Hollywood lined up behind Gary Hart, or in 1992, when Bill Clinton charmed many of the same people, there was no clear favorite. The only candidate who had the potential to approach that kind of consensus was the US senator from California, Kamala Harris, who attracted early support from Jennifer Garner, Sally Field, Ben Affleck, Michael Douglas, Chris Rock, Steven Spielberg, and Sean Penn, although some of them hedged their bets by also donating to other candidates. However, in December 2019 Harris dropped out of the race due to poor poll numbers.

Former Montana governor Steve Bullock welcomed an enthusiastic endorsement from Jeff Bridges. Andrew Yang ran an idiosyncratic campaign that demonstrated a rare comfort level with the digital age, attracting support from Donald Glover (aka Childish Gambino), Dave Chappelle, and Rivers Cuomo of the band Weezer. Even so, there was never a moment during the race when either Bullock or Yang polled high enough to have a real shot at the nomination.

Although Minnesota senator Amy Klobuchar performed well in the early debates, she did not develop traction in the entertainment community. Former New York City mayor Michael Bloomberg's brief appearance in the race was self-financed, though he did receive rhetorical support from Robert De Niro. Alec Baldwin, who also knew Bloomberg, was less enthusiastic, posting on Twitter, "Bloomberg is bright, a gentleman, an enormously successful business leader. And, like others with a lot of cash on hand, a collector . . . Bloomberg was a Republican when it suited his purposes, became a Democrat when it suited his purposes. When he wants something, he simply buys it."

Like Democrats across the country, most artist-activists in California were divided between left-leaning candidates like senators Elizabeth Warren and Bernie Sanders and centrist candidates like former South Bend mayor Pete Buttigieg and former vice president Joe Biden. In the shadow of a possible second Trump term, many older lefties made it clear that, if necessary, they would forego their ideology and go all in for whoever emerged as the nominee. David Simon, creator of *The Wire*, told me, "I am for Warren with Sanders as my number two, but I am uninterested in running down anyone in the Democratic field and creating a rhetorical path for the GOP to use after the primaries. If the Democrats at this point nominate a petri dish laced with smallpox, I'm voting for the pathogen."

Shepard Fairey, the artist who created the iconic "Hope" poster for Barack Obama's 2008 campaign and who had been an Occupy Wall Street supporter, also grappled with this conflict. He told me, "In an ideal scenario, I'd want a hybrid of Bernie and Pete . . . I think Dems attacking each other could be disastrous since Trump repeats criticisms endlessly and exaggeratedly. I'm quite nervous about the circular firing squad on our side." Fairey collaborated with the ACLU to create large murals in battleground states. He said that instead of using a condescending tone—which often crept into conventional exhortations when Democrats encouraged young people to vote—he hoped his images would suggest something more positive: "Voting is an act of defiance. I don't say it's a duty to vote, but that it's something they are trying to take *from* you. They are putting messages out there to make you feel it's all corrupt. The people in control now don't want you to vote. The way to be true to your rebel self is to vote while you still can."

In February 2020, the son of a prominent TV showrunner in LA sent a widely circulated e-mail to his "moderate" parents explaining why he and his friends were campaigning for Bernie Sanders, whose celebrity supporters included Ariana Grande, Emily Ratajkowski, Susan Sarandon, Danny Glover, Tim Robbins, Steve Skrovan, Chuck D, and rock bands like the Strokes and Vampire Weekend.

The most popular performer who supported the Vermont senator was a New York rapper fifty years younger than he: twenty-seven-year-old Cardi B (born as Belcalis Marlenis Almánzar). Cast as a member of the VH1 reality show *Love & Hip Hop*, Cardi B gained a larger following after independently releasing two mixtapes entitled *Gangsta Bitch Music Vol. 1* and *2*, which grabbed the attention of the record industry. In 2018, she released her first major label album, *Invasion of Privacy*, which debuted at number one on the *Billboard* 200. The album spawned three number one singles and won the Grammy for Best Rap Album, making her the first solo female artist to win the award. That same year, *Time* magazine included Cardi B on their annual list of the one hundred most influential people in the world.

As soon as she had a public platform, Cardi B became politically outspoken. She criticized Trump's immigration policies, opposed police brutality, and supported gun control and Medicare for All. In an endorsement video for Sanders in 2016, she told her fans, "Vote for Daddy Bernie, bitch." She supported Hillary Clinton in the general election. At the 2018 Grammy Awards, Cardi B appeared in a video with Clinton to narrate a portion of Michael Wolff's anti-Trump tell-all book, *Fire and Fury*, exclaiming, "Why am I even reading this shit? I can't believe this . . . this is how [Trump] lives his life."

In August 2019, Cardi B again supported Sanders for president, recording a video conversation with him at the TEN Nail Bar in Detroit. She told the senator that Franklin Roosevelt was her favorite president: "He helped us get over the Depression, all while he was in a wheelchair. Like, this man was suffering from polio at the time of his presidency, and yet all he was worried about was trying to make America great—make America great again for real . . . If it wasn't for him, old people wouldn't even get Social Security."

Cardi B told Sanders that she had requested questions for him from her forty-nine million Twitter followers and "the topic that was mentioned the most . . . was about raising the minimum wage," a long-standing Sanders priority. She added that before she got famous she "felt like no matter how many jobs I got, I wasn't able to make ends meet. Like, I wasn't able to pay my rent, get transportation, and eat." She also praised Sanders's plan to eliminate student debt, citing her own financially tumultuous time attending college in New York City.

Finally, the rapper lamented that when "the Democratic debate was going on . . . I just got so upset with Trump tweeting out 'boring' because it's just—this is not a reality show. This is not supposed to be fun. This is not supposed to be entertainment." The ten-minute clip of Sanders and Cardi B was viewed by twenty-two million people, more than any 2020 Democratic presidential debate.

Senator Elizabeth Warren also attracted many among the Hollywood left. She was endorsed by *Transparent* producer Joey Soloway and *The Handmaid's Tale* writer and producer Dorothy Fortenberry, as well as Martin Sheen, John Legend, Chrissy Teigen, Melissa Etheridge, and Jane Fonda, who said, "We cannot be moderate in a radical time. The problems are radical. What the president is doing is radical. Elizabeth is brave, bold, understands all of the problems, and will deal not just from pragmatism but with humanity and compassion."

Sanders's early lead in California polls had some centrists in a panic. TV mogul Haim Saban, a leading Democratic fundraiser who amassed a fortune producing *Mighty Morphin Power Rangers*, told the *Hollywood Reporter* that he "profoundly dislikes Bernie Sanders . . . He thinks that every billionaire is a crook." (What Sanders had actually been saying was that billionaires should pay more taxes and that some of their business should be more regulated.)

Saban's aversion to economic populism was not shared in most of the creative community, but the campaigns of both Warren and Sanders were undermined by a nagging anxiety that animated many Democrats, that victory over Trump was by no means a foregone conclusion and that a more moderate candidate might have a better chance of winning a general election. This was why Steve Earle, who had supported Sanders in 2016, endorsed Biden in 2020. Progressives tried to make the case that a moderate nominee would dampen the engagement of younger voters, but as things turned out, the left lost the electability argument.

Biden received early support from Rob Reiner, Tom Hanks, and Scarlett Johansson, among others. The moderate who earned the most passionate Hollywood support, however, was Buttigieg, the first openly gay politician with a shot at a presidential nomination. At thirty-seven years old, he was also the youngest candidate by far. Buttigieg gained endorsements from David Geffen, Laurie David, Seth MacFarlane, Michael J. Fox, and Kevin Costner, who introduced Buttigieg at an Iowa rally not far from where he'd shot the movie *Field of Dreams*.

Sanders won the California primary by 400,000 votes but it didn't make any difference; Biden won ten other states on Super Tuesday. Jimmy Kimmel joked that "Super Tuesday was like Easter Sunday for Joe Biden, who staged the biggest comeback since Robert Downey Jr." The most pivotal endorsement was not from a performer but from Congressman James Clyburn of South Carolina, where Biden's primary victory four days before Super Tuesday was driven by the overwhelming support of older African American voters, a result that was replicated in enough other states to make Biden the presumptive nominee.

AWARDS SEASON

As Democrats coalesced around Biden, the major movie awards were being handed out. The 2020 Golden Globe Awards attracted eighteen million viewers, more than any other broadcast in its time slot. The show was hosted by British comedian and actor Ricky Gervais, who ridiculed Hollywood activists in his monologue. "You say you're woke, but the companies you work for, I mean, unbelievable: Apple, Amazon, Disney," he said. "If ISIS started a streaming service, you'd call your agent, wouldn't you? So, if you do win an award tonight, don't use it as a platform to make a political speech. You're in no position to lecture the public about anything. You know nothing about the real world. Most of you spent less time in school than Greta Thunberg."

I thought Gervais was an entertaining host and his tone was in keeping with a long show business tradition of performers taking the piss out of each other. When done right, this style of insult comedy comes across as charming candor. But his argument was flawed. If no one who did business with multinational companies could criticize systemic injustice, then most journalists and politicians would be eliminated from such discussions too. The only result of such absolutism would be to exclude artists from dissent while leaders in every other business would continue supporting politicians and policies that served their self-interest.

Gervais's snarky perspective inspired *Washington Post* writer Megan McArdle to write a piece about her own problems with award show activism, singling out Patricia Arquette's 2015 Oscars acceptance speech, which she used to call for wage equality for women. McArdle opined, "Arquette might be right, but is there anything less brave than supporting a liberal cause in a room full of fervent liberals? . . . Gervais neatly illustrated exactly why so many people so resent the increasingly ritualized ceremonial sanctimony. Because it turns out that this may be exactly what makes people hate hypocrites so much: they fool us into giving them credit for holding potentially costly moral beliefs without actually paying those costs."

In her zeal to dismiss the political legitimacy of performers, McArdle missed the point of Arquette's remarks. The actress was not merely supporting a "liberal cause" that was popular in the room—she was directly criticizing the people who controlled her salary on national TV. The equivalent would be for a *Washington Post* writer to publicly rebuke the paper's owner, Jeff Bezos, in the pages of the paper. Despite McArdle's contention that Hollywood anti-Trumpers took positions without "paying the costs" for progressive beliefs, it was clear that if any of the Democrats were elected president, they would roll back the tax breaks for the wealthiest Americans, which would include the supposedly hypocritical superstars.

On January 19, 2020, the Screen Actors Guild held their annual award ceremony. Robert De Niro used his lifetime achievement award acceptance speech to underline his support for the union. He called on voters to look for candidates who support the labor movement: "Political leaders who support unions are more likely to support the Affordable Care Act, equitable taxes, humane immigration regulations, a safe environment, a diverse citizenry, reproductive rights, sensible gun control, and fair wages and benefits. We owe them our support, and we owe them our vote." Anticipating anti-Hollywood carping, he added, "I can imagine some of you are saying, 'All right, all right, let's not get into the politics,' but we are in such a dire situation, so deeply concerning to me and to so many others, I have to say something . . . If I have a bigger voice because of my situation, I'm going to use it whenever I see a blatant abuse of power."

The Academy Awards ceremony took place a few weeks later, on February 9, 2020. Brad Pitt won an Oscar for Best Supporting Actor for his performance in Quentin Tarantino's film *Once Upon a Time . . . in Hollywood*, in which the director imagined an alternate history to the Manson family's murder of Sharon Tate. Pitt noted that he had forty-five seconds for an acceptance speech, which was "more than the Senate gave John Bolton" (a reference to the recent impeachment trial, when the Republican majority in the Senate refused to call Trump's former national security advisor to verify the charges made against the president). Pitt concluded with another cutting remark: "I'm thinking maybe Quentin does a movie about it [the impeachment trial] and in the end the adults do the right thing."

When Joaquin Phoenix won an Oscar for Best Actor for his performance in *Joker*, the actor gave a characteristically rambling but earnest speech that defended animal rights and opposed the plunder of the natural world, racism, and infringements on "queer rights [and] indigenous rights."

The Oscar for Best Documentary went to *American Factory*, which was made by the company that Barack and Michelle Obama set up with Netflix. The film centers around a failed attempt to unionize an auto parts factory in Moraine, Ohio, owned by a Chinese company, Fuyao Glass Industry. Upon accepting the award, directors Steven Bognar and Julia Reichert invoked Karl Marx's famous exhortation: "Workers of the world unite."

Before presenting the Oscar for Best Picture to *Parasite*, Jane Fonda pointedly remarked that "nothing is more important than raising awareness right now." Two weeks later, at a rally in Colorado Springs, Donald Trump rhetorically asked his fawning admirers, "How bad were the Academy Awards this year? Did you see? And the winner is a movie from South Korea. What the hell was that all about? We've got enough problems with South Korea, with trade. On top of it they give them the best movie of the year? Was it good? I don't know." Trump contrasted the foreign film to an old American classic that romanticized the Confederacy: "Can we get *Gone with the Wind* back, please?" In response, Bette Midler tweeted,

"#Trump complained about #Parasite winning the Oscar. I'm more upset that a parasite won the White House."

At the age of eighty-two, Jane Fonda had a lot more on her mind than giving out awards. A singular figure in American culture, she was in her sixth decade as a star with seven Oscar nominations and two victories to her credit. Fonda first established a strong connection with millions of women through popular 1980s home exercise videos. As shown in the recent HBO documentary *Jane Fonda in Five Acts*, her personal life had long been public. Many of Fonda's admirers had the intensity of rock and roll fans. They felt as if they actually knew her.

In August 2019, shortly after her brother Peter died, Fonda asked Rosanna Arquette and Catherine Keener to join her on a road trip to help clear her head. As Arquette told me, "Jane had been inspired by Greta Thunberg's environmental activism and she was reading Naomi Klein's book *On Fire: The (Burning) Case for a Green New Deal*. She was all fired up."

Fonda called Greenpeace USA's executive director, Annie Leonard, to brainstorm ways to channel her fire. Leonard told me that Fonda was so determined to make an impact that she initially considered camping outside of the White House in a tent to dramatize the crisis, but was ultimately persuaded that there was a more effective way to build a movement. Within weeks, Fonda initiated weekly protests in Washington, DC, against practices that exacerbated climate change, such as issuing new fossil fuel licenses and the proliferation of plastics in the ocean. Fonda dubbed the protests "Fire Drill Fridays" and they included civil disobedience. Arquette and Keener were among those who got arrested with her over Labor Day weekend.

Fonda reflected on Fire Drill Fridays in her book *What Can I Do?: My Path from Climate Despair to Action*: "Whether we like it or not, our society is very celebrity focused and having a famous person join a movement helps bring the press out and expands the reach of the message." Given America's limited ability to effectively combat corporate opposition to meaningful action on climate change, Leonard enthusiastically welcomed the actress's engagement. The

Greenpeace leader says that in addition to being a media magnet, Fonda is "an incredible learner" who devoured books and briefing materials.

In recent years, pundits have analyzed political ideas via the so-called "Overton window," a concept created by political scientist Joseph Overton in the 1990s to define the range of policies that have a practical chance at being actualized at any given moment. Leonard wanted to shift the Overton window on climate issues to include the reduction and/or cessation of fossil fuel usage. "Most environmental organizations and even the Green New Deal don't mention this," she told me. "It's much more popular to advocate for solar, electric cars, and the green economy. But stopping the use of fossil fuels is the other half of the equation. This is what gets us into issues like Standing Rock, the Keystone XL pipeline, and challenging corporate power. We needed Jane to inject this into the conversation." Specific policy issues included ending government subsidies to oil companies and halting drilling permits, especially on publicly owned land.

Leonard provided several examples of how Fonda uniquely contributed to climate change activism. She attracted the media and knew how to garner mainstream attention. While in public, she wore a stylish bright red coat that was easy for cameras to find and insisted, whenever possible, that a "No New Fossil Fuels" banner or poster hang in the backdrop of her photos. When asked by reporters, "Are you scared of jail?" she'd fiercely respond, "I'm scared of climate change."

Moreover, Leonard explained to me how "Jane opens doors." While Leonard had been unable to speak to the Climate Change Senate Task Force, the group asked Fonda to give them a briefing. When the Congressional Progressive Caucus wanted to meet Fonda, she insisted that Leonard come with her. In the wake of Fire Drill Fridays, Fonda was asked to speak at the National Press Club, where she gave a forty-five-minute talk with what Leonard described as "perfect scientific complexity."

On January 10, shortly before she resumed shooting the last season of *Grace and Frankie*, Fonda led her final Fire Drill Friday to the steps of the Capitol building. One hundred and forty-seven protesters, including Joaquin Phoenix and Martin Sheen, were arrested for obstructing access to the government building (they were released a few hours later). At the rally beforehand, Sheen called Fonda "one of my heroes nearly all my adult life," and added that "the world will be saved by women. Thank God they outnumber men." He then read Rabindranath Tagore's poem "Where the Mind Is Without Fear."

In earlier Fire Drill Fridays, Lily Tomlin, Sam Waterston, Ted Danson, Diane Lane, and Sally Field were arrested. Fonda was detained five times, and on one occasion spent a night in a jail in Washington, DC. Predictably, Trump mocked her at one of his rallies: "They arrested Jane Fonda. Nothing changes. I remember thirty, forty years ago they arrested her. She's waving to everybody with the handcuffs."

MISS AMERICANA

On January 31, 2020, Netflix premiered *Miss Americana*, a documentary about Taylor Swift. While still in her twenties, Swift scored four number one albums, two of which won Grammys for Album of the Year. During her first several years of superstardom, Swift's persona was defined by the commercial brilliance of her hit songs and a series of public romances and feuds. Having recently turned thirty when most of *Miss Americana* was made, she reflects in the film on her initial entry into the public sphere as a country music artist at the age of nineteen: "When you're living for the approval of strangers . . . one bad thing can cause everything to crumble . . . I've been trained to be happy when you get a lot of praise . . . Like, those pats on the head were all that I lived for. I was so fulfilled by approval that that was it. I became the person everyone wanted me to be."

In 2012, when she was twenty-three years old, Swift told a *Time* magazine interviewer that she didn't "talk about politics because it might influence other people," and that she didn't know "enough yet in life to be telling people who to vote for." On the *Late Show with David Letterman* she reiterated that she didn't think it was her role "to tell other people what to do." Swift's political opacity and platinum-blond hair led many white supremacists to assume that she was one of their own. In 2016, Andrew Anglin, founder of the neo-Nazi blog the *Daily Stormer*, wrote, "Taylor Swift is a pure Aryan goddess, like something out of classical Greek poetry. Athena reborn."

By 2018, Swift was appalled at this misconception, and by Trump's policies. During the Tennessee Senate race, she publicly endorsed Democrat Phil Bredesen and let fans use her social media platforms to organize political activities. Within forty-eight hours, 65,000 of her fans registered to vote. Trump quipped, "I like Taylor's music about 25 percent less now." It seemed unlikely that the president had ever actually listened to her music, but the gentle nature of his rebuke showed a wary respect for the breadth of Swift's eighty-eight million Twitter followers, three million more than he had at the time.

Swift's fan base included a much higher percentage of Republicans than most other artist-activists. *Miss Americana* features a conversation in which the singer explains her newfound activism to her parents. Her father tells her that he's "terrified" of her political involvement, to which Swift recites a litany of grievances against Republican senator Marsha Blackburn, who voted against fair pay for women and the Violence Against Women Act, and believed that there was nothing wrong with kicking gay couples out of restaurants. Swift says, "I can't see another commercial [with] her disguising these policies behind the words 'Tennessee Christian values.' I *live* in Tennessee. I *am* Christian. That's not what we stand for. I need to be on the right side of history . . . Dad, I need you to forgive me for doing it, because I'm doing it."

There is something contrived about filming a family conversation for the public to see. It's hard to know where the courage ends and career calculation begins. Swift subtly acknowledges in the documentary, "Women in entertainment are discarded in an elephant graveyard by the time they're thirty-five . . . Female artists have reinvented themselves . . . more than the male artists. They have to or else you're out of a job . . . Live out a narrative to be interesting enough to entertain us, but not so crazy that it makes us uncomfortable." She then candidly explained that her "moral code, as a kid and now, is a need to be thought of as good." Those six words, *to be thought of as good*, may validate the suspicion of some cynics. However, there are a lot of other ways that celebrities can get attention and acclaim. Very few of them at Swift's level of fame chose a path that also incurred the wrath of Trump's vindictive base.

Despite the singer's support, Bredesen lost and Blackburn was reelected. The next year, however, Swift told *Rolling Stone* that she was now "obsessed" with politics and that white supremacy was "disgusting." She explained that one of her lyrics—"American stories burning before me"—is "about the illusions of what I thought America was before our political landscape took this turn." Another one of her lyrics, "I see the high fives between the bad guys," refers to "really racist, horrific undertones now becoming overtones in our political climate."

The issue that connected to the songs that made Swift a superstar was female empowerment. In 2017, she won a lawsuit against a Denver disc jockey who was accused of groping her at a postconcert meet and greet. As a result, the DJ was fired and he angrily sued Swift. The judge dismissed the DJ's lawsuit and the jury sided with Swift in her symbolic one-dollar countersuit.

In *Miss Americana*, the singer said that she was striving "to deprogram misogyny in my own brain . . . There is no such thing as a slut, there is no such thing as a bitch. We don't want to be condemned for being multifaceted . . . [I can] love glitter and also stand up for the double standards that exist in our society. I want to wear pink and tell you how I feel about politics. I don't think those things have to cancel each other out." At the end of the film, Swift displayed a petition urging the Republican Senate to pass the Equality Act, which would explicitly ban discrimination based on sexual orientation and gender identity, a law already passed by the Democratic House.

By March 2020, however, every subject but one took a backseat in American consciousness.

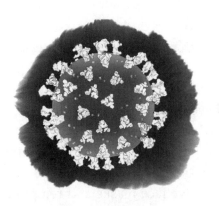

CHAPTER 6
SHIT IS REAL!
MARCH 11-30, 2020

On March 11, 2020, the NBA announced the suspension of its 2020 basketball season. That same day, Tom Hanks and Rita Wilson revealed that they had tested positive for COVID-19. Cardi B posted a video on Instagram in which she screamed at fever pitch, "Let me tell y'all something! I ain't even gonna front, a bitch is scared . . . Coronavirus! Coronavirus! I'm telling you, shit is *real!* Shit is gettin' *real!*" A few days later, DJ iMarkkeyz interpolated her rant over a beat, a mash-up that was soon streamed millions of times and spawned several homages, including a popular remix by DJ Snake and a video in which Cody Simpson said "coronavirus" and his girlfriend, Miley Cyrus, chimed in, "It's getting *real!*"

March 11 was also the day that Harvey Weinstein was sentenced to twenty-three years in prison for rape. Although the conviction was a triumphant culmination of justice undertaken by many of Weinstein's victims, the world's eye had now singularly turned their focus toward the alarming and novel coronavirus.

Historians will long discuss why Donald Trump didn't use his reality television craftsmanship to dramatize the peril of COVID-19 and make himself the front man for a federal response and posture as a unifying wartime president. All he had to do was cloak himself with the advice of doctors and scientists, empathize with the families of the dead, take credit for the most effective strategies, and he would have undoubtedly benefited from the kind of popularity that other presidents have received in times of war or national emergencies. He would have had a much better chance of reelection.

Instead, for whatever reason, Trump politicized the issue by belittling the peril of COVID-19. He made himself, and his supporters, enemies of those who advocated for common sense actions like wearing protective face masks and temporary shutdowns that would mitigate mortality rates. He perversely abdicated federal leadership and delegated most of the response to individual states, then battled with governors who didn't pander to his outrage du jour. Like cartoon villains, Trump and his political enablers behaved as if it were a weakness to be vigilant about health, to express sympathy for victims, and to call for more aggressive public heath responses to the disease.

As Barbra Streisand wrote on Twitter, "The United States had three months to prepare for the coronavirus. Donald Trump and the conservative media like Fox News have downplayed its threats. Now we will face the consequence of this negligence."

While most of America quarantined, much of the population was glued to their phones, laptops, and TVs. Sports leagues were canceled. Cable news networks focused on the pandemic almost to the exclusion of anything else. It was surreal to watch TV shows and movies—what entertainment executives call "scripted drama"—depicting a pre-COVID world. Episodes which had been shot just a few weeks earlier felt like instant nostalgia; it would be impossible to film or produce anything new for many months. There was a sudden demand for entertainment that connected to the new reality, and within days dozens of entertainers improvised performances from home without the kind of lighting, makeup, and rehearsal they were accustomed to. Yet these performances captivated audiences with a new level of intimacy.

Patrick Stewart released daily videos of himself reading Shakespearean sonnets. Keith Urban, John Legend, and Chris Martin of Coldplay, among others, performed stripped-down concerts from their living rooms. Michael Stipe sang the R.E.M. classic "It's the End of the World as We Know It (And I Feel Fine)." After the final chorus, Stipe looked at his computer webcam and said, "I *do* feel fine . . . We are going through something that none of us have ever encountered before . . . Please take this seriously and don't leave your house unless you have to . . . I'm quarantining . . . I don't want to be responsible for getting someone else sick . . . I don't think I am [infected with coronavirus], but none of us know if we are."

Several rock and roll elders weighed in with acoustic performances, including Neil Young (seventy-four years old), Joan Baez (seventy-nine), Graham Nash (seventy-eight), John Fogerty (seventy-four), and Bonnie Raitt (seventy). Neil Diamond (seventy-nine) updated his lyric in the bridge of "Sweet Caroline" from "holding hands" to "wash your hands." For the baby boomer audience that had been following these artists for a half a century, there was something deeply moving about members of an at-risk demographic singing to a quarantined online audience, as if for the last time. After Paul Simon posted an at-home rendition of "American Tune," one YouTube commenter remarked, "He does a fine job of pulling that off with that 79-yr-old voice, by God. And watch his face, he isn't 'performing,' he is consoling and testifying and storytelling . . . Makes me proud of him and proud to have been a fan all these years."

During the first week of April, the American musical community was shaken by the COVID-related deaths of Adam Schlesinger (fifty-two years old) of Fountains of Wayne, producer Hal Willner (sixty-four), and singer-songwriter John Prine (seventy-three).

After a brief hiatus, late-night TV personalities began hosting their shows from home. On March 12, recently withdrawn presidential candidate Pete Buttigieg guest-hosted *Jimmy Kimmel Live* and quipped, "When you don't have a real audience, you have to fake one, just like Trump's inauguration."

On other late-night shows, jokes focused on Trump's recent Oval Office speech, which featured a number of glaring errors, including the suggestion that all travel from Europe had been suspended, when in reality, Americans and others were exempt from this rule. Trump also said that insurance companies would waive copayments for COVID-19 treatment, which was false; the waiver was just for testing, not for treatment.

The president referred to the virus as "foreign." In an exasperated tone, Trevor Noah said, "It isn't a *foreign* virus. It's just a virus, okay? Trump makes it sound like corona doesn't speak English. We can blame Europe for many things—colonialism, skinny jeans, Piers Morgan—but this virus is worldwide, all right? It was going to get here no matter what Europe did." The following week, Noah aired an interview with Dr. Anthony Fauci where he asked Fauci for basic information, such as how the virus spreads and whether it was safe to go to the grocery store, pick up a package, or walk into an elevator. Within a week, a clip of the conversation had more than ten million views on YouTube.

As Kathy Griffin had noted, Trump's "show" required conflict. Within days, the right-wing echo chamber made it clear that for their tribe, it was not cool to listen to doctors and scientists instead of stock market analysts. Pro-Trump media included Fox News, its website, and the *New York Post*—all owned by Rupert Murdoch. But the most reliable barometer of Trump-think was *Breitbart News*. One tactic of the website's entertainment coverage was to cherry pick the most outrageous comments of celebrities. However, since many Trump supporters paid more attention to stars than they did to the political world, *Breitbart* sometimes shifted from mocking performers to taking them seriously and then providing opposing talking points. For example, on March 12, 2020, *Breitbart* reported that "Chelsea Handler repeated the false claim that President Trump suggested that people who have 'tested positive for coronavirus can still go to work and get better there.'" *Breitbart* then defended their leader: "But president Trump never said or suggested what Handler claims he did. The president described some situations in which people who have contracted coronavirus only experience a mild case of the illness and quickly recover."

The same week, *Breitbart's* Jerome Hudson wrote that the pandemic gave Hollywood elites an "opportunity to trash the president." Hudson gave the example of Rosanna Arquette, who had tweeted that Trump's "psychosis has become normalized this is more dangerous than ever the evil empire must go . . . vote blue no matter what." He also cited former *West Wing* star Bradley Whitford, who tweeted, "It's an Al Anon situation. We've been forced into a relationship with a lethally destructive narcissist. Daddy's hammered and wants to drive, but Mommy (GOP/Fox News) is too scared to confront him."

Breitbart's David Ng indignantly reported, "Cher . . . claimed that President Trump is lying, adding that he kept quiet about the coronavirus because 'he knew we weren't prepared.'" Lest readers trust the singer's criticism, Ng added, "Cher omitted the fact that President Trump restricted entry to the US from China as early as February 1, a decision that was widely reported at the time."

Several performers publicly questioned Vice President Mike Pence's qualifications for heading the national response to COVID-19 in light of his previous political positions. Bradley Whitford tweeted, "He doesn't believe in evolution. He doesn't believe that cigarettes cause cancer. He does believe that gay people are going to hell." John Leguizamo wrote, "He said smoking doesn't kill! In Indiana he treated HIV like it was somebody else's problem! Why are we letting him deal with a medical emergency?" Chelsea Handler wrote, "Trump is . . . unable to answer any real questions on the matter, and then turns it over to Pence, who then praises Trump for what a great job he's been doing. How stupid do we have to be before we get rid of this moron?" Rob Reiner rhetorically asked, "How far has Mike Pence flown up the Trump's ass?" Chris Evans, who was best known for his portrayal of Captain America in the Marvel films, criticized one of Trump's initial COVID-19 press briefings on Twitter, writing, "The president just ran off stage after his rambling press conference without answering a single question. America wants answers. America wants leadership."

Some artists focused on humanitarian themes. On Facebook, Lady Gaga posted, "It's so important to acknowledge that we are and must be a global . . . community . . . We can create healing by learning how to be kind and take care of each other." Justin Timberlake wrote, "This is a crazy time, but remember we're all in it together. Start small and support your local communities by getting food out to those in need. I'm donating to @midsouthfoodbank . . . an organization in my hometown this is helping . . . families . . . Every. little. thing. helps." Ben Affleck wrote, "During these times of uncertainty, I'm thinking about our most vulnerable populations . . . Join me in supporting @FeedingAmerica, the nationwide network of 200 food banks working tirelessly to feed our neighbors around the country."

In an interview for the *New Sun*, Michael Douglas discussed the pandemic's surprising silver linings: "With this vulnerability, we have a chance to be a little more open, or to discuss more clearly, what's going on . . . I think we've all been struck by how much clearer the skies have become—in such a very short period of time. So we actually get to see a real result—by accident—just how we can affect our climate."

On Twitter, Miley Cyrus cautioned, "Be thoughtful. Respectful. Compassionate. HUMAN . . . NO ONE needs every soup in the store. The more we hoard, the more expensive and sparse necessities will become . . . There is enough to go around if we take care of one another." Justin Bieber provided a list of organizations his followers could support and pleaded for people to "stay home" and not to go out "in groups [to] . . . bars . . . clubs . . . [and] restaurants."

By the end of March, there were several videos on YouTube that showed young people partying, particularly in Florida, due to previously planned spring break activities. Hilary Duff begged her followers to "go home." One of actor Michael Rapaport's YouTube videos was harsher. "To all you young millennial assholes that keep going out partying . . . stop killing old people. This is the *real* March madness. Survive and advance. Get in the fucking house. Follow the rules." These exhortations weren't a substitute for national leadership on health issues, but they didn't hurt.

The pandemic soon spawned several multi-artist telethons. On March 22, 2020, Rosie O'Donnell hosted an online benefit for the Actors Fund. Guests included Morgan Freeman, Lin-Manuel Miranda, Bernadette Peters, Matthew Broderick, Sarah Jessica Parker, Kristin Chenoweth, and Harvey Fierstein. Within the first twenty-four hours, the webcast attracted 340,000 views on YouTube and raised $90,000. O'Donnell, a longtime Trump nemesis, kept political comments to a minimum but did remark, "We deserve a leader who tells the truth." Harvey Fierstein reminded the Broadway audience that "we have a lot of election work to do."

On April 18, 2020, the three major TV networks broadcast the final two hours of a marathon entertainment special called *One World: Together at Home*, which was cohosted by three men usually competing for the same audience: Fallon, Colbert, and Kimmel.

Lady Gaga, who curated the music for *One World*, sang the inspirational tearjerker "Smile," which Charlie Chaplin originally wrote for his anticorporate classic film *Modern Times* (1936) at the height of the Great Depression. Among those who performed from home were Lizzo, Billie Eilish, Stevie Wonder (who began his set with "Lean on Me," written by the recently deceased Bill Withers), Elton John, Celine Dion, Jennifer Lopez, Taylor Swift, Paul McCartney, John Legend, Keith Urban, and Andrea Bocelli.

The vibe was similar to other feel-good celebrity events that have taken place in the wake of disasters. Comedian Jerry Lewis hosted telethons for the Muscular Dystrophy Association that were first broadcast nationally in 1966 at the height of the Vietnam War. Such televised extravaganzas had traditionally been apolitical, but temporary unity was impossible in the Trump era.

One World raised $127.9 million from corporate sponsors, half of which was donated to "local and regional responders," and the other half to the World Health Organization (WHO). The previous day, Trump had announced that he was suspending US funding of the WHO, so its status as a beneficiary was perceived by Trumpists as a sign of disrespect, as were appearances by New York mayor Bill de Blasio and London mayor Sadiq Khan, both of whom had a history of public disputes with the president. Former first ladies Michelle Obama and Laura Bush made appearances on *One World*, but no Melania and no Ivanka.

The Rolling Stones performed an acoustic version of "You Can't Always Get What You Want," which not only featured a lyric that was relevant to the crisis, but also had the distinction of having been played without permission by the Trump campaign at 2016 rallies until the Stones objected to its use.

Non-singing appearances were made by Bill Gates (the subject of numerous COVID-19-related conspiracy theories), David Beckham, Oprah Winfrey, Idris Elba (who was recovering from COVID-19), and Beyoncé, who reminded her fans that "this virus is killing Black people in alarming rates here in America." She hailed "those in the food industry, delivery workers, mail carriers, and sanitation employees who are working so we can be safe in our homes, we thank you."

The pro-Trump media predictably hated the event. A review by the *New York Post's* Johnny Oleksinski began: "One world together, pulling our hair out." Oleksinski added that the concert "achieved the impossible: It made us feel even worse about our already miserable circumstances. The insufferable show . . . pieced together saintly speeches from A-list celebrities and somber United Nations officials . . ."

Breitbart's Simon Kent complained that "Lady Gaga applauded Tedros Adhanom Ghebreyesus, the embattled director general for the World Health Organization, calling him a 'superstar' barely 48-hours [sic] after President Donald Trump announced the US will pause funding of the UN body over its handling of the Chinese coronavirus pandemic . . . Tedros was effusive in his unrestrained regard for the 33-year-old singer."

There were two meta-disputes playing out in popular culture. One was to what extent people should trust scientists and doctors. This was not a new divide in America. In the 1960s, opposition to the fluoridation of drinking water was a popular hobby horse in right-wing subculture, an attitude which was satirized in *Dr. Strangelove* during a demented rant by General Ripper (played by Sterling Hayden). This is not to suggest that every argument about the role of government in medicine was laughable. On the one hand, it was the obligation of a government to protect its citizens. On the other, there was a strain of American individualism that considered any mandate from authorities on the subject of health an infringement of personal freedom. The question was where to draw the line. Yet politicizing a common sense health measure like wearing a mask during a pandemic was tribal insanity.

The other political subtext that the president and his minions tried to exploit was informed by the fact that, in the early months of the pandemic, when New York City had coffins stacked in Central Park, many people in rural America did not know anyone who had actually fallen ill with the disease. *Vanity Fair's* Katherine Eban described how this played out during White House deliberations under the direction of Trump's son-in-law, Jared Kushner: "The political folks believed that because [COVID-19] was going to be relegated to Democratic states, that they could blame those governors, and that would be an effective political strategy." "Democratic states" were also where most artists and entertainers lived.

In real life, the virus did not observe political or demographic boundaries. Trump, however, with a political attention span limited to the twenty-four-hour news cycle, downplayed COVID to the point where many of his followers believed that the disease was a hoax or merely an urban problem for people of color. For those whose news diet was provided exclusively by right-wing media, entertainers were among the few who could penetrate the bubble with political messages. A billboard erected in New Jersey showed pictures of Bruce Springsteen, Jon Bon Jovi, and Jon Stewart exhorting their fans to "wear a friggin' mask!"

The pandemic also refocused attention to a number of economic issues that had long been central to American political debates. Bernie Sanders supporters like Mark Ruffalo felt that the pandemic underlined the need for a Medicare for All system. Britney Spears, who had been a vocal supporter of George W. Bush after 9/11, wrote on Instagram, "Redistribute wealth. Strike." Spears was praised by the Democratic Socialists of America, who affectionately referred to her as "comrade." Fran Drescher, the former star of the sitcom *The Nanny* and not known as an idealogue, tweeted, "Capitalism has become another word for Ruling Class Elite! When profit is at the expense of all things of true value, we gotta problem."

Video streams were up by more than 30 percent in March, mostly for escapist entertainment. That month, the number one Netflix show was *Tiger King*, a docuseries about a controversial zookeeper named Joe Exotic serving a twenty-two-year jail sentence for hiring an assassin to murder one of his enemies and for killing five tigers, which violated the Endangered Species Act. Trevor Noah joked about the similarities between Joe Exotic and Trump, noting that, like the president, Exotic made everything about himself and saw conspiracies everywhere. According to Noah, the most Trumpian thing about Exotic was that "he has the delusion that he's an expert in his field."

Dramatic films about pandemics, such as *Outbreak* (1995) and *Contagion* (2011), also trended heavily on Netflix. The latter, directed by Steven Soderbergh and written by Scott Z. Burns, imagined an even more fatal disease than COVID-19 infecting the globe. In mid-March, Soderbergh and several of *Contagion's* stars reunited to produce a series of public service announcements about how people could minimize the chance of contracting COVID. Matt Damon assured viewers that "everything you're going to hear from us has been vetted by public health experts and scientists." The actor emphasized that everyone was at risk for COVID, including young people, and he urged everyone to stay home and practice social distancing, concluding, "We can all do this by staying apart. Please do your part."

Kate Winslet, who played an epidemiologist in *Contagion*, said, "I spent time with some of the best public health professionals in the world . . . who told me: Wash your hands like your life depends on it." Screenwriter Burns published an open letter in the voice of the virus, in which he referred to Trump as "Captain Handshake":

Hello, America:

My name is SARS-CoV-2—but you probably know me by my disease name, COVID-19 . . .

Yes, I am talking to you, U.S.A.

Sort of crazy that I came to your country and South Korea on pretty much the exact same day—South Korea wound up with drive-thru testing and .0002 cases per capita . . .

Seriously, imagine how excited I was when I got here only to find that nobody had bothered to come up with a test to track me or a way to distribute the tests you didn't bother to make, or a way to get test results back to people in a timely fashion. And when you finally did get around to it, the first test you produced didn't actually work. I'm not sure why you didn't just use the one the World Health Organization came up with? . . .

On March 13, the guy with the orange face—Captain Handshake— said you were going to have drive-thru tests like they have in South Ko- rea at Walmart stores by the end of the next week. Beautiful tests! I was right there in the Rose Garden when he said it. It's late April now, and I spend a lot of time at Walmart stores playing with your kids and on credit cards—and out of 5,000 Walmart stores across the country, only three have drive-up testing.

PSAs could be pulled together within a few days. Jokes could be written and delivered within a twenty-four-hour news cycle. With rare exceptions, songwriting usually took longer; the average gap between albums by singer-songwriters was two years. The greatest of them all, Bob Dylan, had not released an album of new songs since *Tempest* in 2012.

On March 27, as his seventy-ninth birthday loomed, Dylan re- leased a new track entitled "Murder Most Foul." It was a seventeen- minute epic about another defining American moment: the assassi- nation of John F. Kennedy. Dylan was twenty-two years old when JFK was killed but he had already written "Blowin' in the Wind" and "Only a Pawn in Their Game," the latter of which he performed in Washington in 1963 before Martin Luther King Jr. made his "I Have a Dream" speech.

The secondary subject of "Murder Most Foul" was the role of music in American mythology. Dylan referenced the 1960s broad- caster Wolfman Jack and dozens of artists in many genres, as if their greatest songs were a cultural cushion against the damage done by the assassination. Dylan reminded his audience, "If you want to remember, you better write down the names."

Although "Murder Most Foul" was written before the pandemic, the song's release in the first few weeks of quarantine felt poetically intentional to many of his older fans, who streamed the song so much that it rose to number one on Billboard's "Rock Digital Songs" chart. In an interview with Douglas Brinkley in the New York Times, Dylan made it clear that the song was connected to currents of American culture that transcended the 1960s and resonated in the Trump era. "I don't think of 'Murder Most Foul' as a glorification of the past or some kind of send-off to a lost age. It speaks to me in the moment. It always did, especially when I was writing the lyrics out."

A few critics considered the song to be a minor work. The New Yorker's Kevin Dettmar called the song "weird" and "disappointing," opining that "all the clichés . . . aren't adding up to much." Others, however, felt that Dylan had tapped a long-buried sliver of the American unconscious mind. Anthony DeCurtis wrote, "It's . . . an implied comment on our current president . . . contrasting the sense of possibility JFK represented to our current moment." Rolling Stone's Simon Vozick-Levinson opined that the song "is really about the ways that music can comfort us in times of national trauma . . . For those of us who often turn to Dylan's catalog for that very purpose, 'Murder Most Foul' has arrived at the right time."

Many artists and performers agreed. Chrissie Hynde posted her praise on Facebook: "The one thing that really lifted me out of my moment of darkness was hearing the new Dylan track. Aren't you glad we have him? He's always been there for us when we need help. It's why I've seen men in their seventies stand up at his gigs in tears . . . because he really has been there in our lives when we're all alone. And he still is." In an e-mail, actor Bobby Canna-vale told me how much the song meant to him: "If you put the song together with the moment and consider that sometimes the timing of something contributes to its artfulness, then Bob is the King. I've listened to ['Murder Most Foul'] every day once since it came out and I have different feelings about it with every new listen . . . I marvel at how he comes back to Kennedy with that section about Jackie catching him in her lap. Sometimes it's the crankiness and truth in 'Hate to tell you mister, but only dead men are free.' When he gets to the part where he tells Wolfman Jack what to play, I'm so fuckin' all in."

Mark Jacobson, who chronicled American culture for decades in the *Village Voice* and *New York*, published *Pale Horse Rider* in 2018; it's a biography about a cult figure named William Cooper who was obsessed with the JFK assassination. Cooper's 1991 book *Behold a Pale Horse* popularized conspiracy theories to disparate audiences, ranging from rap icons like Tupac Shakur and the Wu-Tang Clan to the young Alex Jones decades before his strident pro-Trump radio broadcasts became a pillar of the right-wing media echo chamber. Jacobson sensed shades of Cooper in "Murder Most Foul" but he loved that "everyone in our crowd is excited about a Dylan song at this day and age. It is a community creator."

There had long been a disconnect between the "serious" academic and political worlds and the minds of many artists on the subject of the Kennedy assassination. Most political pundits accepted the official findings of the Warren Report, which concluded that Kennedy was killed by a lone assassin. In Washington, DC, anyone who suggested otherwise was considered a kook. But for many Americans, the official history was unconvincing. Over the years, several artists had tried to fill the knowledge vacuum around Kennedy's death.

In Woody Allen's 1977 film *Annie Hall*, the protagonist, Alvy Singer, played by Woody Allen, is obsessed with discrepancies in the Warren Report. It was not made clear if Allen, who also wrote and directed the Oscar-winning film, doubted the official version of the assassination or was parodying conspiracy theorists. It was probably a little bit of both. There was no such ambiguity in Oliver Stone's 1991 epic *JFK*, the script of which dramatizes many of the facts that fueled the widespread belief that Kennedy's murder was not the work of a lone assassin but of a conspiracy that involved several others.

Implicit in Stone's vision is the idea that if JFK had lived, been reelected, and served as president for eight years instead of three, then the Vietnam War would not have escalated as it did under his successors. As Dylan sings in "Murder Most Foul," "The soul of a nation is torn away and it's beginning to go into a slow decay."

Scripted dramas took even longer to germinate than did songs.

David Simon's six-part miniseries *The Plot Against America*, based on the Philip Roth novel, was green-lit shortly after Trump's election but premiered on HBO on March 16, 2020. The story is an alternative history in which Charles Lindbergh, the aviation hero and Nazi sympathizer, is elected president in 1940, leading to the widespread persecution of Jews in the United States. Soon after Lindbergh takes office, federal policies are implemented to disperse Jews from urban communities and into the American "heartland." *The Plot Against America* is told from the point of view of several characters: a ten-year-old boy from New Jersey named Philip Levin (played by Azhy Robertson), Philip's anti-Lindbergh father, Herman (Morgan Spector), and his mother, Bess (Zoe Kazan). Much of the drama revolves around arguments within the Jewish community between those who are scared and horrified by Lindbergh's ascendance to power and a few who naively cooperate with the new president, including a rabbi named Bengelsdorf (John Turturro) and Philip's aunt, Evelyn (Winona Ryder), who falls in love with Bengelsdorf to the horror of the rest of her family.

The *New Yorker's* film critic Richard Brody succinctly captured the essence of *The Plot Against America*: "[It] dramatizes two vast and contradictory principles simultaneously: on the one hand, the susceptibility of American individualism to the cult of celebrity, and of American faith in democracy to a tyranny of the majority, leading to a particular vulnerability to unscrupulous politicians who win widespread popular support . . . and, on the other, the distinctively American sense of freedom . . . the will to resist such political depravities, a will that's integral to the country's values, heritage, and history."

In 2018, a few months before he died, Roth told the *New York Times'* Charles McGrath that he never intended for his novel to be a political allegory. In the context of the Trump administration, however, he realized that the parallels between the world he had invented and what was happening in contemporary America were hard to ignore.

The Plot Against America had a particular impact on American Jews because aspects of the plot echoed arguments between those Jews for whom all issues are subordinate to support for Israel's Likud government (whose leader Benjamin Netanyahu was a Trump ally) and those whose core identity is intertwined with the tradition of progressive Jewish activism on issues like labor and civil rights (and who were thus among Trump's harshest critics).

Simon was in the latter category. Many of the family photographs shown on the fictitious Levin family's walls were actually those of Simon's own relatives. His mother "had that sensibility of always having to step off the sidewalk because the Cossacks were coming." The producer's goal was for "people to take from the book at this moment that all of us should be judged on what we accept and don't accept. The book is about . . . a family arrayed against an ugly political moment and what each of them does. What's the cost of that and what's the effect? Every one of us should be asking ourselves that question right now."

Roth's novel ended with FDR defeating Lindbergh in 1944, but Simon's dramatization leaves the outcome of the 1944 election ambiguous in order to reflect the uncertainty of the 2020 presidential election. He rhetorically asked the *Times*' McGrath, "Do you think we can go back to normal after Donald Trump? I don't. I'm very frightened. Something has shifted in our whole political demeanor . . . We're having this argument: is Donald Trump good or bad? As if the argument ends with him."

Around the same time that *The Plot Against America* first aired, the fourth season of *The Good Fight* premiered on CBS. The initial episode showed the alternative history in which Hillary Clinton won the 2016 election. In a long fantasy sequence, lawyer Diane Lockhart (played by Christine Baranski) "remembers" Trump's presidency. Talking it over with her law partner Liz Reddick-Lawrence (Audra McDonald), Diane concludes that this memory was really a nightmarish dream. She describes the horrors of kids in cages at the border, America's withdrawal from international agreements, and the president's sympathetic words about neo-Nazis. Liz asks in shock, "Where were the Obamas during all this?" to which her partner replies, "They had an overall deal at Netflix."

CHAPTER 7
QUARANTINE AS THE NEW NORMAL
APRIL 1–MAY 26, 2020

BERNIE WITHDRAWS

On April 2, 2020, Bernie Sanders supporter Sarah Silverman tweeted, "To my wonderful friends who are passionate about Biden . . . allow me to continue to fight with all I have for the person who has unflinchingly fought for the rights of every American his whole life. Who understands the existential threat of climate change . . . I will vote for the nominee with gusto. But please don't call it yet. Not now. Thanks."

Six days later, Sanders formally withdrew from the race and endorsed Joe Biden. Silverman lamented, "I'm heartbroken about Bernie. In all this darkness, he made me believe that people, together, could be the light . . . Thank you, Bernie. For me, you're right up there [with] Mr. Rogers." Emily Ratajkowski tweeted, "I feel so hopeless and devastated and powerless." Rosie O'Donnell wrote, "thank u bernie." Nancy Sinatra tweeted, "Bravo Bernie." Rosanna Arquette joined in too: "Gratitude Bernie Sanders for waking many Americans up."

Cardi B blamed some of her own fans for not turning out for Bernie: "Y'all young motherfuckers . . . I'm about to start hanging out with my grandma's friends because they vote . . . Y'all be like,

'We *looove* Bernie.' I be seeing all over Twitter, y'all love Bernie. But y'all wasn't voting! Y'all wasn't voting! . . . And because of that . . . Bernie is out of the motherfucking race. And now we gotta vote for Biden." Cher resignedly wrote, "You have to vote for the one side you hate the least."

On April 14, 2020, Cardi B filmed another conversation with Sanders. Sporting purple hair and long light-green nails, the rapper told Sanders, "Since I've been so focused on you, I haven't really done my research well on Joe Biden . . . The youth don't really rock with Joe Biden because he's conservative . . . I want you to tell my platform: Why are you endorsing him?" Sanders made his support for Biden crystal clear: "When I announced that I was running for president . . . what I said is, 'If I don't win'—and I tried hard to win—'I will endorse the Democrat who wins.' Because Donald Trump is, to my mind, the most dangerous president in the history of America. This is a guy who lies all the time. He doesn't believe in science. He downplayed the coronavirus . . . He doesn't believe in the Constitution . . . This is a bad-news guy who has got to be defeated . . . I'm trying to work with Joe to see that he becomes a more progressive candidate . . . to raise the minimum wage . . . to cancel student debt . . . He is moving in the right direction on immigration reform . . . and criminal justice." Cardi B was sold: "I'm excited and I'm nervous . . . and I hope that all of the viewers have a better sense of what's going on . . . Joe Biden for 2020!"

John Cusack, one of Sanders's most stalwart celebrity supporters, also argued Biden's case to unconvinced lefties. One tweet read, "Do not let Trump get exactly what he wants—a low election turnout . . . that's his wet dream." In another tweet, Cusack reiterated, "Nobody loathes neoliberalism more than me . . . [but] 4 more years of Trump = unimaginable cruelty . . . Suffering will happen."

On April 11, 2020, *Saturday Night Live* aired its first episode since the onset of the pandemic. Tom Hanks hosted the show and his monologue took place in his kitchen. "Good to be here, though it is also very weird to be here hosting *Saturday Night Live* from home. It is a strange time to try to be funny . . . There is no such thing as Saturdays anymore—every day is *today*. And we're not really *live*, but we are doing everything we can to make this feel like the SNL you know and love." The actor was still quarantined in Australia and Hanks acknowledged that he had "been the celebrity canary in the coal mine for the coronavirus . . . We are in this for the duration and we will get through this together. We are going to thank the hospital workers, our first responders, and all the helpers, the supermarket stockers, the people who deliver our food . . . the men and women who are keeping this country going."

The first sketch satirized a small company's initial Zoom meeting, showing employees fumbling over the new technology. It was one of the first televised parodies of a practice that became ubiquitous within days of the quarantine. Kate McKinnon impersonated the eighty-seven-year-old Supreme Court justice Ruth Bader Ginsburg doing one of her famous workouts. Larry David revived his grumpy Bernie Sanders impersonation, chiding, "Let's just say I'm voting for Joe Biden as enthusiastically as he voted for the Iraq War." Alec Baldwin played Trump and referred to the virus as "a giant hoax that we should all take very seriously . . . America, now number one in coronavirus! . . . TV ratings through the roof!" Chris Martin performed an acoustic version of Bob Dylan's "Shelter from the Storm," and the episode ended with a heartfelt tribute to Hal Willner, the music producer and SNL consultant who had died days earlier from complications due to COVID-19. With Lou Reed's song "Such a Perfect Day" playing in the background, SNL regulars past and present reflected on Willner's encyclopedic knowledge of culture.

CLIMATE CHANGE THROUGH A COVID LENS

In the early stages of COVID, the news media primarily fixated on Trump's daily behavior, as well as on the local and state health issues related to COVID. Yet the relentless effects of climate change did not pause in deference to other crises. Several artists used their public platforms to frame the pandemic in the context of long-standing environmental issues. On her blog, Drew Barrymore wrote, "What if one day, you had been married for many years, and your wife comes home and tells you she is unhappy . . . You don't go back to business as usual . . . Run to her! . . . Your wife's name is Mother Earth. And she is worth it! . . . If you take care of her, she will love you back."

An op-ed in *Le Monde,* coauthored by French actress Juliette Binoche and astrophysicist Aurélien Barrau, linked COVID-19 to the longer-term issue of climate change. Entitled "No to a Return to Normal," the piece argued that "consumerism and an obsession with productivity have led us to deny the value of life itself: that of plants, that of animals, and that of a great number of human beings. Pollution, climate change, and the destruction of our remaining natural zones has brought the world to a breaking point . . . The COVID-19 pandemic is a tragedy. This crisis is, however, inviting us to examine what is essential." The letter was cosigned by dozens of performers including Adam Driver, Cate Blanchett, Rooney Mara, Penélope Cruz, Madonna, Marion Cotillard, Javier Bardem, Jeremy Irons, Robert De Niro, Joaquin Phoenix, Barbra Streisand, and Willem Dafoe, as well as directors Alfonso Cuarón, Spike Jonze, Pedro Almodóvar, and Alejandro González Iñárritu.

On Michael Moore's podcast, he suggested that the pandemic is the earth "trying to tell our species to back off, slow down, and change your ways." Spike Lee told radio host Joe Madison that "pollution is clearing up. Skies are clear. Animals are coming out . . . People may think I'm crazy [but] I believe it in my heart and soul that we had gone too far and Earth said, 'Hold up, we gotta change this.'" In an interview with *Vice,* filmmaker David Lynch said, "For some reason, we were going down the wrong path and Mother Nature just said, 'Enough already.'"

Pearl Jam made a music video for their song "Retrograde" which starred Greta Thunberg as a fortune-teller warning of imminent climate destruction. On April 22, 2020, the fiftieth anniversary of Earth Day, several environmental organizations produced a three-day virtual celebration that included Joaquin Phoenix, Moby, Patricia Arquette, Jane Fonda, Robby Romero, Al Gore, Stacey Abrams, Questlove, and Jason Mraz. The message of the event was simple: "In the midst of a global pandemic, Earth Day Live aims to spur collective action to protect our communities and our planet, through performances, conversations, and training sessions curated by climate activists."

Alicia Keys tweeted, "Mama needs all of our love and she's making sure we slow down and pay attention. Let's take care of each other and our home." Paul McCartney tweeted, "Happy Earth Day everyone. Let's take care of this beautiful place." Ellen DeGeneres joked, "It's the 50th anniversary of #EarthDay. You don't look a day over 49."

Breitbart's Alana Mastrangelo wrote with predictable contempt, "The leftist, millionaire Hollywood elite took to their social media accounts to celebrate Earth Day on Wednesday, with some posting actually tree-hugging photos. Alyssa Milano used the Chinese coronavirus to push green energy policies, while others honored and gave thanks to 'Mama' earth."

Some artists felt that their role was to provide perspectives missing in the twenty-four-hour news cycle. On March 29, John Krasinski launched a show on YouTube that was dedicated to exposing positive stories in a difficult time. It was called *Some Good News*. Krasinski had recently starred as a CIA agent in *Jack Ryan*, but on *SGN* he exuded the sunny personality that had first made him a star in *The Office*.

SGN included footage of crowds cheering for health care workers in Spain and the United Kingdom. A feature called "Love in the Time of Quarantine" showed grandparents trying to emotionally connect with grandkids without risking exposure to the virus. Krasinski also presided over a Zoom wedding of two fans of *The Office* which included a reunion of the cast, who celebrated the occasion with silly dances. The first episode of *SGN* received ten million views.

Spanish director Pedro Almodóvar wrote a piece for IndieWire that observed, "The new global and viral situation seems to come out of a fifties sci-fi story, the Cold War years. Horror films with the crudest anticommunist propaganda. I'm also thinking about *The Day the Earth Stood Still, D.O.A., Forbidden Planet, Invasion of the Body Snatchers*, and any other film with martians in it. Evil always came from the outside (communists, refugees, martians) and it served as an argument for the crudest populism. (Nevertheless, I ardently recommend all the films I've mentioned; they are still excellent.)"

MRS. AMERICA

On April 15, 2020, *Mrs. America*, a nine-episode series about the struggle in the early 1970s to ratify the Equal Rights Amendment (ERA), premiered on FX. Although the series had a feminist point of view, the main character and villain was Phyllis Schlafly, the real-life conservative activist who orchestrated the defeat of the ERA. In addition to activism through her group Eagle Forum, Schlafly was periodically involved with Republican presidential politics. In 1964, she published *A Choice Not an Echo*, a book that lionized Barry Goldwater. In 1980, she became an influential ally in Reagan's presidential campaign and in 2016 she cowrote *The Conservative Case for Trump*, which was published a day before her death that fall. Trump gave a eulogy at her funeral.

Cate Blanchett, who played Schlafly, was also the show's executive producer. She told the *New York Times*, "I was reverse engineering my understanding of her grassroots influence over how we got where we are today."

The full text of the Equal Rights Amendment read, "Equality of rights under the law shall not be denied or abridged by the United States or by any state on account of sex." It passed both houses of Congress in 1972 and was endorsed by President Nixon. By 1977, the legislatures in thirty-five of the thirty-eight states required for ratification had approved the amendment. It was at this point that Schlafly organized Eagle Forum with the agenda of preventing the ERA from passing in the remaining states.

Mrs. America portrayed an array of feminist leaders in the seventies, including Gloria Steinem (played by Rose Byrne,) Bella Abzug (Margo Martindale), Betty Friedan (Tracey Ullman), pro-ERA Republican Jill Ruckelshaus (Elizabeth Banks), and Congresswoman Shirley Chisholm (Uzo Aduba), who ran in the 1972 Democratic presidential primaries.

The drama accurately depicted the left's perennial infighting. In the show, Abzug is eager to hitch the ERA fight to George Mc-

Govern's presidential candidacy and she admonishes Chisholm for continuing her symbolic campaign. Chisholm replies, "I didn't get anywhere in this life waiting on someone's permission." After McGovern secures the nomination, Steinem tartly calls him "the best white male candidate."

One episode included a scene where Schlafly meets with former Trump advisors Paul Manafort and Roger Stone. Dahvi Waller, the series showrunner, writer, and producer, acknowledged to *Slate* that the conversation was fabricated: "While we know [Manafort and Stone] helped run Reagan's campaign, we do not know if they crossed with Phyllis . . . but it was a shorthand way to dramatize the parallels between the 1980 election and 2016."

As Katha Pollitt observed in the *Nation*, *Mrs. America* raises "issues that are still with us: pragmatism versus revolution, compromise versus purity, winning power inch-by-inch within the system versus raising your battle cry outside it . . . Although Abzug supports lesbian rights, she has to be argued into fighting for them." In one episode, Friedan refers to lesbians and queer women as "the lavender menace." Pollitt also points out that although Schlafly's anti-ERA rhetoric was "about drafting women and unisex bathrooms, the real issue was not these things. It was that many women raised to be traditional homemakers, supported by their husbands and respected in their communities, found their pedestals knocked out from under them practically overnight."

Mrs. America ends with a montage from the 2017 Women's March. One demonstrator outside of the White House holds a sign that reads, "RESIST." Another says, "I cannot believe we still have to protest this shit."

Gloria Steinem was not happy with the series. She told the *Guardian*'s Laura Bates that *Mrs. America* "gives you the impression that [Schlafly] was the reason [the Equal Rights Amendment] was defeated. In actuality, I don't believe she changed one vote . . . The insurance industry here opposed the Equal Rights Amendment because if they stopped segregating their actuarial tables it would cost them . . . millions of dollars."

OLD MUSIC, NEW MUSIC, AND TV FINALES

The pandemic had an immediate impact on the way people listened to music. R.E.M.'s 1987 hit "It's the End of the World as We Know It (And I Feel Fine)" was streamed 5.6 million times in April 2020, a 110 percent increase from the previous month. The Police's "Don't Stand So Close to Me," originally released in 1980, was streamed 3.4 million times in April 2020, an 81 percent increase from March. The Five Stairsteps' 1971 hit, "O-o-h Child," with a chorus that promises "things are gonna get easier," was streamed 3.2 million times, a 72 percent increase from March.

The Rolling Stones scored their first number one record on iTunes when they released the new song "Living in a Ghost Town," which was written before the pandemic but contained the prescient lyrics, "Life was so beautiful, then we all got locked down / Feel like a ghost, living in a ghost town."

Lucinda Williams released the anti-Trump song "Man Without a Soul," which included the lyric, "You bring nothing good to this world / Beyond a web of cheating and stealing." She told *Pitchfork* that she had "spent a lot of time writing these songs from a place of being really frustrated and angry about what's been going on in the country since we lost Obama."

In the years leading up to the pandemic, Steve Earle had written songs for a Public Theater play called *Coal Country*, which he appeared in until the pandemic shut it down. The songs were also on his album *Ghosts of West Virginia*, which was released in the spring of 2020. Both the play and Earle's songs focused on a lethal accident that occurred in the Upper Big Branch coal mine in West Virginia in 2010, killing twenty-nine men. In speaking to relatives of the victims, Earle, a native Texan, was reminded of the huge cultural divide between the Greenwich Village creative milieu he called home and the huge sections of America that had voted for Trump. He hoped that his songs and the play would sensitize his audience to the shared humanity of America's conflicting cultures, emphasizing that one thing urban liberals and West Virginia miners had in common was a belief in labor unions, a dozen of which collaborated with Earle to stream songs during the pandemic.

In April, the ABC prime-time comedy series *Modern Family* aired its final episode. It had started its run eleven years earlier during the first year of Obama's presidency, before Netflix, Hulu, and Amazon Prime were creating original programming, at the end of an era when prime-time network TV shows were still culturally dominant.

Modern Family was one of the first TV series to have two of its main characters, Mitch and Cam (played by Jesse Tyler Ferguson and Eric Stonestreet), be a married gay couple. When fans of the show noticed that the couple eschewed public displays of affection, an online petition objecting to the inhibition obtained thousands of signatures; the couple kissed in a subsequent episode. When the Supreme Court legalized gay marriage nationally in 2015, the *Daily Beast's* Kevin Fallon opined, "With its palatable, matter-of-fact progressiveness, [*Modern Family*] may very well have been the show that finally tipped the scale."

Two weeks after the *Modern Family* finale, *Homeland* wrapped up its eighth and final season with the denouement of a professional relationship between the brilliant bipolar CIA agent Carrie Mathison (Claire Danes) and her mentor and friend, CIA director Saul Berenson (Mandy Patinkin). *Homeland* was originally created in the wake of 9/11, offering a more sophisticated perspective on the war on terror than *24*. (Howard Gordon was an executive producer of both shows.)

Homeland's final seasons were informed by Trump's occupation of the White House. Executive Producer Alex Gansa told the *Hollywood Reporter*, "If we had a more global message, it was to try to dramatize what a precarious position we are in. An accident or a misinterpretation of an event, or another actual attack on the homeland, could bring us to our knees . . . With leadership that is either inexperienced or misguided, that becomes an even greater possibility."

The *Washington Post's* Hank Steuver wondered, "What sort of contemporary hero would be the natural successor to . . . Carrie Mathison? Who or what is the enemy—domestic terrorism? Vladimir Putin? Climate change deniers? Is it, perhaps, an FBI agent who thwarts American hate crimes and fake-news kooks, in a show about a divided nation rotting from within? . . . Could it be a show about . . . a special-ops team of former diplomats, tasked with restoring a previous administration's global damage? Is it about an epidemiologist who fights disinformation campaigns?"

Between *Homeland* ending and the quarantine beginning, Mandy Patinkin and his wife Kathryn Grody were motivated to elevate their presence on social media. The couple had long been humanitarian activists. In the years leading up to 2020, they worked with the International Rescue Committee (IRC). Patinkin explained, "When I was filming the fifth season of *Homeland* in Berlin, the very first episode was centered around the Syrian refugee camp. At that moment, 125,000 refugees were trying to make it across the Balkan route into Germany. I looked at those photos and I saw my grandparents and ancestors who fled to the United States and the United States welcomed them with open arms." Patinkin and Grody visited several refugee camps and regularly fundraised for the IRC.

Referring to the character he played on *Homeland*, Patinkin recalled, "What Saul Berenson has on his desk, in every single scene, in every single season . . . was the phrase from the Mishnah, 'Destroy a life, and it's as though you have destroyed the entire world. Save a life, and it's as though you have saved the entire world.'"

Patinkin and Grody's thirty-four-year-old son, Gideon, hunkered down with them in quarantine and started making videos in which he would ask his parents personal questions. In one of the first videos, they recalled that they'd had a big argument on their first date forty years earlier. That video got more than 400,000 views and the couple's posts for the IRC began drawing more traffic. Gideon told me, "In a world of artifice, people like seeing a real connection. The honesty of the answers was heightened by the pandemic and an awareness of mortality."

SEAN PENN TO THE RESCUE

In mid-April, volunteers in Los Angeles helped administer thousands of COVID-19 tests in low-income neighborhoods under the auspices of Community Organized Relief Effort (CORE), an organization started several years earlier by Sean Penn, after Haiti's earthquake.

In 2008, when Penn accepted the Academy Award for Best Actor for his performance as the slain gay politician Harvey Milk, the actor thanked his cheering peers with a wry grin: "You commie, homo-loving sons of guns." Yet Penn's presence in America's political conversations had become defined as much by his personal volunteer work in the midst of disasters as by his movies. Hunter S. Thompson, no slouch when it came to putting himself in harm's way, once said, "Sean is batty as a loon and is prone to taking extraordinary risks in foreign towns."

Penn visited Iraq in 2002 and 2003, both before and after the United States attacked the country, and wrote about his travels in the *San Francisco Chronicle*. The actor was so visible as an activist that he was mockingly depicted in Trey Parker and Matt Stone's parody of the Hollywood left, *Team America: World Police*.

Undaunted, Penn traveled to Iran in 2005, where he met with dissidents and former president Rafsanjani. Later that year, after Hurricane Katrina decimated New Orleans, Penn braved the floodwaters in a small motorboat and pulled stranded people off roofs after the levees broke.

More recently, in an interview with *Deadline*'s Mike Fleming, Penn explained his rationale for focusing on COVID-19 testing: "It seemed very sensible for us to relieve highly skilled first responders, [like] the Los Angeles Fire Department, from having to man these sites. We were able to take their training at the directing of [Los Angeles mayor] Garcetti . . ." At each site where CORE set up, twenty-five firefighters were able to return to their usual duties. Los Angeles fire chief Ralph Terrazas acknowledged that "the volunteers from CORE have been doing an excellent job." By the end of the year, CORE had administered more than three million COVID tests.

TWITTER ABIDES

Tweet-to-tweet combat during every news cycle continued unabated during the pandemic. On April 6, 2020, in the wake of sexual harassment accusations by former Biden staffer Tara Reade against Joe Biden, Rose McGowan, who had been one of the most prominent voices in exposing Harvey Weinstein, wrote that American media was a "complicity machine . . . hard at work covering up for Creepy Joe Biden." She criticized fellow Me Too activist Alyssa Milano for sticking with Biden. Milano tweeted in response, "I just don't feel comfortable throwing away a decent man that I've known for 15 years, in this time of complete chaos, without there being a thorough investigation." Recalling the tense moment several months later, Rosanna Arquette told me that she agreed with Milano: "Biden was not my choice. Warren was. But we were in danger of real-time dictatorship. I felt we could lose all of our rights. People were dying. I wanted to do everything to make sure Trump was not reelected."

On May 5, 2020, when Trump visited a mask-making facility in Phoenix, the president's handlers blasted the Guns N' Roses version of "Live and Let Die" without the band's permission. The following day, singer Axl Rose tweeted about his disgust with Treasury Secretary Steve Mnuchin's suggestion that Americans should travel more while their places of work were closed: "Whatever anyone may have previously thought of Steve Mnuchin he's officially an asshole." Mnuchin responded, "What have you done for the country lately?" followed by what was apparently supposed to be an emoji of the American flag but was actually the similar-looking flag of Liberia. Rose retorted, "My bad I didn't get we're hoping 2 emulate Liberia's economic model but on the real unlike this admin I'm not responsible for 70k+ deaths n' unlike u I don't hold a fed gov position of responsibility 2 the American people n' go on TV tellin them 2 travel the US during a pandemic."

Brandon Friedman, who had been deputy assistant secretary at the Department of Housing and Urban Development during the Obama administration, tweeted about the members of Guns N' Roses, "There is a 100% chance America would be better off with Axl Rose as Secretary of the Treasury, Slash as Secretary of State and Duff McKagan as Secretary of Commerce instead of Steve Mnuchin, Mike Pompeo and Wilbur Ross."

Meanwhile Joe Biden's general election campaign was underway. In an interview on Charlamagne tha God's radio show, *The Breakfast Club*, the Democratic candidate made an unforced error when he blurted out that if anyone supported Trump, "you ain't Black." Sean "Diddy" Combs was appalled, tweeting, "I already told you the #BlackVoteAintFree." Wanda Sykes did damage control: "Biden feels at home speaking to the Black community. He made a joke . . . I would not . . . say that voting for Trump means you're not *Black*. I would say it means you're not *smart*."

Rob Reiner tweeted: "In 2016, a mentally deranged Con Man colluded with an enemy power to steal an election. He's abused women. He's praised Nazis. He's taken babies from mothers. He's decimated the Rule of Law. He's turned his back as tens of thousands of US die. In 2020 he must be gone." David Ng felt the need to give *Breitbart* readers a bullet-point refutation of the director's indictment while recapitulating his assertions in boldface type: "Reiner alleged that Trump **is mentally deranged**—There is literally no evidence whatsoever to support this claim . . . **is a con man**—Democrats cling to this claim, though Trump has never been prosecuted for any fraud or 'con,' **colluded with an enemy**—100% false, as proven by the report of Special Counsel Robert Mueller . . . **abused women**—Trump has faced (and denied) accusations of sexual impropriety, but never of 'abuse,' **praised Nazis**—In fact, he condemned them 'totally.'"

Not everything was about Trump. On May 27, 2020, Larry Kramer died at the age of eighty-four. He was a legendary gay rights and AIDS activist, an Oscar-nominated screenwriter (*Women in Love*), and a playwright best known for *The Normal Heart*. Reiner was one of many artists who tweeted in tribute to Kramer: "We shared the stage in Lance Black's play '8' which highlighted our fight for marriage equality." Lin-Manuel Miranda tweeted, "Don't know a soul who saw or read *The Normal Heart* and came away unmoved, unchanged." Elton John wrote, "We have lost a giant of a man who stood up for gay rights like a warrior. His anger was needed at a time when gay men's deaths to AIDS were being ignored by the American government."

LATE NIGHT

On late-night TV, Samantha Bee focused on pols who used the pandemic as an excuse to restrict abortion rights. Producer Kristen Bartlett explained to *New York* magazine, "What is something that Sam could say that other hosts wouldn't say? What is something from her viewpoint, or specifically as a woman, she would want to talk about?"

Trevor Noah mocked Trump's boast that his daily coronavirus briefings got high ratings: "The ratings aren't high because of Trump. People are watching TV because of the virus." Noah added that the president's grandstanding was "as if the guy on *Friends* who owns the coffee shop [took] credit for the success of the show."

Jimmy Kimmel lamented the politicization of wearing masks: "Of all the fights we've had over the last few years, this one makes the least sense. This is the dumbest standoff ever. We all want to go back to work, we all want to go back to eat, we all want to hang out, none of us want to see people die. So if wearing a mask can help slow the virus and get us back to normal sooner, why not wear a mask?" Stephen Colbert joked, "*Of course* Trump is the guy saying he doesn't want to wear protection."

Trump and Pence staged a photo op at a Michigan Ford factory that was manufacturing face masks, yet neither the president nor the vice president wore a mask. Seth Meyers commented on the scene's absurdity: "Put aside the fact that Trump and Pence are ignoring their own government's guidelines on mask-wearing, or the stupid conservative culture war over masks: why do you guys have to be such dicks about everything? Just be polite. If you go over to someone's house and they ask you to take your shoes off, you take your shoes off . . . You don't make a big show of leaving them on and tracking mud everywhere."

After Trump was criticized for suggesting that disinfectant might be a cure for COVID, he claimed that he had been speaking "sarcastically." Seth Meyers said, "If there's one thing people want from leadership during a pandemic, it's sarcasm. And that was me . . . using sarcasm." Stephen Colbert wondered if Trump was also being sarcastic when he took his oath of office. Jimmy Kimmel asked, "Can we claim *we* were being sarcastic when we elected him?" Trevor Noah focused on the original remark: "I love that people were actually calling their local health departments to ask if they should try to cure themselves with disinfectants . . . That means that even the people who are dumb enough to drink bleach are still smart enough not to trust something Donald Trump said."

Trump took the bait. In a *New York Post* interview, the president complained, "Seth Meyers, he was nasty . . . The guy's got no talent whatsoever. Zero. How do these guys get jobs? I don't get it." He also went after Colbert: "There's nothing funny about him." Colbert responded: "It's nice to know that Trump is staying laser-focused on the ball during a crisis."

New York governor Andrew Cuomo asked Chris Rock and Rosie Perez to join one of his daily COVID briefings. Cuomo acknowledged, "I am not cool enough. They are going to use their voice, their skill, their talent to communicate better than I have." The performers announced a PSA campaign that urged New Yorkers to wear masks. Rock said, "People need . . . to posse up for testing. If you love your grandmother, you should get tested."

CO-OPTING HOLLYWOOD

Despite right-wing attacks on the president's critics in the entertainment business, his acolytes made persistent efforts to cloak Trump in the totemic trappings of Hollywood, as if art could be irrevocably severed from artists.

In early May, a digitally altered clip from the 1996 film *Independence Day* was posted by Trump supporters on social media. The plot of the movie centered on an alien invasion, where flying saucers hover over major cities. President Thomas J. Whitmore, played by Bill Pullman, orders evacuations of New York, Los Angeles, and Washington, DC, but before most people can escape, beams from the saucers kill millions. In the film's denouement, American scientists and the military figure out the aliens' weak spot and destroy the invaders.

In the film clip distorted by MAGA supporters, Trump's face was superimposed on Pullman's when the fictitious president makes his climactic inspirational speech. The video also replaced the faces of other actors so that Donald Trump Jr., Ted Cruz, and

Fox News personalities Sean Hannity and Tucker Carlson appear to bask in the glow of the president's cinematic eloquence.

Trump tweeted a link to the clip and it was retweeted fifty thousand times. An appalled Pullman told the *Hollywood Reporter*, "My voice belongs to no one but me . . ." *Independence Day* costar Vivica A. Fox tweeted to Trump, "Cant believe U would insult our classic film this way! But hey! Typical POS behavior! U never had the leadership or courage to do this role! Never!"

On May 15, when Trump announced a public–private partnership to develop a COVID-19 vaccine, he named the operation "warp speed," a phrase coined by science-fiction writers in the 1960s and popularized on *Star Trek* to describe the fictitious notion of traveling faster than the speed of light.

The following day, Elon Musk, while urging the California government to let him reopen a Tesla factory despite the quarantine, co-opted a plot device from *The Matrix*, suggesting that his followers "take the red pill." Ivanka Trump retweeted it, adding the word "taken." Lilly Wachowski, who cowrote and codirected *The Matrix*, promptly replied, "Fuck both of you."

The Matrix, first released in 1999, was about a dystopia in which human beings are placed in a coma while the energy from their bodies is used by a tyrannical ruling class. Neo, the protagonist played by Keanu Reeves, is awakened by rebel leader Morpheus (Laurence Fishburne), who offers him a choice: "You take the blue pill, the story ends, you wake up in your bed and believe whatever you want to believe. You take the red pill, you stay in Wonderland, and I show you how deep the rabbit hole goes."

In the years since the film's release, the "red pill" metaphor had been periodically co-opted by alt-right groups and libertarians like Musk. Yet Wachowski explained to the *Hollywood Reporter* that "*The Matrix* was born out of a lot of anger and a lot of rage . . . at capitalism and corporatized structure and forms of oppression." Wachowski, who came out as a transgender woman in 2016, also indicated that the "red pill" was a metaphor for being true to herself.

In early May, Trump's 2020 campaign manager Brad Parscale invoked *Star Wars* by comparing Trump's reelection apparatus to the

"Death Star." Parscale said that they were ready to "start pressing fire." Molly Jong-Fast of the *Daily Beast* tweeted a reference to the climactic destruction of the Death Star in the film: "Didn't make it till the end of Star Wars, huh?" NBC legal analyst Barb McQuade wondered, "Who chooses to portray themselves as the Death Star?" But *Politico*'s Derek Robertson saw a method to the madness: "The president has favorably likened himself to the vile Captain Bligh of *Mutiny on the Bounty* . . . and [Trump's] campaign . . . posted a video with the president's head bizarrely photoshopped onto Thanos, the genocidal alien despot of the Marvel Cinematic Universe. Each instance elicited the same response from a certain set of liberals: *Don't they get it? Don't they understand they have it all wrong?* The real explanation is . . . Parscale and his ilk . . . understand those characters' morality perfectly well . . . Behavior that makes one a villain in fiction—deceit, wanton rule-breaking, a willful disregard for collateral damage—is, in real life, more likely to get one branded a 'winner.'"

Most artists had a very different perspective of what "winning" meant. On April 15, 2020, James Cromwell, who would be nominated later in the year for an Emmy for his appearances in *Succession*, posted a video on YouTube in which he said, "You wanna do something? Try this. Choose an issue. Inform yourself. Discern the truth. Communicate it. Organize in your community. Think globally, act locally. Dare to take effective action. Listen to your conscience and follow your heart. Question the prevailing wisdom. Resist. Goddammit. Resist."

There would soon be more resistance than the actor could have imagined.

CHAPTER 8
BLACK LIVES MATTER
MAY 27–JUNE 12, 2020

GEORGE FLOYD

The sadistic murder of George Floyd by a Minneapolis police officer on May 27, vividly captured on video, triggered a reaction that was much broader than had occurred after previous incidents, in part because millions of people had more time on their hands as a result of the pandemic, in part because of the uniquely grotesque nature of the killing, but also because of the mysterious rhythms of America's long-delayed reckoning with racism in the criminal justice system. It was time.

The mixed feelings that some white progressives had about political entertainers were not shared by most Black leaders. Artists had long played a uniquely prominent role in African American struggles for equality, from Harriet Beecher Stowe's novel *Uncle Tom's Cabin* to Marian Anderson's appearance in front of the Lincoln Memorial in 1939 to Harry Belafonte's pivotal role in Martin Luther King Jr.'s mission. John Lewis called rhythm and blues music "the soundtrack to the Civil Rights Movement." During the last decade of civil rights leader Julian Bond's life, he delivered lectures about the political importance of popular music.

At a press conference related to the investigation of Floyd's murder, Minnesota attorney general Keith Ellison said, "We need arts and entertainment to help inspire us toward justice." In an interview with *Variety* that week, Black Lives Matter cofounder Patrisse Cullors said, "We need every single musician . . . to show up right now."

After Floyd's funeral, Cornel West told CNN's Anderson Cooper that it was "in the great tradition of the best of Black people . . . You saw John Coltrane's *A Love Supreme* in that church service. You saw . . . Marvin Gaye's *What's Going On* and Toni Morrison's *Beloved*."

Shortly after Floyd's death, Spike Lee released a ninety-second film called *Three Brothers* that began with the graphic "Will History Stop Repeating Itself?" The director interspersed video clips of Floyd's murder with the fatal police choking of Eric Garner in New York and the fictitious strangulation of the character Radio Raheem in Lee's *Do the Right Thing*. On Don Lemon's CNN program, a shaken Lee explained that he had based Raheem's cinematic death on the real-life police killing of the unarmed Michael Stewart by New York City transit cops in 1983 after they apprehended him for spraying graffiti in a subway station. The director said that when he saw the Floyd video he thought, "Oh my God, that's the same thing." Lee added, "This guy we got in the White House—he ain't helping."

Time magazine began crafting a special issue about race relations that would be published in August under the title "The New American Revolution." It would include pieces from Congresswoman Barbara Lee, activist Angela Davis, and musician Tyler, the Creator, among others. The issue was edited not by a journalist or historian, but by Pharrell Williams, a thirteen-time Grammy Award–winning artist, writer, and producer.

X Clan's 1992 song "F.T.P." references several police victims including Yusef Hawkins, Eleanor Bumpurs, and Gavin Cato. Ice Cube's 1992 "We Had to Tear This Muthafucka Up" focuses on the reaction to the acquittal of the Los Angeles officers who had beaten Rodney King. In the 2004 track "My Hood," Maino expresses outrage at the police killing of an unarmed man in his Brooklyn apartment. On Papoose's 2007 track "Change Gon' Come," the rapper begins by acknowledging several victims of police killings: "R.I.P.

to Sean Bell, R.I.P. to Kathryn Johnston, R.I.P. to Amadou Diallo." The unarmed Johnson was killed in her home in Atlanta by police in a botched drug raid. The unarmed Bell was killed by plainclothes police who shot him fifty times outside of a strip club in Queens. The unarmed Diallo was shot forty-one times by police outside his Bronx home in 1999, a killing that was also the subject of Wyclef Jean's "Diallo" and Bruce Springsteen's "American Skin (41 Shots)."

Contemporary rappers who released tracks in the wake of Floyd's murder included Lil Baby ("The Bigger Picture") and DaBaby ("Rockstar"). R&B singer H.E.R. wrote and released "I Can't Breathe," which includes the words: "All of the names you refuse to remember / Was somebody's brother, friend / Or a son to a mother that's crying, singing, 'I can't breathe, you're taking my life from me.'" (The song won a Grammy Award in 2021.)

Several relevant older tracks had a big resurgence. Between May 26 and June 2, 2020, Childish Gambino's "This Is America" (2018) increased its weekly streams from 273,000 to 1,826,000. Kendrick Lamar's "Alright" (2015) increased from 131,000 to 1,162,000. Public Enemy's "Fight the Power" (1989) increased from 19,000 to 178,000 and N.W.A's "Fuck tha Police" (1988) increased from 77,000 to 579,000.

The most dramatic spike was for Killer Mike's "Don't Die," a track originally released in 2016 which jumped from 2,000 to 547,000 streams in a single week. A former MC for the group Run the Jewels, Killer Mike had become as well known as a Bernie Sanders surrogate as for his recordings. In the wake of the protests following Floyd's murder, Killer Mike, whose father had been an Atlanta police officer, gave a moving speech at a press conference with Atlanta's mayor Keisha Lance Bottoms (whose own father was Major Lance, an R&B star in the sixties and seventies).

Killer Mike told the assembled media, "I got a lot of love and respect for police officers . . . [but] I'm mad as hell. I woke up wanting to see the world burn down yesterday, because I'm tired of seeing Black men die. He casually put his knee on a human being's neck for nine minutes as he died like a zebra in the clutch of a lion's jaw . . . So that's why children are burning it to the ground.

They don't know what else to do. And it is the responsibility of us to make this better right now . . . We want to see four officers prosecuted and sentenced . . . It is your duty *not* to burn your own house down for anger with an enemy. It is your duty to fortify your own house so that you may be a house of refuge in times of organization, and now is the time to plot, plan, strategize, organize, and mobilize."

Shortly after Floyd's murder, CNN's Don Lemon rhetorically asked, "What about Hollywood? Strangely quiet . . . Why aren't they helping these young people? These young people are out there standing on a platform at the edge of an abyss by themselves . . . Get on television or do something and help these young people instead of sitting in your mansions and doing nothing. Have some moral courage and stop worrying about your reputation and your brand."

On June 6, 2020, Dave Chappelle filmed a performance before a small socially distanced audience in Yellow Springs, Ohio. The show was titled "8:46," a reference to the length of time that Floyd had been strangled. (We later learned that it was even longer than that.) The comedian lashed out at Lemon, mocking CNN as "that hotbed of reality." He asked his audience, "Do you want to see a celebrity right now? Do we give a fuck what Ja Rule thinks? Does it matter about celebrity? No, this is the streets talking for themselves." Yet Chappelle agonized about the grotesque murder: "I don't want to see this because I can't unsee it." His monologue has received almost thirty million views on YouTube.

Lemon acknowledged Chappelle's eloquence but defended his original remarks: "The reason I said that is because there's a vacuum of leadership in this country and we live in a very celebrity-driven society and people listen to artists of all kinds." He need not have worried.

Seth Rogen posted a large "Black Lives Matters" image on Instagram and wrote, "If this is a remotely controversial statement to you, feel free to unfollow me." Beyoncé, Rihanna, Cardi B, Lizzo, Machine Gun Kelly, Cynthia Erivo, Selena Gomez, and Dwayne Johnson also posted pro-BLM social media images and videos. Madonna wrote on Instagram, "Watching this cop suffocate George Floyd with his knee on his neck, handcuffed and helpless, crying for his life with his face in the street, is the most sickening, heartbreaking thing I've seen in a long time. This officer knew he was being filmed and murdered him with arrogance and pride. This has to stop!! . . . I pray to GOD it does one day. Until then—Fuck The Police!"

In a message posted to her social media platforms, Lady Gaga wrote:

> I am outraged by the death of George Floyd as I have been by the deaths of . . . too many Black lives over hundreds of years that have been taken from us in this country as a result of systemic racism and the corrupt system that supports it . . .
>
> We have known for a long time that President Trump has failed. He holds the most powerful office in the world, yet offers nothing but ignorance and prejudice while Black lives continue to be taken . . . He is fueling a system that is already rooted in racism, and racist activity . . .
>
> We MUST show our love for the Black community. As a white, privileged woman, I take an oath to stand by that. And I will use the words that I can find to try to communicate what needs to change in as an effective and nonviolent way as possible for me.

Billie Eilish expressed frustration with those who insisted on saying "all lives matter," posting, "If your friend gets a cut on their arm are you gonna wait to give all your friends" a Band-Aid first "because all arms matter? NO you're gonna help your friend because THEY ARE BLEEDING!"

Dolly Parton told *Billboard*, "I understand people having to make themselves known and felt and seen. And of course Black lives matter. Do we think our little white asses are the only ones that matter? No!" Steve Earle dedicated an episode of his show *Hardcore Troubadour Radio* to protest music, beginning with Paul Robeson's performance of "The House I Live In," an aspirational song about

American unity that Frank Sinatra had popularized in the 1940s just before blacklisting stigmatized Robeson and the song's writers.

Neil Young performed on his porch for *Fireside Sessions*, singing a cover of Dylan's "The Times They Are A-Changin'," and his own songs "Ohio," "Southern Man," and "Lookin' for a Leader," the latter of which Young added new lyrics to: "America has a leader building walls around our house / Who don't know Black lives matter, and it's time to vote him out."

Taylor Swift wrote, "As a Tennessean, it makes me sick that there are monuments standing in our state that celebrate racist historical figures who did evil things . . . Taking down statues isn't going to fix centuries of systemic oppression, violence and hatred that Black people have had to endure but it might bring us one small step closer to making ALL Tennesseans and visitors to our state feel safe—not just the white ones." She also took a shot at a recent Trump tweet, which said, "When the looting starts the shooting starts." Swift responded, "After stoking the fires of white supremacy and racism your entire presidency, you have the nerve to feign moral superiority before threatening violence? We will vote you out in November." Over the next twenty-four hours, it was retweeted over 390,000 times and became Swift's most "liked" post ever.

Jamie Foxx marched alongside activists in Minneapolis. Ariana Grande posted photos from a protest in West Hollywood, captioning, "We were passionate, we were loud, we were loving." Emily Ratajkowski tweeted a photo in which she held a sign that read, "Dismantle power structures of oppression." Lana Del Rey, Miley Cyrus, and Billie Eilish also joined protesters in Los Angeles, as did Kendrick Sampson, who was hit by rubber bullets.

John Cusack filmed a protest (or as *Breitbart* called it, a "riot") in Chicago. He said, "Cops didn't like me filming the burning car so they came at me with batons." Kanye West established a $2 million fund to help the families of Ahmaud Arbery and Breonna Taylor, and also set up a college fund for George Floyd's daughter, Gianna. Drake donated $100,000 to the National Bail Out fund, a group that supports Black mothers and caregivers.

In 2016, when Trevor Noah first began hosting *The Daily Show*, viewership declined 32 percent compared to Jon Stewart's final year as host. By 2019, however, Noah had found his footing, and by 2020 the show's viewership had risen by 35 percent. Paramount announced that Noah's memoir, *Born a Crime: Stories from a South African Childhood*, would be adapted into a feature film starring Lupita Nyong'o as Noah's mother, Patricia.

In the wake of the pandemic, Noah's at-home broadcasts looked more like YouTube vlogs than a professional TV studio, yet the sparse presentation added an emotional intensity. His signature pandemic look was a pullover hoodie, and for weeks after Floyd's death, Noah wore a black one, explaining, "I didn't feel like color." After George Floyd's murder, Noah's status as the only major late-night host who was also a person of color took on a greater significance.

Reflecting on the multiracial composition of the protests, Noah said, "One ray of sunshine for me in that moment was seeing how many people instantly condemned what they saw." Yet Noah also explored the broader context of systemic racism, acknowledging concern about property damage and looting: "What is society? When you boil it down, society is a contract we sign as human beings amongst each other . . . But if you think of being a Black person in America who is living in Minneapolis, or any place where you're not having a good time, ask yourself this question when you watch those people: what vested interest do they have in maintaining the contract? . . . When you are a 'have' and when you are a 'have not,' you see the world in very different ways . . . A lot of people say, 'Well, what good does this do?' Yeah, but what good doesn't it do? How does it help you to *not* loot Target?"

After the first day of protests, the white late-night hosts turned most of their shows over to African American guests. Seth Meyers told Amber Ruffin, one of the show's writers, "As a white man, I can't speak of the deep-rooted and justified fear African Americans have when encountered by police." Ruffin disclosed that when she was a teenager, she was pulled over by a cop who objected to her playing Busta Rhymes at full volume: "I think: This is how I die. This man is going to kill me." Conan O'Brien interviewed W. Kamau

Bell, whose CNN show, the *United Shades of America*, had repeatedly explored American racism during the Trump years. Bell suggested that the host look into his own television culture: "Evaluate how many Black people work at TBS and on *Conan* and whether those people are at the top or bottom levels of the corporate ladder."

Wanda Sykes told Jimmy Kimmel, "We can't do it alone. We're out there marching and asking for change. You know, we need white people to do it. We need white people to tell white people to stop being racist because when we do it, obviously it's not working . . . Just because it's Black Lives Matter doesn't mean we don't want you involved. We need you involved . . . I had to go to the grocery store and it was a bunch of white kids on the corner, and some Black kids too, and they were out protesting and it's just beautiful."

Stephen Colbert told his viewers, "Take it upon yourself to be a leader and set an example of the kind of country you want to live in. That might mean going to a protest or making a donation or having a tense conversation about race. But you're not going to get that from the White House, so we need to step up and provide it ourselves. America is now officially B.Y.O.P.: Be Your Own President."

Inevitably, some activist expressions created a backlash. A group of white performers participated in an "I Take Responsibility" video, in which Aaron Paul, Bryce Dallas Howard, Debra Messing, Kristen Bell, Julianne Moore, Justin Theroux, Stanley Tucci, and others apologized for any unconscious racism and "every not-so-funny joke." According to several critics on Twitter, the video was primarily an exercise in virtue signaling. The *New Yorker*'s Jordan Coley used the mini-controversy about "I Take Responsibility" to indulge in the contempt that some old-school journalists had long harbored about entertainment activists in general, opining that the video "joined the ever-growing canon of the unsought celebrity PSA . . . Hollywood is perhaps one of the last places to look for inspiration—practical, emotional, or otherwise—in times of crisis."

On his Fox News show, Tucker Carlson predictably ridiculed the protesting celebrities. He stared on in disgust as part of the screen showed flames juxtaposed with a scroll of pictures of performers who Carlson implied were stoking unrest, including Steve Carell, Don Cheadle, Harry Styles, Seth Rogen, Patton Oswalt, Cynthia Nixon, Rob Delaney, and Chrissy Teigen.

DEFUND?

There was a widespread sense among protesters that although it was important to prosecute police officers who broke the law, there were systemic problems in American policing that needed to be resolved. The phrase that showed up on many protest signs was "Defund the police." Republicans immediately exploited the phrase and dishonestly insisted that without Trump in office, police would disappear from American cities and criminals would run rampant.

John Legend, Lizzo, Natalie Portman, Jane Fonda, Common, Brie Larson, Taraji P. Henson, and ACLU executive director Anthony Romero signed a letter that spelled out the actual intent of the slogan. It pointed out that in 2017, $194 billion was spent on the police by America's various governments, even as "Black communities are living in persistent fear of being killed by state authorities like police, immigration agents, or even white vigilantes who are emboldened by state actors." This letter suggested that *some* of the money allocated to police would be better spent on "building healthy communities . . . to the health of our elders and children, to neighborhood infrastructure, to education, to childcare, to support a vibrant Black future."

Portman elaborated upon the letter on her Instagram: "When I first heard #defundthepolice, I have to admit my first reaction was fear. My whole life, police have made me feel safe. But that's exactly the center of my white privilege: the police make me as a white woman feel safe, while my Black friends, family, and neighbors feel the opposite: police make them feel terror."

In a Twitter thread, John Legend explained his position on the issue: "I know this word 'defund' has caused some controversy, even from some who are inclined to agree with a lot of the underlying arguments . . . Police funding takes up a huge portion of our local budgets. Budgets are moral documents which spell out in black and white what our priorities are. We have finite amounts of money to spend and right now we spend far too much on policing . . . This doesn't mean there will be no police; it means there should be significantly fewer police and more professionals of other types with expertise in their fields." Legend argued that the word "defund" is useful because "it says we're taking away some funding from one budget item and moving it to higher priorities. 'Reform' or 'retrain' does not at all suggest the same thing. We've been supposedly doing the latter for decades." In the same thread, Legend also noted that artists serve a different public function than those running for office. "It's not the job of grassroots activists on the left to craft political messaging for mainstream Democratic candidates. I'm almost 100 percent sure Biden won't be tweeting #DefundThe Police. It's the job of activists to push these politicians toward meaningful change."

On his weekly HBO show *Last Week Tonight*, John Oliver observed, "America loves nothing more than a renegade cop who doesn't play by the rules . . . Defunding the police absolutely does not mean that we eliminate all cops . . . Instead, it's about moving away from a narrow conception of public safety that relies on policing and punishment, and investing in a community's actual safety, things like stable housing, mental health services, and community organizations. The concept is that the role of the police can then significantly shrink because they are not responding to the homeless or to mental health calls or arresting children in schools, or really any other situation where the best solution is not someone showing up with a gun."

Spike Lee, however, was worried about the real-life political impact of the phrase. On Al Roker's *Today Show Radio*, Lee said that activists "have to be careful with the words because already this guy is running with that. You know the guy I'm talking about. Agent Orange . . . We've got to be careful what we say because one or two wrong words, they'll twist that thing around and the narratives change . . . I think there [could] be better terminology."

DRAMATIC SUBTEXT

Streaming services quickly took note of the change in the national mood. Netflix created a "Black Lives Matter" section, which featured films directed by or starring African Americans. In January, Warner Bros. had released *Just Mercy*, a feature film about Bryan Stevenson's fight against the death penalty and the disproportionate number of African Americans who were executed. In the wake of the protests, the studio made the film available for free on several streaming services.

There was resurgence of interest in the HBO series *Watchmen*, which had first aired at the end of 2019. Executive produced and written by Damon Lindelof, the show derived from a 1980s DC Comics series of the same name. Despite using some characters from the original comic, Lindelof introduced new ones for the revamped series. The updated narrative takes place decades after the comic book and the plot integrates contemporary America into a science-fiction and fantasy world where bigotry is confronted by superhuman resistance.

The series imagines a white supremacist group called the Seventh Kavalry taking up arms against the police department in Tulsa, Oklahoma, after deeming their policing to be anti-white. On Christmas Eve, during an event that comes to be known as the "White Night," the Kavalry attacks the homes of forty police officers. Detective Angela Abar (played by Regina King) investigates the murder of police chief Judd Crawford (Don Johnson) and discovers the depth of the plot against the government. Most of *Watchmen* is set in the future, by which time the embattled police must conceal their identities with masks to prevent the racist militia from targeting them in their homes. In July 2020, *Watchmen* received twenty-six Emmy nominations, the most of any series that year.

Part of *Watchmen's* relevance after the Floyd killing was that it underlined the threat of white supremacist cults. As the *New Yorker's* Emily Nussbaum noted, "Lindelof's *Watchmen* reorders the fictional universe, writing buried racial trauma—from slavery to lynching—back into comic-book mythology, as both its source and its original sin, stemming from the Ku Klux Klan, a group reawakened, back in

1915, by the original masked-hero blockbuster, *The Birth of a Nation*." Once Americans had watched the eight-and-a-half-minute sadistic killing of Floyd, the comic book world seemed like it had a grasp on America's most disturbing elements.

THE BOSS

To older rock and roll fans, no one had more credibility than Bruce Springsteen, who told me: "When the pandemic hit, you could see Trump wasn't prepared for any national emergency and had no real interest in it or in the job itself. COVID made concerts impossible. I couldn't go and play. It wasn't my style to do a press conference so I started a radio show." Six weeks after Springsteen started *From My Home to Yours* for Sirius/XM, George Floyd was killed. Springsteen devoted several episodes to racial justice, telling his audience, "The politics of paranoia, division, prejudice, intolerance, fear—all that's antithetical to the American idea . . . We are in deep trouble, my fellow citizens." He played his own "American Skin (41 Shots)," Bob Dylan's "Political World," Patti's Smith's "People Have the Power," Bob Marley's "Burnin' and Lootin'," Kanye West's "Who Will Survive in America," Billie Holiday's rendition of "Strange Fruit," and Paul Robeson's version of "Go Down Moses."

Springsteen also included an excerpt from a speech that Martin Luther King Jr. gave, after which he explained, "The Birmingham movement was organized . . . to bring attention to the integration efforts of African Americans . . . Now, almost sixty years later, we wake again to an America who burned our buildings, torched police cars, and shattered shop windows, a cost that we're paying for another half of a century of unresolved fundamental issues of race. We have not cared for our house very well. There can be no standing peace without the justice owed to every American, regardless of their race, color, or creed . . . We need systemic changes in our law enforcement departments and in the political will of our national citizenry to once again move forward to the kind of changes that will bring the ideals of the Civil Rights Movement once again to light and into this moment."

I first met "the Boss" forty years ago while codirecting the political music documentary *No Nukes* with Julian Schlossberg. The film included several of Springsteen's performances from benefit concerts to support MUSE, a foundation created by Jackson Browne, Bonnie Raitt, John Hall, and Graham Nash to help grassroots groups oppose nuclear power plants. Springsteen's participation in those shows was his first public political statement.

By the time he appeared in the *No Nukes* shows, Springsteen had already released four albums, most recently the widely celebrated *Born to Run* and *Darkness on the Edge of Town*. The awareness that his twenties were drawing to a close impelled Bruce to broaden his persona to include social consciousness. He told me, "I'm capable of drawing attention to things and capable of raising capital. I'm not a frontline activist, but I have no problem putting these other things to use." On September 23, 1979, Springsteen celebrated his birthday onstage at Madison Square Garden during one of the *No Nukes* shows. "I was turning thirty," he recalled wistfully. "A half a life ago."

Springsteen headlined a 1981 benefit for the Vietnam Veterans of America. In the mid-eighties, he began raising money at concerts for the Second Harvest network of food banks. During that same period, as he toured the country, he was shaken by how many communities had been devastated by the loss of manufacturing jobs. Reflecting on this time, he said, "I wrote about the importance of work in people's lives and the tragedy of not having work. I wrote about that for most of my career. It's an essential subject of mine, the pain that was being felt from the loss of having work in your life." In 1984, when he released his most successful album, *Born in the U.S.A.*, both presidential candidates professed to identify with him: Democrat Walter Mondale, who cited the plight of the workingman, and incumbent Ronald Reagan, who glommed onto the patriotic chorus of the album's title song but conveniently ignored the verses that described the disillusionment of a Vietnam vet. At the time, Springsteen refrained from making an endorsement but he did remark that Reagan was probably not familiar with all of his lyrics.

For the most part, Springsteen avoided electoral politics until the 2004 presidential campaign, when he headlined a series of concerts to support John Kerry's attempt to prevent George W. Bush's reelection. He said, "I don't think people get opinions from musicians, but if you have some two cents of credibility, you choose your spots and you use what small cred you have." Although by 2020 his views were well known, Springsteen's periodic political expressions had a measured tone and he had many Republican fans, most famously the former New Jersey governor Chris Christie. When I saw Springsteen's Broadway show shortly after Trump became president-elect, Christie was in attendance but not invited backstage. Springsteen's manager Jon Landau told me, "We let him meet Bruce *once* after he was publicly seen with Obama in the aftermath of Hurricane Sandy, but that's it." Despite such calculations, Springsteen's motives seemed to arise from a place beyond politics; he insisted, "I'm not an activist; I'm a concerned citizen."

In an interview with David Brooks after George Floyd's murder, Springsteen said, "I think any time there is a fifty-foot Black Lives Matter sign leading to the White House, that's a good sign. And the demonstrations have been white people and Black people and brown people gathering together in the enraged name of love." Referring to soldiers who tear-gassed demonstrators so that Trump could have a photo taken in front of a church, Springsteen said, "We may have finally reached a presidential tipping point with that Lafayette Square walk, which was so outrageously anti-American, so totally buffoonish and so stupid, and so anti–freedom of speech." He added, "I want to go back to my neighborhood, and I want to understand the structural issues, personal issues, social issues that are pressing down hard on the people I'm writing about and still living among. That's where what I'm looking for resides. And so that's kind of where my politics really began to develop, out of concern for my own moral, spiritual, emotional health, and that of my neighbors."

RESISTANCE CONTINUES

It wasn't as if America's renewed preoccupation with racism made COVID-19 go away. On *The Tonight Show*, Robert De Niro told Jimmy

Fallon that the death of more than 100,000 Americans "could have been avoided if Trump had listened to the people in the intelligence community. They kept telling him something was coming. What scares me is that people just were afraid to tell him the truth."

On Lawrence O'Donnell's MSNBC show, De Niro said, "I can't help thinking there are people like [Rupert] Murdoch who have enabled this person . . . and when this guy is in power as the president, saying the most absurd, ridiculous things that you could ever imagine . . . we all have to sit there with straight faces and listen to him and take what he says."

By 2020, a significant percentage of younger audiences were preoccupied with an entirely different universe of entertainment: low-cost productions that showed up on YouTube and TikTok, the latter of which was launched in 2016 as a platform for short videos. Although many of the content creators on TikTok were teenagers, there were also older comedians and performers who found success on the app, such as Sarah Cooper, who became one of the most politically influential American performers in the spring of 2020.

The forty-three-year-old Cooper was born in Jamaica but then moved to New York, where she found modest success as a stand-up comedian and the author of humorous books. In April 2020, she posted a video on TikTok where she lip-synched Donald Trump's statement about light and Lysol being potential cures for COVID-19. Something about Cooper's facial expressions created a devastating satire of the president, while the audio consisted solely of his words. Between TikTok and Twitter, the clip was watched more than twenty million times.

Cooper told *InStyle*, "Black women usually don't get the luxury of faking their way through life and still succeeding, but when a white guy does it, he may even get to be the president of the United States . . . The first sound bite I did is still one of my favorites. In it, I, as Trump, say, 'We're gonna form a committee. I'm gonna call it a committee. And we're gonna make decisions. And we're gonna make decisions fairly quickly. And I hope they're going to be the right decisions.' Absolute nonsense. But it was exhilarating to play the most powerful man in the world and expose him as the clueless snake-oil salesman he is. I had taken away the suit and the podium and the people behind him smiling and nodding and calling him 'sir,' and all that was left were his empty words, which, in reality, were not the best. It felt like the antidote to the gaslighting."

America had many ethnic dramas playing out simultaneously, and the lingering tension between American Muslims and the broader domestic culture was explored in the second season of *Ramy*, which premiered on Hulu on May 29, two days after the Floyd murder.

Ramy Youssef starred as the title character, a twentysomething son of Egyptian immigrants living in New Jersey. Rather than focusing on terrorism, as had been the case with many dramas involving Muslims, *Ramy* revolved around the tension between spiritual traditions and sexual modernity. Mahershala Ali played an African American Muslim spiritual leader, Sheikh Ali Malik, who becomes Ramy's mentor. In one of the few overt references to 2020 politics, an episode depicted Ramy's mother (played by Hiam Abbass) trying to pass a written test to qualify her for American citizenship before the 2020 election so she could vote against the architect of the "Muslim ban." After succeeding, she says to herself with a triumphant smile, "Fuck Donald Trump! I am here to stay." In January 2020, Youssef won the Golden Globe for best actor in a comedy.

The global environment was still a huge concern to millions of people. The day after George Floyd was killed, there was a previously scheduled telethon called *Artists for Amazonia* which included pretaped segments from Jeff Bridges, Barbra Streisand, Carlos Santana, Jane Fonda, Morgan Freeman, Jane Goodall, Peter Gabriel, Dave Matthews, Peter Coyote, Alfre Woodard, Sting, and Trudie Styler. It was hosted by Oona Chaplin, an actress whose credits included *Game of Thrones*, and who was the granddaughter of Charlie Chaplin.

Julie Bergman produced the event because she felt that in the wake of the pandemic, she could "use this moment to be intimate; to talk to individuals which you don't feel at rallies." Jeff Bridges explained that the Amazon rainforest has "four hundred billion trees . . . [and] helps regulate our climate. It is home to most of the world's terrestrial biodiversity and gives us 20 percent of the world's oxygen." The event was intended to support efforts by environmental activists in response to massive deforestation in Brazil, after the country's authoritarian president Jair Bolsonaro (a Trump ally) removed environmental regulations on logging and mining companies.

One of the sponsoring groups for *Artists for Amazonia* was the Amazon Conservation Team (ACT), which provided medical help to indigenous tribes near the Amazon, among whom COVID had rapidly spread. ACT's leader, Dr. Mark J. Plotkin, had personally worked with fifty-five tribes. He explained that, as a result of the destruction of large portions of the rainforest, ninety other tribes have disappeared since the end of the twentieth century. At the virtual event, Plotkin called for an urgent response to "preserve the wisdom of elders who are at risk. These people hold secrets to healing we have yet to understand."

As important as environmental issues were to many Americans in the summer of 2020, the reverberations of George Floyd's murder continued to dominate much of America's inner dialogue in the weeks to come.

CHAPTER 9
SHOWBIZ LOOKS IN THE MIRROR
JUNE–JULY 2020

In another century, in another country, in another context, Vladimir Lenin had said that a single revolutionary day could seem like ten years. In the wake of Black Lives Matter's resurgence, a wide array of long-festering problems in America suddenly came to the fore, one of which was racism within the entertainment community. Trump notoriously said that "when you're a star they let you do it. You can do anything." Now, Hollywood was finally trying to expunge that attitude when it came to race. Although some of the responses seemed more like virtue signaling than anything substantive, the effort still mattered.

In his first TV appearance after Floyd's death, Jimmy Fallon began *The Tonight Show* with an apology for wearing blackface in a 2000 *SNL* skit in which he impersonated Chris Rock. "I thought about it and I realized that I can't *not* say I'm horrified. I'm sorry and I'm embarrassed." It turned out that there were quite a few TV series in recent years that had blackface moments. Within days, episodes with such scenes in *30 Rock*, *The Office*, *It's Always Sunny in Philadelphia*, *Scrubs*, and *Community* were removed from streaming services.

In late June, Kendrick Lamar, Tessa Thompson, and Black Lives Matter cofounder Patrisse Cullors wrote an open letter urging the entertainment community to "prove that Black Lives Matter to Hollywood by taking bold moves to affirm, defend, and invest in Black lives . . . Due to Hollywood's immense influence over politics and culture, all of the racism, discrimination, and glass ceilings Black people in Hollywood experience on a regular basis have direct implications on Black lives everywhere . . . This gives us less control over our narratives, continues the legacy of white supremacy's influence over our stories, and makes Black people in Hollywood and all over America less safe." It was signed by more than three hundred Black actors, artists, and executives, including Issa Rae, Michael B. Jordan, and Viola Davis.

Lady Gaga told *Billboard*, "I am in the process of learning and unlearning things I've been taught my whole life . . . When you're born in this country, we all drink the poison that is white supremacy. Social justice is not just a literacy, it's a lifestyle."

On June 2, 2020, most entertainment companies closed for "Blackout Tuesday," an idea which originated with Atlantic Records executive Jamila Thomas and Brianna Agyemang of Apple Music's Platoon division. The hashtag #TheShowMustBePaused linked to an extensive list of books, articles, and movies filed under the category of "antiracism resources." In advance of the event, the executives wrote a statement that read, "Tuesday, June 2, is meant to intentionally disrupt the workweek. The music industry is a multibillion-dollar industry . . . that has profited predominantly from Black art." The concept quickly spread to talent agencies, producers, and companies like Viacom, whose networks include MTV, BET, and Comedy Central. A solid black square appeared on the websites of the companies that participated.

Bad Robot Productions, which had produced *Lost* and the most recent *Star Wars* film, issued a statement that read, "Enough police brutality. Enough outsized privilege. Enough polite conversation. Enough white comfort. Enough lopsided access . . . In this fragile time, words matter, listening is critical, and investment is required." The company announced a five-year commitment to donate $2 million annually to organizations with "antiracist agendas that close the gaps, lift the poor, and build a just America for all," including grants to Black Lives Matter LA, the Community Coalition, Bryan Stevenson's Equal Justice Initiative, and Colin Kaepernick's Know Your Rights Camp.

The celebrated country music group Lady Antebellum announced that they would change their name to Lady A. The band explained that their eyes had been opened to "blind spots we didn't even know existed" and "the injustices, inequality, and biases Black women and men have always faced." The group immediately encountered a PR nightmare, however, when they were sued by blues singer Anita White, who had performed as Lady A for twenty years, and whose most recent album was called *Lady A: Live in New Orleans*. As the singer bitterly voiced, "Lady A is my brand . . . They're using the name because of a Black Lives Matter incident that, for them, is just a moment in time . . . It shouldn't have taken George Floyd to die for them to realize that their name had a slave reference to it." In the immediate aftermath of the conflict, both artists continued to use the name pending a final legal resolution.

The Dixie Chicks changed *their* name to the Chicks before releasing their new album, *Gaslighter*. Singer Natalie Maines told *Rolling Stone* that it was about Trump: "He was told what was going to happen months ago and he was too worried about his money to prepare our country . . . His denial, greed, and inaction are going to kill hundreds of thousands of people."

COPS AND COPS

In the reality television world, Paramount announced the cancellation of the long-running reality TV shows *Cops* and *Live PD*, whose critics accused them of reinforcing the stereotype that African Americans are inherently criminal. But fictional crime series still made up more than 60 percent of prime-time drama programming on the major four networks.

As Alyssa Rosenberg explained in the *Washington Post*, "Purely from a dramatic perspective, crime makes a story seem consequential, investigating crime generates action, and solving crime provides for a morally and emotionally satisfying conclusion. The result is an addiction to stories that portray police departments as more effective than they actually are; crime as more prevalent than it actually is; and police use of force as consistently justified. There are always gaps between reality and fiction but given what policing in America has too often become, Hollywood's version of it looks less like fantasy and more like complicity." She suggested that the closest thing to a "reformist police show" was *Brooklyn Nine-Nine*, whose cocreator Dan Goor was aiming to model "what a good police-community interaction would be like." (Goor and the cast also donated $100,000 to the National Bail Fund Network.)

Todd Boyd, a professor of race and popular culture at the University of Southern California, told the *Hollywood Reporter* that "when you look at Hollywood movies and you see the threatening, Black, menacing thug, he's like a monster, and I think a lot of people, particularly people who don't spend much time around Black people, believe that . . . Hollywood has not been innocent in creating and circulating the images that many people come to believe really exist. And thus, when someone is killed in this manner, it's not as though you've killed another human being, but you've killed a monster." The professor pointed out that in films like Clint Eastwood's *Dirty Harry*, "you start to get the image of these cops whose job it is to take on criminals that are being represented as having taken over society and the cops are going to take back control . . . There's been this false sense that politicians are tying police officers' hands behind their back, that they can't do their job because of politics and bureaucracy . . . You have the rogue cop . . . who rejects the politics . . . and instead decides to go on their own in pursuit of catching what is regarded as the bad guy. And in so doing, people embrace this idea that the end justifies the means."

Regarding the widespread support for Black Lives Matter, Boyd suggested that "a lot of it's fueled by hip-hop culture . . . One of the reasons we are seeing so many white people in the street now speaking up, finally, for Black people has to do with their connection to Black culture. We now have multiple generations of people who have come into the world when Black culture has been at the center of American culture . . . One of the things we've seen consistently are people saying some version of 'You need to love Black people as much as you love Black culture' . . . You can't talk about race and policing anymore without having the image of George Floyd, Eric Garner, or someone else being killed by a police officer."

THE SHOWRUNNERS' DILEMMA

On June 16, 2020, the *Hollywood Reporter* published a dialogue among several of the most successful TV showrunners in America whose series addressed racial issues, including *Power's* Courtney Kemp, *Watchmen's* Damon Lindelof, *The Good Fight's* Michelle King, *The Terror: Infamy's* Alexander Woo, and *Little Fires Everywhere's* Liz Tigelaar.

Lindelof explained that since *Watchmen* was "about race," he decided that, in the writers room, "I have to reject tokenism and create a balance where I can literally be overwhelmed by the consensus . . . which happened myriad times, to the show's benefit." Lindelof was influenced by Ta-Nehisi Coates's essay "The Case for Reparations," in which Lindelof first learned of the 1921 Tulsa race massacre. When he was putting together his writers room, he reached out to Coates's agent because he wanted "to acknowledge that he inspired this work. And he's a comics writer, so maybe he has ideas for *Watchmen*." Lindelof received no reply, but a few of months later he heard Coates on a podcast seemingly address the invitation: "All these white people in Hollywood are trying to reach out to me so that I will give them the approval stamp for their projects, and I'm not interested in doing that." Initially, Lindelof was shocked. "At first I was like, 'That's not what I was doing!' And then I was like, 'That is *exactly* what I was doing.' And this is part of the culture of appropriation that the show was trying to first shine a light on but then criticize. And having those moments . . . where you realize that you're a part of the system . . . it's depressing."

Tigelaar said that in the writers room for *Little Fires Everywhere*, Robin DiAngelo's book *White Fragility* was required reading. "What we set out to explore with the show was this idea of white liberal women who feel like they are 'postracial.' That they have it all figured out and that they've done their part because they see the world in this binary way, you're either racist or you're not racist . . . And what we hoped is that by exploring that white liberal woman who legitimately doesn't see herself as racist, or the experience of a Black, queer artist, or a Chinese immigrant who is in this country illegally and has to fight for her daughter, they are jumping-off points for dialogue."

The Terror: Infamy was a story about Japanese American internment camps during World War II. Woo, a Chinese American, acknowledged, "My experience is not literally that of what Japanese Americans went through during World War II. But I plugged into it as an immigrant story, and the feeling of coming to this country with hopes and dreams and embracing a country that doesn't always embrace you back is something that I . . . was very familiar with. And then I knew I needed writers who could tap into it from a specifically Japanese American perspective." Until rehearsals, Woo said, he "didn't realize every Japanese American actor we cast has some connection to the internment . . . We had people dropping everything to come work on our show because this was their parents' story or their grandparents' story."

The feature film business had similar issues. Stephanie Allain, a producer and studio executive who had been involved with *Hustle & Flow* and *Boyz N the Hood*, and who had also produced the most recent Oscar telecast, elaborated in the *Hollywood Reporter*, "For the last thirty years in Hollywood, we have been talking about diversity and inclusion, and I have been saying the gatekeepers need to be inclusive and represent all voices . . . People who are sitting at the table must be representative of the folks who are buying tickets."

Even amid the intensity of 2020's issues, America's past was intertwined with its present. At the end of June, Spike Lee released his new film *Da 5 Bloods* about four African American Vietnam vets who, decades after the war, return to Vietnam. In an opinion piece for the *New York Times*, Viet Thanh Nguyen wrote, "All wars are fought twice, the first time on the battlefield, the second time in memory . . . Born in Vietnam but made in America, I have a personal and professional interest in Hollywood's fetish about this war . . . For Americans, Hollywood turns a defeat by Vietnamese people into a conflict that is actually a civil war in the American soul, where Americans' greatest enemies are actually themselves."

Nguyen pointed out that while the film began with a famous quote by Muhammad Ali—"No Viet Cong ever called me n*****"—the character played by Delroy Lindo refers to the Vietnamese as "gooks." Addressing this juxtaposition, Nguyen wrote, "I stand with Black Lives Matter and against anti-Black racism, but still, as I watched the obligatory scene of Vietnamese soldiers getting shot and killed for the thousandth time, and as I felt the same hurt I did in watching *Platoon* and *Rambo* and *Full Metal Jacket*, I thought: Does it make any difference if politically conscious Black men kill us?"

CANCEL CULTURE

In the wake of George Floyd's murder, John Ridley, the screenwriter of *12 Years a Slave*, wrote an op-ed in the *Los Angeles Times* asking HBO Max to temporarily remove *Gone with the Wind* from their streaming platform. "It is a film that glorifies the antebellum South . . . When it is not ignoring the horrors of slavery, [the film] pauses only to perpetuate some of the most painful stereotypes of people of color . . . I don't believe in censorship . . . I would just ask . . . that the film be reintroduced to the HBO Max platform along with other films that give a more broad-based and complete picture of what slavery and the Confederacy truly were."

HBO Max quickly complied. A company spokesperson told CNN Business that *Gone with the Wind* was "a product of its time and depicts some of the ethnic and racial prejudices that have, unfortunately, been commonplace in American society. These racist depictions were wrong then and are wrong today, and we felt that to keep this title up without an explanation and a denouncement of those depictions would be irresponsible." The following month, *Gone with the Wind* returned to HBO Max accompanied by a discussion of its historical context. The film could be viewed "as it was originally created, because to do otherwise would be the same as claiming these prejudices never existed."

Others in the creative community saw free speech as a vital moral issue as well. On July 7, 2020, *Harper's* magazine published a letter under the headline "A Letter on Justice and Open Debate." It was a vague but impassioned plea for the increased tolerance of controversial speech, as well as an attack on so-called "cancel culture." Originally conceived by Thomas Chatterton Williams, author of *Self Portrait in Black and White* (2019), the letter was signed by 153 writers and intellectuals, many of them with storied progressive accomplishments such as Noam Chomsky and Gloria Steinem. Other signatories included Wynton Marsalis, Katha Pollitt, Atul Gawande, Todd Gitlin, Michelle Goldberg, Greil Marcus, Fareed Zakaria, Orlando Patterson, Garry Wills, Margaret Atwood, Bill T. Jones, Martin Amis, J.K. Rowling, Salman Rushdie, and Malcom Gladwell.

The letter began: "Our cultural institutions are facing a moment of trial. Powerful protests for racial and social justice are leading to overdue demands for police reform, along with wider calls for greater equality and inclusion across our society, not least in higher education, journalism, philanthropy, and the arts. But this needed reckoning has also intensified a new set of moral attitudes and political commitments that tend to weaken our norms of open debate and toleration of differences in favor of ideological conformity. As we applaud the first development, we also raise our voices against the second." The letter went on to caution that "institutional leaders, in a spirit of panicked damage control, are delivering hasty and disproportionate punishments instead of considered reforms. We need to preserve the possibility of good-faith disagreement without dire professional consequences."

There was an immediate outcry from other voices on the left. Some critics of the *Harper's* letter focused on the perceived flaws of some of the signatories rather than on the letter itself. For example, J.K. Rowling had recently been engaged in a highly publicized dispute with the transgender community. A more thoughtful response came from a tweet thread by Anand Giridharadas: "I have no problem with serious discussion of cancel culture. Can we make sure we spend at least as much time talking about greenlight culture—which is a form of preemptive cancellation many voices must deal with? I am minorly interested in which people with platforms should not have them. I am majorly interested in which people without platforms should have them . . . Cancellation takes many forms. Layoffs cancel. Private-equity media ownership cancels. Unpaid internships cancel. Educational disparity cancels. Publishing's insularity cancels. Agent gatekeeping cancels. Lack of connections cancels. Mysterious hiring processes cancel. Race and gender privilege cancels. So let's face the problem you speak of. But I doubt your seriousness if you do not speak of these cancellations too."

As Mary McNamara recalled in the *Los Angeles Times*, "When I was a young feminist, the pejorative term applied to those calling for change in a way that upset the establishment was 'politically correct.'" McNamara paraphrased the condescending attitude of such critics: "You want diversity in the workplace, equal pay, a nonbrutal police force, rapists brought to justice? How 'politically correct' of you."

Some "cancel culture" critics invoked free speech battles of the past. In the mid-sixties, Lenny Bruce, one of comedy's largest influences, had been relentlessly persecuted by law enforcement for using language that would become routinely accepted just a few years later. The publisher of Allen Ginsberg's *Howl* had been prosecuted for obscenity, though the ACLU successfully defended them.

When I worked with the ACLU, I had no trouble supporting their controversial decision to defend the right of Nazis to peacefully march or the rights of rappers like Public Enemy or N.W.A to resist pressure from politicians to change their lyrics. But these were all classic First Amendment cases in which the government tried to limit free speech. I was opposed to any kind of systemized pressure that would create a cultural version of blacklisting, but the portentousness and timing of the *Harper's* letter seemed disproportionate to me. I agreed with Mary McNamara's conclusion: "I have no idea why those who wrote and signed it thought that the middle of a global pandemic and a worldwide uprising against law enforcement's long history of racist brutality was an ideal moment to give young people a stern talking to about the moral and societal risks of cancel culture."

It didn't take long for right-wingers to co-opt the notion of "cancel culture" as a way of delegitimizing criticisms of racism, sexism, and Trump. They claimed that the real victims of prejudice were white conservatives. At a speech at Mount Rushmore on July 4, 2020, the president decried protests aimed at removing Confederate statues from display on public land: "One of their political weapons is cancel culture, driving people from their jobs, shaming dissenters, and demanding total submission from anyone who disagrees." In a guest editorial for Cleveland.com, Republican congressman Jim Jordan warned that "if Joe Biden and the Democrats win in November, 'cancel culture' will only get worse."

Meanwhile, the reverberations of both COVID-19 and the struggle for racial equality continued unabated.

CHAPTER 10
SUSPENDED ANIMATION
JUNE 13–JULY 11, 2020

S ummer had arrived. Schools and their virtual classes were out. Sports arenas, movie theaters, and concert venues were empty. Biden had yet to pick a running mate.

To some artists, Trump's continued denial of COVID's gravity, as well as his insistence that America "open up," suggested analogies to several cinematic bunglers from Steven Spielberg's oeuvre. On Instagram, musician Ben Lee wrote, "You know what else opened too early? *Jurassic Park.*" Jim Carrey tweeted, "Trump is willing to risk countless lives to save his economic record. He has fully become the mayor from *Jaws.*"

Trump scheduled a rally in Tulsa on June 19, a date better known in the African American community as Juneteenth. On that day in 1865, Texas read the Emancipation Proclamation into the state's official record; it was the final former Confederate state to do so.

Katy Perry tweeted, "#Juneteenth is a day to celebrate freedom, culture, and the progress achieved through activism and voting." Actress Lupita Nyong'o retweeted a story about Opal Lee, who led a national effort to make Juneteenth a national holiday. Pharrell Williams participated in Virginia governor Ralph Northam's announcement that made Juneteenth a state holiday. Taylor Swift revealed that she made the day a paid holiday for her employees.

In a rare show of deference to forces outside of their bubble, the Trump campaign delayed the Tulsa event by a day. When the program did occur, the venue was only one-third full, perhaps because even some MAGA supporters were worried about getting COVID in an indoor arena. On social media, photos of empty seats were promptly attached to a series of sarcastic posts. Jordan Peele tweeted, "Looks like they're social distancing after all!" Ava DuVernay's post read, "Happening now in #Tulsa at Trump MAGA outdoor stage. A lot of silent. Not much majority."

Footage of a clearly dispirited Trump returning to Washington after the sparsely attended rally circulated around the media. Jimmy Fallon observed that he looked like "a guy coming home from a bar where all his buddies met girls except for him." George Takei tweeted, "The digital brains behind Trump's campaign, Brad Parscale, got punked by an army of TikTok teens who registered for tickets to Trump's rally but never showed." Takei was referencing reports that fans of the Korean dance music genre K-pop had claimed credit for tricking the Trump campaign into thinking that far more people would be attending the Tulsa rally. As Joe Coscarelli explained in the *New York Times*, "A spokeswoman for Twitter said that K-pop was the most tweeted about music genre worldwide, with more than 6.1 billion tweets in 2019 . . . In recent weeks, K-pop devotees . . . disrupted a Dallas police app seeking intelligence on protesters, flooded would-be white supremacist hashtags, while also announcing that they had matched a $1 million donation from the Korean boy band BTS for Black Lives Matter groups."

On June 16, 2020, Jenifer Lewis, one of the stars of *Black-ish*, appeared on Ari Melber's MSNBC show wearing a T-shirt that read, "All hands on deck. Get your knees off our necks." Lewis explained, "I speak to the millennials, those kids grew up with me as the aunt on *Fresh Prince* . . . and I have a special relationship with them. I'm here to say to the protesters: continue peacefully protesting . . . There has to be reform."

Melber's fellow MSNBC host Joe Scarborough, who was also a solid rock guitarist, released a song called "Lift Me Up," sung by

Steven Hayden and Roz Brown, along with a music video that included a montage of protest scenes.

Ava DuVernay announced that she and her *When They See Us* cowriter Michael Starrbury were producing *Colin in Black & White*, a six-episode series for Netflix about the story of Colin Kaepernick, the former NFL quarterback whose decision to kneel during the playing of the national anthem was a critical turning point in the Black Lives Matter movement.

On June 28, 2020, the BET Awards began with Chuck D, Nas, YG, Black Thought, and Rapsody performing a new arrangement of "Fight the Power," the Public Enemy song that famously played during the opening credits of *Do the Right Thing*. The performance was juxtaposed with a montage of images from Black Lives Matter protests. Host Amanda Seales paid tribute to Breonna Taylor during her opening monologue, calling for justice for the twenty-six-year-old woman, who was killed during a police raid in her Louisville home months earlier. Alicia Keys performed her new song "Perfect Way to Die," after which she took a knee as the camera pulled overhead and showed the names of Black people killed by cops written in chalk on the street below. Later in the program, Michelle Obama presented Beyoncé with the BET humanitarian award.

A few days later, on the Fourth of July, Kanye West tweeted that he was running for president on an independent ticket using the slogan #2020Vision: "We must now realize the promise of America by trusting God, unifying our vision and building our future." West's ten-point policy agenda was headlined by "creating a culture of life," and featured a Bible verse for each item. The number one priority was restoring school prayer. West promised support for faith-based groups, a strong national defense, and an "America First" diplomacy. Also mentioned were progressive goals like equitable policing, funding of the arts, and protecting the environment. Lest there be any doubt that West's third-party run was a gimmick to help Trump, it was soon reported that Jared Kushner had met with him and that the staff trying to get the famous rapper's name onto ballots were longtime Republican operatives. Their theory was that West would take far more votes from Biden than from Trump. If the 2020 election turned out to be as close as 2016, a small number of West voters could permit the president to be reelected.

In an interview with the *Daily Mirror*, will.i.am said of West's candidacy, "It's a dangerous thing to be playing with." But Chance the Rapper rhetorically asked on Twitter, "Are u more pro biden or anti ye and why? I get that you'll want to reply that you're just tryna 'get trump out' but in this hypothetical scenario where you're replacing Trump, can someone explain why Joe Biden would be better??"

The *Atlantic's* Spencer Kornhaber weighed in: "If [West] has had a consistent message in the past four years, it's that Black people should not vote for Democrats in the overwhelming numbers that they have historically . . . Some say it's because Obama called him a jackass" (an epithet the ex-president had used to describe the rapper after West went onstage and interrupted Taylor Swift as she was accepting a Video Music Award in 2009).

John Legend was more diplomatic than some of West's critics but just as clear. He tweeted, "Part of an artist's job is to imagine a different future. I appreciate the desire to break free from the strictures of the 2-party system in America. But you can't divorce that conversation from the real world implications of rooting for a futile 3rd party bid."

At the same time, Legend offered cautionary advice to young artists about political activism: "It ain't for everybody. If you're more comfortable just making bops, do that. We need that in our lives too! . . . If you are going to speak out, try to do your home-work. Read about it. Talk to activists and organizers and people impacted. Be open to evolution and changing your mind. Be intentional and strategic. And think about the impact of your words on the real lives of real people."

Despite the primacy of race and the pandemic in the national conversation, other issues were still circulating in the news. After the president commuted his longtime advisor Roger Stone's sentence for lying to the FBI during the Mueller probe, Mark Hamill tweeted out a series of vomiting emojis. Rob Reiner wrote, "You can free Stone, Flynn, fire prosecutors. It won't help. You're going down. You're a Sociopath, a Criminal and a Moron. You're gonna lose in a landslide then go to jail." Bette Midler called the president a "little stinker" and Stone a "little shit." George Takei compared the president to the villain Voldemort from the *Harry Potter* novels.

It is difficult to determine how valuable these daily anti-Trump tweets were. There is an argument that they perpetuated tribal polarization, yet the counterargument is that without daily pushback, Trump's thuggish behavior would have become normalized. In any event, a number of activist entertainers chose this time to make longer, more thoughtful comments on the upcoming election.

REDFORD SPEAKS

Robert Redford had produced and starred in *All the President's Men* in the seventies, and in the ensuing years had been an environmentalist and advocate for LGBT and Native American rights. He rarely weighed in on national elections, however, and in recent decades had twice supported Republicans in his home state of Utah. Although he had endorsed Obama's reelection effort in 2012, Redford's name had appeared below a blurb on Trump's 2015 book *Crippled America* which read "I'm glad he's in there because him being the way he is, and saying what he says the way he says it, I think shakes things up, and I think that's very needed." (After the book was published, a Redford spokesperson said that those words had been excerpted from a televised conversation Redford had with Larry King and were not intended as an endorsement of the book or Trump's 2016 campaign.)

On July 8, six weeks before his eighty-fourth birthday, the actor issued a statement about the 2020 election that began with Redford's memory of growing up in Los Angeles and listening to President Roosevelt on the radio with his parents. He explained that although he was too young to follow much of what FDR was saying, he recalled that it was "something about World War II" and that even kids like him had a role to play, participating in paper drives, collecting scrap metal, etc. The young Redford was convinced that FDR cared about his family's well-being and he felt that the president's voice had both authority and empathy. "Americans were facing a common enemy—fascism—and FDR gave us the sense that we were all in it together . . . That's what it was like to have a president with a strong moral compass."

This was, in the actor's view, a dramatic contrast to 2020. "Instead of a moral compass in the White House, there's a moral vacuum. Instead of a president who says we're all in it together, we have a president who's in it for himself. Instead of words that uplift and unite, we hear words that inflame and divide." Redford felt that when Trump retweeted a video of a supporter shouting "white power," or when the president called journalists "enemies of the state," or made mask-wearing during a pandemic fodder for a culture war, or ordered the military to tear-gas peaceful protesters, "he sacrifices . . . any claim to moral authority."

Although in the past he had rarely revealed his voting preferences, Redford was convinced that 2020 was a unique moment and believed that "Biden was made for this moment. Biden leads with his heart. I don't mean that in a soft and sentimental way. I'm talking about a fierce compassion—the kind that fuels him, that drives him to fight against racial and economic injustice, that won't let him rest while people are struggling." The actor was encouraged by peaceful protests against racism and the way that communities were pulling together during the pandemic, "even if the White House has left them to fend for themselves . . . These acts of compassion and kindness make our country stronger. This November, we have a chance to make it stronger still—by choosing a president who is consistent with our values, and whose moral compass points toward justice."

SUMMER ENTERTAINMENT

On July 9, 2020, Amy Schumer debuted her new series, *Expecting Amy*, which documented her pregnancy. It began with a scene of the comedian speaking at a rally in 2018, where she asked the Senate not to confirm Trump's appointee, Brett Kavanaugh, to the Supreme Court. She was then arrested for civil disobedience in front of the Hart Senate Office Building and later told reporters, "I want to be able to say I did everything I could to stop him even though I know the outcome may not be what we wanted."

Borat actor/creator Sacha Baron Cohen continued his long-running practice of creating news-related stunts as performance art that depicted right-wingers in a negative light. In June, wearing a fake beard, he infiltrated a pro-gun rally in Olympia, Washington, as the lead singer of a band that supposedly supported the event. He sang lyrics about injecting Obama, Fauci, and anyone caught wearing a mask with the "Wuhan flu" or chopping them up "like the Saudis do." The crowd cheered.

Despite the suspension of production since the spring, new dramas and comedies that had been produced before the quarantine made their way into the culture. In June, Netflix announced a fourth and final season of writer/director Justin Simien's *Dear White People*. Like Simien's 2014 feature film of the same name, the series followed several Black college students at an Ivy League institution, discussing issues surrounding modern American race relations.

In the context of a discussion about the show by African American writers in the *Atlantic*, Ta-Nehisi Coates expressed mixed feelings: "Blackness in Netflix's *Dear White People* is largely a mode of protest. Nearly everything revolves around racism and the pariah-like feelings it inspires. The show is much less concerned with the interior lives of Black people. Is there a single scene of a Black party in the series?" At the same time, Coates acknowledged some elements of the show he enjoyed: "I think *Dear White People* is a tremendous artistic achievement. It's always hinting that there is something beyond the pleading and wokeness, something that the show's more militant characters can't see."

Simien saw *Dear White People* as a diary of the Black experience in modern America and he used several African American directors for episodes including Barry Jenkins, Cheryl Dunye, and Salli Richardson-Whitfield. In the weeks after George Floyd's murder, streams of *Dear White People* increased by 329 percent.

On June 21, 2020, the third season of *The Chi* premiered on Showtime. The series centered around an African American neighborhood on the South Side of Chicago. Executive producer Justin Hillian told *Parade*, "The reason this show exists is because we see so many statistics on the news but each one of these statistics represents a real person. And that person is someone's entire world—someone's mother, daughter, son, brother, father . . . We do our best to showcase the humanity of a community that has been much-maligned and within that, we explore every emotion from the highest high, to the lowest low." While the first two seasons had a heavy police presence, Hillian explained that in the new season "we are highlighting the ingenuity of Black mothers and their power to rally armies and demand action in times of crisis." *Breitbart* wasn't buying it. According to Warner Todd Huston, "*The Chi* veered into the anti-cop narrative currently being pushed by the political left when a teenaged character disappears and her family and friends attack the police for ignoring the case."

Debuting in 2019, the Netflix series *The Politician* was a scripted comedy with dramatic overtones. Produced by *Glee* cocreator Ryan Murphy, the series spotlighted high school student Payton Hobart (played by Ben Platt), whose obsession with becoming president of the United States plays out in a high school election. The second season, which premiered on June 19, 2020, focused on Payton's plan to run for state senator in New York.

In a campaign speech, Payton expresses concern with the "climate catastrophe that threatens all of civilization as we know it . . . [the] greatest long-term threat to human existence . . . Every one of us here today knows that we are in a generational fight that will determine our species' future on this planet . . . I do not want my children and grandchildren living in a New York City with twenty-foot seawalls holding back a dying ocean on a scorched earth with tens of millions of climate refugees."

Meanwhile, Payton's mother, Georgina (Gwyneth Paltrow), mounts her own election campaign for governor of California, telling CNN's Jake Tapper (playing himself), "California should be its own independent country. Most of our federal tax dollars go out of state to people who think we are pot-smoking, Satan-worshipping, abortion doctors—or something—who can't shut up about how our high taxes are strangling the private sector. And yet somehow

California manages to remain the world leader in growth, industry, innovation, and culture."

The conservative website MRC wrote that *The Politician* was "determined to remind us of everything we hate about election season . . . It's filled with lies, smug liberals, and countless scandals . . . It is shoved with progressive politics to the point where the term 'right wing' is used as a pejorative."

THE ROOM WHERE IT ACTUALLY DID HAPPEN

On July 4, 2020, a live stage recording of the Broadway show *Hamilton* debuted on Disney's new streaming service. Lin-Manuel Miranda wrote the musical after finding inspiration from Ron Chernow's biography of Alexander Hamilton. Miranda incorporates rapping and singing to tell the story of the American Revolution through the prism of Hamilton's life.

With a cast consisting almost entirely of people of color, *Hamilton* opened during the latter part of the Obama administration at the Public Theater in New York before moving to Broadway, where it became one of the most successful theatrical musicals in history. Other than the inherent power of racial minorities depicting the Founding Fathers, the political subtext was limited to its celebration of immigration (Hamilton was born on the Caribbean island of Nevis), most famously in the lyric, "Immigrants, we get the job done," which became an applause line after Trump's campaign was launched with anti-immigrant rhetoric.

When vice president–elect Mike Pence and his wife attended *Hamilton* two weeks after the 2016 election, they were booed by the audience as they approached their seats. At the end of that performance, Brandon Victor Dixon, the actor who played Aaron Burr, read a statement to Pence, thanking him for attending, but noting, "We are the diverse America who are alarmed and anxious that your new administration will not protect us." (The next day, Trump tweeted that the *Hamilton* cast had "harassed" Pence and been "very rude." He demanded that they "apologize!")

The phenomenal success of the show catapulted Miranda into the epicenter of American artistic culture. His parents were born in Puerto

Rico, and after Hurricane Maria devastated the island, Miranda raised millions of dollars in aid and criticized Trump for his negligence.

Trump's former national security advisor, John Bolton, appropriated one of *Hamilton's* song titles, "The Room Where It Happened" (which, in the context of *Hamilton*, is about the compromise of 1790), as the title of his White House memoir. Miranda made a short video mocking Bolton's attempt to cloak himself in *Hamilton's* relevance, singing a rewritten version of another *Hamilton* song, "Who Lives, Who Dies, Who Tells Your Story," which laments the lack of one's control over life and death, or, per the rewritten version, one "who borrows your song title to write a cash-in book when they could have testified before Congress."

Bolton's book reported that Trump spent weeks trying to send Kim Jung-un an Elton John CD that Trump had autographed himself. Trevor Noah commented, "You know, this might actually explain why nuclear negotiations between America and North Korea broke down, because can you imagine being Kim Jong-un and then getting a signed CD from Elton John, but it's signed by Donald Trump? . . . It's also weird that Trump thinks Kim Jong-un listens to CDs. Dude, he's the president of North Korea—the man listens to *cassettes*." Jimmy Fallon also had fun with Bolton's reveal: "Giving someone a CD isn't diplomacy; it's how you tell someone you have a crush on them in the eighth grade."

JON STEWART RETURNS

The Jon Stewart–directed feature film *Irresistible* premiered in select theaters in late June 2020. Other than the Obamas, there was no one whose absence from the public conversation had been lamented by Democrats more during the Trump years than Stewart's. From 1999–2015, as host of *The Daily Show*, he had expanded the idea of political satire to the point that his "comedy news show" competed with regular news outlets as a source of political information and ideas, especially among younger viewers. He was also a great curator of talent. Future talk show hosts Stephen Colbert, Samantha Bee, Hasan Minhaj, and John Oliver were brought to public attention after appearing on *The Daily Show*.

The politics Stewart espoused on the show were primarily progressive, yet he also focused on systemic problems in American politics, especially ones that had polluted the integrity of both parties. That concern had impelled Stewart and Colbert to host the "Rally to Restore Sanity and/or Fear" at the National Mall in Washington, which was held on October 30, 2010, attracting 200,000 people. Stewart was also a critic of cable news culture and he supported a writers' union while working at Comedy Central. Since leaving the show, Stewart had fiercely advocated for better benefits for 9/11 first responders, many of whom had developed health problems as a result of their work.

The protagonist of *Irresistible* is Democratic political strategist Gary Zimmer (played by Steve Carell, another *Daily Show* alumnus). Despondent after Hillary Clinton's election loss, Zimmer sees a clip on YouTube of a small-town meeting in Wisconsin, where retired Marine colonel Jack Hastings (played by Chris Cooper) berates his fellow townspeople for their lack of support of local undocumented immigrants. Zimmer is blown away by Hastings's eloquence and decides to try to persuade him to run for mayor of his hometown as a Democrat. Zimmer theorizes that if Hastings wins in a Republican town, he can also become a new national voice for Democrats, specifically targeting a portion of the electorate where the party's unpopularity helped produce Trump's victory. A Republican consultant, played by Rose Byrne, also notices this possibility and tries to stop it. The movie shows massive fundraising and advertising campaigns wildly out of proportion with the size of the town. Ultimately, it turns out that Hastings and his Republican opponent were merely pretending to compete in order to attract money into their small town to help pay for school and other vital social services.

Although it was well-acted and generally entertaining, *Irresistible* was suffused with a reverse snobbery that suggested that small-town people were inherently more authentic than those from big cities. Notwithstanding the perverse incentives of the money-driven American political system, the portrayal of the major political parties as moral equivalents was hard for a lot of progressives to swallow given the behavior of Trump-era Republicans.

While promoting the film, Stewart reverted to his progressive voice, addressing the compelling moral issues of the moment. He told David Marchese of the *New York Times* that "the police are a reflection of a society. They're not a rogue alien organization that came down to torment the Black community. They're enforcing segregation. Segregation is legally over, but it never ended. The police are, in some respects, a border patrol, and they patrol the border between the two Americas. We have that so that the rest of us don't have to deal with it."

Stewart had been supportive of Bernie Sanders and Elizabeth Warren during the primaries, but told Stephen Colbert, "We are a country in terrible anguish right now. We are in pain . . . And when I see Biden . . . I see a guy who knows what loss is, who knows grief. And I think that that kind of grief humbles you . . . There's a humility to the randomness of tragedy that brings about a caring that can't be faked, and it can't be contrived. And what I think in this moment this country needs is a leader of humility."

On July 3, Netflix premiered a ten-episode reinvention of *The Baby-Sitters Club*. The series was based on novels written by Ann M. Martin, which had sold more than 170 million copies. The concept was previously adapted as a short-lived TV series in the early nineties and a film in 1995.

The Baby-Sitters Club revolved around the ups and downs of a group of high school girls as they operate a babysitting business. While the lead characters were originally portrayed as white on book jackets and in earlier dramatizations, Rachel Shukert, the showrunner of the reboot, explained their decision to diversify the cast: "We wanted a Latina to play Dawn Schafer because she's supposed to be the quintessential California girl." Shukert cast Mexican American Xochitl Gomez for the role and African-born Canadian Malia Baker as Mary Anne Spier. The role of Claudia went to Japanese Canadian actress Momona Tamada. Eight of the episodes were directed by women, and all ten were written or cowritten by women, including African American, Latina, and Asian writers.

In one scene at a summer camp, when two of the main characters discover that the poorer kids aren't allowed to participate in art lessons (which cost extra), they barricade themselves in their cabins and demand equality.

In the weeks leading up to the *Baby-Sitters Club* premiere, several cast members participated in Black Lives Matter protests. In Los Angeles's Echo Park, Gomez, then thirteen years old, was seen wearing a mask and holding a "Latino 4 Black Lives Matter" sign. Baker gave a speech at a rally, saying, "I am an African-born Canadian. I am Black youth. I have experienced racism that comes from unawareness and targeted racism, as well. We need change." Another cast member, Shay Rudolph, a white fourteen-year-old who played Stacey McGill, changed the link in her Instagram bio to direct her followers to a Black Lives Matter resource site and added her own message: "Although posting black screens may feel like solidarity and activism, it is not enough . . . BLACK! LIVES!! MATTER!!!"

Meanwhile, back in Trump world, the campaign decided that if they couldn't attract artistic energy, they would appropriate it.

CHAPTER 11
DOG DAYS OF SUMMER
JULY 22–SEPTEMBER 5, 2020

LOOK WHAT THEY DONE TO MY SONG

There were no summer movies to speak of, and although basketball and baseball started up again, the news was dominated by Black Lives Matter 2.0, COVID 3.0, and the grinding day-by-day conflict between the president and the resistance.

As Trump resumed appearances at rallies, his campaign continued its practice of cloaking him with music by artists who were appalled by his regime. During the 2016 campaign, Pharrell Williams, Queen, Rihanna, Aerosmith, Adele, Elton John, the Rolling Stones, R.E.M., and the estates of Tom Petty and Prince publicly complained after their music was used at Trump rallies. In July 2020, Mick Jagger, Michael Stipe, Regina Spektor, Steven Tyler, Sheryl Crow, Lionel Ritchie, Elvis Costello, Blondie, Green Day, and Pearl Jam were among those who signed a letter that read in part, "No artist should be forced to compromise their values or be associated with politicians they don't respect or support . . . We're calling on campaigns to get permission before using music at political events."

Although the status of copyright law at political rallies was murky, prior to the Trump era, campaigns usually asked for permission from the songwriters and artists. If they neglected to do so and artists objected, they refrained from using the music in the future. But as was the case in dozens of other spheres, Trump and his minions ignored previous norms.

Music can uniquely trigger emotional associations. This is why film directors and advertisers pay substantial sums for the rights to license classic recordings and why approval rights are so highly prized by songwriters and artists. The documentary *Alive Inside* shows Alzheimer's patients with seemingly dead eyes suddenly coming alive with joy when they hear big band numbers that were on the hit parade during their formative years. In the film, neurologist Oliver Sacks quotes Immanuel Kant's observation that "music is the quickening art."

In August 2020, Eddy Grant filed a lawsuit to stop Trump's use of "Electric Avenue" in a minute-long campaign video. Neil Young filed a lawsuit to stop Trump's persistent use of "Rockin' in the Free World," claiming that it implied an endorsement, which was not the case in other public settings like sporting events, in which most arenas had blanket licenses with performing rights societies. Young complained, "Plaintiff in good conscience cannot allow his music to be used as a 'theme song' for a divisive, un-American campaign of ignorance and hate."

Other artists whose work was appropriated limited themselves to public statements. After Republicans played Leonard Cohen's "Hallelujah" over a visual of fireworks at an event, the lawyers for the Cohen estate voiced their displeasure: "We are surprised and dismayed that the RNC would proceed knowing that the Cohen Estate had specifically declined the RNC's use request." They were appalled by the Trump campaign's "rather brazen attempt to politicize and exploit in such an egregious manner 'Hallelujah,' one of the most important songs in the Cohen song catalogue . . . Had the RNC requested another song, 'You Want It Darker,' for which Leonard won a posthumous Grammy in 2017, we might have considered approval of that song."

In a similar vein, Eric Burdon tweeted, "Even though nobody asked my permission, I wasn't surprised to learn that #Trump used

#HouseoftheRisingSun for his rally the other day . . . A tale of sin and misery set in a brothel suits him so perfectly! Far more appropriate for this time in our history might be #WeGottaGetOutofThisPlace. This is my answer: . . . #bidenharris2020."

Trump retweeted a fan-made reelection campaign ad that used Fleurie and Jung Youth's cover of Linkin Park's 2002 hit song "In the End." Over the music, the video was interspersed with audio from Trump's inaugural address. Before his death in 2017, Linkin Park's front man and songwriter Chester Bennington said that Trump was "a greater threat to the USA than terrorism." After the unauthorized use of "In the End," surviving band members said that "Linkin Park did not and does not endorse Trump, nor authorize his organization to use any of our music." Jung Youth also chimed in on Twitter: "Fuck Trump!!!! Def do not approve this usage of my music just FYI."

The president's reelection campaign also caught flak from Betty Buckley for repeatedly using her rendition of "Memory" from the original *Cats* cast album. In 2017, Buckley asked the song's composer, Andrew Lloyd Webber, to send a cease-and-desist letter to the campaign. When Trump refused to stop playing the song at his rallies, Buckley urged the president to "stop this misappropriation of music that has nothing to do with the representation of your regime. Your presidency, completely devoid of empathy or humanity, is the very antithesis of art."

In late August 2020, an article in the *Atlantic* revealed that Trump had expressed contempt for military volunteers. The week it was published, Trump's campaign played Creedence Clearwater Revival's "Fortunate Son" as the president disembarked Air Force One en route to a Michigan rally. John Fogerty originally wrote the song in 1969 to shine a light on the fact that while wealthy young Americans were able to avoid service in the Vietnam War (as Trump did), thousands of poor and middle-class people were required to fight. One lyric in the song is, "I ain't no millionaire's son." Fogarty said he found the campaign's use of the song "confounding." It almost seemed that they wanted to boast that Trump *was* a fortunate son. What was anyone going to do about it?

In September, Monty Python's Eric Idle called the Republican National Congressional Committee (RNCC) "lowlife reprobates" after they blatantly violated copyright law when using the group's most popular melody, from "Lumberjack Song," without permission. The original lyrics were about a cross-dressing woodsman, but the RNCC rewrote the lyrics for an attack ad against Representative Cindy Axne, a Democratic incumbent House member from Iowa. Around the same time, a group of Floridian Trump supporters created a disturbance in a Target store, playing Twisted Sister's anthem "We're Not Gonna Take It" as they called for customers to take off their face masks. The band's lead singer, Dee Snider, tweeted that the song should not be used to promote a "moronic cause" and called the protesters "selfish assholes."

In mid-September, Robert Davi, one of Trump's few celebrity supporters, released a cover of "The House I Live In." The song was written by Earl Robinson and Abel Meeropol, two outspoken left-wingers who were blacklisted during the McCarthy era. On *Breitbart News Tonight*, although Davi acknowledged that the lyrics opposed racism and antisemitism, he brazenly pretended that Trump was in sync with those ideas: "It's an inspiring song talking about America's greatness . . . not about people on their knees, and the Hollywood media telling you how awful the country is . . . Don't believe the left's version of America." Presumably, Davi meant that American bigotry had magically ended after World War II and that the "left" had invented the idea that racism was endemic to our country's law enforcement. As Bill Maher had said on his show *Real Time*, "Denying that there is racism is the new racism."

Perhaps the most surreal Trumpist co-option came from Michael Caputo, the assistant secretary of public affairs in the Department of Health and Human Services. In a speech attacking career professionals who were truthful about the pandemic, Caputo said, "There are scientists who work for this government who do not want America to get well, not until after Joe Biden is president." He further suggested that his staff should listen to the Grateful Dead; perhaps he meant the song "Friend of the Devil."

KAMALA'S BACK

Biden announced Kamala Harris as his running mate on August 13, 2020. Some Trump supporters predictably resorted to smearing her with racist and sexist remarks.

Harris received immediate support from the TIME'S UP Legal Defense Fund, which was created in the wake of the Me Too movement by three hundred women in the entertainment business. After Harris's nomination, they issued a statement that read, "We unequivocally have Harris's back . . . We are calling on the media to stamp out the kind of unfair coverage, double standards, and coded language that have held women—and especially women of color—from positions of power, across party lines, for far too long." Charlamagne tha God called for the African American community to defend Harris in the wake of "disgusting" attacks.

Alyssa Milano tweeted, "Sexist and racist political attacks on @kamalaharris have already begun. Let's demand that the media keep these ignorant, bad-faith attacks out of their 2020 election coverage." Reese Witherspoon wrote, "During this historic time of having a female vice-presidential candidate, ALL media outlets have a responsibility to watch the editorializing about Female Political Candidates. So important to evaluate candidates using respectful language." Kerry Washington, Julianne Moore, Amy Schumer, Rosanna Arquette, and Sarah Paulson also made statements, as did former Sanders supporter Mark Ruffalo, who posted, "Let's get this party started," above a video clip of Harris dancing with school kids.

Ava DuVernay wrote an impassioned Instagram post on the subject: "There is no debate anymore . . . We either make this happen. Or literally, more of us perish. People are dying . . . This virus is real. If it hasn't visited your doorstep, it will." Mocking the unenthusiastic leftists who criticized Harris's record as attorney general, DuVernay added, "Oh but, Kamala did this or she didn't do that. I hear you. I know. And I don't care. Because what she DIDN'T DO is abandon citizens in a pandemic, rip babies from their mother's arms at the border, send federal troops to terrorize protesters, manufacture new ways to suppress Black and brown votes, actively

disrespect Indigenous people and land, traffic in white supremacist rhetoric in an effort to stir racist violence at every turn, attempt to dismantle most American democratic systems of checks
and balance, degrade women all day every day, infect the Supreme
Court with another misogynist hack, demolish America's standing
on climate, actively cultivate and further white supremacist structures and systems across all aspects of American daily life. I mean,
that's what she DIDN'T do . . . Vote them in and then let's hold
them accountable. Anything other than that is insanity."

JOE BIDEN MEETS CARDI B

There were various reasons why Trump won in 2016, but one major
factor was that more than six million people voted for third-party
candidates, mostly for the Green Party's Jill Stein and the Libertarian candidate Gary Johnson. Those voters accounted for 5.7 percent
of the total ballots cast in 2016, which was far greater than the 1.7
percent of voters who chose a third-party candidate in 2012. That
differential of 4 percent was decisive. Trump's share of the popular
vote in 2016 was only 46.1 percent, a percentage point *less* than what
Mitt Romney had received four years earlier in his loss to Obama.
If the four-point increase in third-party votes had instead gone to
Clinton, she would have easily won the swing states, securing an
electoral vote majority.

For Biden to defeat Trump in 2020, he would have to claw back
most of that third-party vote. Biden would have to convince young
people, many of whom were turned off by conventional political
campaign tactics. The entertainment audience included millions of
people who did not respond to political media coverage. As John
Legend told me, "We are closer to people's hearts. We can speak
to them in a way that is stripped of some of the political rhetoric."

On August 17, 2020, Cardi B talked to Joe Biden for *Elle* magazine. Ten days earlier, she and Megan Thee Stallion had released
an erotic song and video called "WAP" (an acronym for "Wet-Ass
Pussy"), which cultural conservatives eagerly attacked. James P.
Bradley, a Republican congressional candidate from California,
complained on Twitter that "Cardi B & Megan Thee Stallion are

what happens when children are raised without God and without a strong father figure." DeAnna Lorraine, another Republican House candidate, tweeted that Cardi B and Megan Thee Stallion "set the entire female gender back by 100 years with their disgusting & vile 'WAP' . . . Remember, Bernie Sanders campaigned with Cardi B. Kamala Harris called her a role model."

Twenty years earlier, during the Gore–Lieberman era of the party, Democrats had joined such censorious choruses. But Biden had resolved to treat young people with more respect than national Democratic leaders had in recent decades. It was a moment when all hands had to be on deck to defeat Trump, and thus the Democratic presidential nominee ignored Republican gaslighting and took advantage of the opportunity to speak to Cardi B's massive young fan base.

After Biden introduced Cardi B to his daughter Ashley (evidently a fan), the rapper focused on the election: "I have a whole list of things that I want . . . our next president to do for us, but first . . . I just want Trump out . . . We're dealing with a pandemic right now and . . . I want to know when this will be over. I want to go back to my job . . . But I don't want someone to lie to me and tell me that it's okay to go outside, it's okay not to wear a mask, that everything is going to be okay . . . I want a president to tell me what are the steps for us to get better . . . And also, I of course want free Medicare . . . I think we need free college education . . . I want Black people to stop getting killed and no justice for it . . . I want laws that are fair to Black citizens and that are fair for cops too."

Biden was all in: "There's no reason why we can't have all of that. Presidents have to take responsibility . . . If I get elected president, anybody with a family [that makes] less than 125 grand, you're going to get free education. And everybody gets free community college."

A few minutes later, Cardi B wrapped up the conversation: "I feel like this country is so hurt, to the point that this year, a lot of people couldn't even celebrate July 4, because not everybody feels like an American . . . We're not asking for sympathy, we're not asking for charity—we are just asking for equality. We are asking for fairness, and we are asking for justice . . . We want to feel like Americans . . . I want the new generation, my fans, my people, to go out and vote."

Cardi B's support of Biden was replicated by the vast majority of Bernie Sanders backers. A few weeks later, even Susan Sarandon announced that despite the many policy disagreements she had with the former vice president, she was voting for Biden "to stop fascism."

CONVENTIONS

Rob Reiner had supported Biden since the beginning of the election cycle. The celebrated director of films such as *A Few Good Men*, *This Is Spinal Tap*, and *The Princess Bride* first entered national prominence in 1971 as a twenty-four-year-old actor playing Mike Stivic in *All in the Family*. In the show, Stivic is the son-in-law of Archie Bunker, a racist from Queens. Now at the age of seventy-three, Reiner was campaigning to defeat Trump, a real-life racist from Queens. The day before the Democratic convention, Reiner was selected as the main speaker on a "Jews for Biden" Zoom conference, wherein he lamented that Trump was "dismantling the pillars of democracy. For Jews, we know what it's like to live under an autocrat, a pharaoh, a czar, or Hitler. We are hanging by a thread. We must get the pathological liar out of the White House."

The 2020 nominating conventions were virtual and thus reporters and delegates were deprived of the networking, gossip, and schmoozing typical of the traditional campaign process. Although much was made of how difficult the new format was, it actually turned out to be substantially simpler for the campaign teams to control their messages.

The Democrats used performers as emcees every night. Former *Desperate Housewives* star Eva Longoria Bastón welcomed the audience before Springsteen's "The Rising" played alongside a montage of scenes from around the US. Lily Adams, who had worked for Kamala Harris in the early primaries and whose grandmother Ann Richards had given the Democratic keynote address at the 1988 convention, tweeted, "Just inject the Springsteen into my veins.

Now it's a convention." Later, a memorial to COVID victims was shown to the accompaniment of "I Remember Everything" by the recently departed John Prine.

The first evening ended with Stephen Stills and Billy Porter performing "For What It's Worth." When Buffalo Springfield first recorded the song in 1966, it was about a clash between cops in Hollywood and teenage hippies on Sunset Boulevard. Over the years, the haunting guitar intro has added drama to protest scenes in dozens of films and cable news montages. During the convention, it helped inject a rebellious energy into a redefinition of the Democratic mainstream.

Porter told the *Washington Post*'s Helena Andrews-Dyer that he "recorded 'For What It's Worth' the day after the Emmys last September . . . My goal was to be in the political arena . . . Historically, the artist has been the conduit for society to heal and to propel change . . . That's why people who are in positions of political power attack the arts first."

Black-ish star Tracee Ellis Ross emceed the convention's second night. John Legend wrapped up the evening by playing his new song "Never Break." In an interview the following night, Ari Melber asked Legend what he would say to progressives uninspired by Biden. With his customary clarity, the singer answered, "I supported Elizabeth Warren in the primaries and she didn't win. Joe Biden won. He wasn't my first choice but he is the representative of our party and we have to rally around him. He has a progressive agenda and the alternative is four more years of Trump."

Scandal star Kerry Washington hosted the convention's third night. The program included an appearance by the eighteen-year-old superstar Billie Eilish, who said, "Donald Trump is destroying our country and everything we care about. We need leaders who will solve problems like climate change and COVID, not deny them, leaders who will fight against systemic racism and inequality . . . someone who's building a team that shares our values . . . Silence is not an option and we cannot sit this one out. We all have to vote like our lives and the world depend on it, because they do." She then sang "my future," after which Dr. Jill Biden tweeted, "Billie

Eilish is breathtaking." As Kamala Harris walked onstage to accept her vice presidential nomination, Curtis Mayfield's "Move On Up" boomed from the speakers.

On the final night of the convention, *Veep* star Julia Louis-Dreyfus emceed and the Chicks performed "The Star-Spangled Banner." Later, *Law & Order* star Mariska Hargitay spoke about the Democratic Party's commitment to combatting violence against women. Jennifer Hudson performed Sam Cooke's classic "A Change Is Gonna Come." Prince Royce sang "Stand By Me" in both English and Spanish. Although the convention was broadly popular, there were a few dissenters. Samantha Bee complained that it was the "first national convention to also feel like a PBS pledge drive."

In the days between the conventions, Trump's secretary of state Mike Pompeo tweeted a picture of *The Simpsons* character Lisa Simpson crying while the Democratic National Convention broadcast a segment featuring domestic violence survivors. Apparently, Pompeo thought that focusing on battered women was a sign of weakness. Pompeo had previously mocked Nancy Pelosi with the same Lisa Simpson photo when the speaker ripped up President Trump's State of the Union speech. Yeardley Smith, who voiced Lisa Simpson on the show, tweeted, "fuck you @mikepompeo for co-opting my character." Bill Oakley, a former *Simpsons* showrunner, tweeted, "Mr. Secretary of State please do not ever ever ever use Simpsons material in your twitter or watch the show or refer to it in any way."

After the first night of the Republican National Convention, *Breitbart's* David Ng wrote, "Alec Baldwin, Bette Midler, Dave Bautista, and anti-Trump comedian Kathy Griffin joined in on the mockery, providing snarky commentary of Monday's virtual convention . . . Rob Reiner asked if anyone else is 'throwing up right now?' Bette Midler . . . falsely claimed that 'Trump delivered zero,' omitting the president's accomplishments in trade, jobs, immigration, the Middle East, and the border wall."

The Republican convention included an appearance by eighteen-year-old Nick Sandmann, who had gained national notoriety when he stood nose-to-nose with a Native American man at an antiabortion "March for Life" rally. Sandmann sued multiple news outlets for misrepresenting the confrontation, claiming that he was being "silenced by the far left." At the convention, Sandmann bemoaned that "many are being fired, humiliated, or even threatened. Often, the media is a willing participant. But I wouldn't be canceled." A *Daily Beast* headline sarcastically observed, "Nothing Says Cancel Culture Like a Prime Time Speaking Slot at the GOP Convention."

Trump delivered his acceptance speech from the White House lawn, departing from a long tradition that excluded the seat of the presidency from electoral politics. "Here comes the asshole," Rosie O'Donnell tweeted as the president began to speak. Bradley Whitford called Trump's speech a "desecration." Wanda Sykes lamented, "I don't have enough weed to watch this foolishness."

During her speech, Melania Trump gave lip service to racial brotherhood, but few Democrats were inclined to give her the benefit of the doubt. After all, Melania had perpetuated the lie that Obama had not been born in America. Yet *New York Times* columnist David Brooks, a Republican who had turned against Trump, chided those criticizing Melania on Twitter: "Stop scoffing. Melania's speech is at least relatively decent and humane." An infuriated David Simon responded, "You placid rube. Amid vast, vicious intolerance and fascism, she is being used as the singular sop to compassion and antiracism, voicing these things for a moment to give white people with even a shard of conscience permission to keep voting for misrule. Is that scoffing enough?"

Cardi B also took a shot at Melania, to which Republican congressional candidate DeAnna Lorraine indignantly tweeted, "America needs far more women like Melania Trump and far less like Cardi B." The rapper promptly posted a seminaked photo of Melania from a 1995 modeling shoot and wrote that the first lady had been "fuckin wit some wet ass pussy vibes," and added a provocative question: "Didn't she used to sell that Wap?"

During Vice President Pence's speech, he said that it was time to "make America great again—again." In his late-night recap of the convention, James Corden mused, with a twinkle in his eye, "It's almost like they never made America great in the first place."

THE BEAT GOES ON

Some artists still yearned for a nonpartisan framework through which to view current events. Chris Evans debuted a website called A Starting Point, a platform attempting to create "a bipartisan channel of communication and connectivity between Americans and their elected officials with the goal of creating a more informed electorate." The site posted videos and articles explaining issues via congresspeople from both parties.

On July 19, 2020, John Oliver launched a website to debunk conspiracy theories under the name TheTrueTrueTruth.com. He showed videos from Alex Trebek, Paul Rudd, and Catherine O'Hara with the message, "Don't believe everything you see on the Internet," suggesting that people should read multiple news sources.

The talent agency ICM urged citizens to vote by mail. Bradley Whitford, John Leguizamo, and Michelle Monaghan appeared in commercials along with Amy Klobuchar, Eric Holder, and Tom Steyer. On July 27, 2020, *Friends* stars Courteney Cox, Jennifer Aniston, and Lisa Kudrow reunited on Cox's Instagram page to encourage their fans to vote in the upcoming presidential election, writing, "Friends don't let Friends skip elections."

Voter registration efforts were nonpartisan. Most artist-activists were not. A virtual Biden fundraiser collected $760,000 with appearances by John Legend, Julianne Moore, Rob Reiner, Kristin Chenoweth, Jay Leno, Sara Bareilles, and Barbra Streisand, the latter of whom said, "Let's face it, Trump is unfit, mentally and morally, to hold this distinguished office . . . Biden is a decent and ethical man with an open mind and open heart . . . The military was designed to protect us, not attack us. But a few weeks ago, Trump called out the troops against peaceful protesters. That's what cowards do when they are scared. Donald Trump has failed us, and we cannot survive four more years of his incompetence."

Trump tweeted that voting by mail "will be a great embarrassment to the USA. Delay the Election until people can properly, securely and safely vote???" *Billions* producer Brian Koppelman, who usually refrained from partisan issues, tweeted, "This is the single scariest thing a president has said in my lifetime." Rob Reiner responded that the president "will lie, cheat, try to stop US from voting." Patricia Arquette called Trump "a pussy . . . trying to destroy our democracy."

Taylor Swift tweeted, "Trump's calculated dismantling of the USPS proves one thing clearly: He is WELL AWARE that we do not want him as our president. He's chosen to blatantly cheat and put millions of Americans' lives at risk in an effort to hold on to power." Jim Gaffigan, a comedian who had previously been publicly apolitical, finally had enough: "Look Trumpers I get it. As a kid I was a Cubs fan and I know you stick by your team no matter what but he's a traitor and a con man who doesn't care about you. Deep down you know it. I'm sure you enjoy pissing people off but you know Trump is a liar and a criminal."

Over the next few weeks, George Clooney and Barack Obama hosted an online fundraiser for the Biden campaign; Piper Perabo, Mark Hamill, Debra Messing, and Rosie O'Donnell participated in a virtual event for No Dem Left Behind to bolster Democrat congressional candidates in rural areas of Wisconsin; and 2 Chainz teamed up with Michelle Obama's "When We All Vote" initiative to educate former and current prison inmates about their voting rights.

Trump's daily outrages kept comedians stocked with fresh material. In an interview with Jonathan Swan for *Axios*, the president said of those dying from COVID-19, "It is what it is." The next night, Jimmy Fallon ranted, "'It is what it is'? You're the president of the United States. You're not Paulie Walnuts delivering bad news to Tony Soprano." Former *Veep* costar Sam Richardson tweeted, "Yes, this is like a scene from *Veep*. Except on *Veep* this scene would have been rewritten . . . because a president being this stupid is too gaggy and unrealistic." When Trump said he might not accept the 2020 election results, Colbert said, "I have a great therapist who helped me accept the results of the 2016 election."

As the first celebrity to publicly test positive for COVID, Tom Hanks took it upon himself to be a messenger for common sense, telling Stephen Colbert's audience in an exasperated tone, "If you can't wear a mask and wash your hands and social distance, I've got no respect for you . . . I think of George Washington's troops at Valley Forge. If you asked them to wear a mask . . . they would have been happy to do that . . . If you drive a car, you think it's your constitutional right not to use your turn signals? . . . You don't want to go 120 miles an hour in a school zone; you slow down."

Although most anti-Trump celebrities got on board the Biden bandwagon, Rose McGowan remained unconvinced, tweeting, "What have the Democrats done to solve ANYTHING? Help the poor? No. Help black & brown people? No. Stop police brutality? No. Help children? No. You have achieved nothing. NOTHING. Why did people vote Trump? Because of you motherfuckers."

Alyssa Milano, who had costarred with McGowan on the TV show *Charmed*, responded with twenty examples of the Democratic accomplishments. "Rose and anyone bleating the same 'dEmOcRaTs DoNt HeLp PeOpLe' nonsense, your lies are going to hurt people less privileged than you. It's the kind of thing an ACTUAL fraud would do. Thousands of people are dying a day but you go on with your hyperbolic attention seeking tweets."

Milano also criticized Ivanka Trump, sharing a 2014 tweet from the first daughter that read, "I'm admitting to a total girl crush on @Alyssa_Milano. She's hilarious! And incidentally, one of the first people I followed on Twitter." Milano explained that she had met Ivanka when she was a guest judge on Lifetime's *Project Runway All Stars*, which Milano hosted. She wrote of the president's daughter: "I'm sad to see what she has evolved into."

On a more somber note, a heartbroken Sharon Stone posted a video explaining that her grandmother had died of COVID-19 and her sister- and brother-in-law had fallen ill and were not doing well. "One of you Non-Mask wearers did this . . . The only thing that can change this is if you vote. Don't vote for a killer."

Rainn Wilson, formerly of *The Office*, hosted *An Idiot's Guide to Climate Change*, a six-part documentary series featuring academics and activists, including Greta Thunberg. Wilson explained that he "took a trip to Greenland with some climate scientists. I knew nothing about global warming and I'd never seen a glacier before. It was my idiotic way of exploring this extremely non-idiotic issue."

Other celebs searched for broader ways to voice their discontents in advance of the election. Chelsea Handler tweeted, "The discord in today's America is being caused by Trump . . . If you are rich, and are thinking about your taxes, remember that a vote for Trump is a vote for white supremacy." The next day she added, "Just a friendly loving reminder that equality does not mean something is being taken away from you. It means when we are all equal, we all benefit and we all win."

Amid COVID's omnipresence, Joan Baez wrote an open letter to Dr. Anthony Fauci, who was arguably the closest thing the US had to a unifying figure. In 1963, Baez sang at the March on Washington before Dr. King's "I Have a Dream" speech. In 1968, at the height of the Vietnam War, Baez and her sisters Mimi and Pauline posed for a poster that was captioned, "GIRLS SAY YES to boys who say NO." The following year, she performed at Woodstock while pregnant with the son of draft resistance leader David Harris, who was then serving a jail sentence for antiwar civil disobedience. Although Baez retired from touring in 2019, she streamed songs for fans during the pandemic, including a poignant version of "Blowin' in the Wind," and she continued her avocation as a painter. Her letter to the nation's most respected medical authority read:

Dear Dr. Fauci,

I've painted your portrait to honor you and all you are doing for us and for the world. It will be a part of my second art exhibit of "Mischief Makers," paintings of people who have made meaningful social change without the use of violence.

I don't imagine you've ever thought of it this way, but you are engaging in nonviolent resistance every time you stand in front of the cameras and attempt to educate the public on how to survive the COVID-19 pandemic. You cheerfully continue your task, surrounded by people who are dreaming up every way possible to discredit you and what you bring *to us: common sense, scientific facts, some warmth, a bit of humor, and towering moral fortitude . . .*

Corragio, Dr. Anthony Fauci!

As Labor Day loomed, however, the general election was about to crowd out all other dramas.

CHAPTER 12
THE CAMPAIGN ACCELERATES
SEPTEMBER 7-29, 2020

Even in the shadow of the pandemic, when *back to school* merely meant back to the screen for millions of families, Labor Day still signaled the end of summer and a two-month countdown to Election Day.

In the old days, the main use of celebrities during the fall was to make remarks or sing before a candidate appeared at fundraisers or rallies. In 2020 the action was on Facebook, Instagram, and Zoom, and one of the most successful gimmicks for the Democrats were cast reunions of popular movies or TV shows.

The original cast of *The Princess Bride* performed a virtual table read, including Cary Elwes, Robin Wright, Carol Kane, Chris Sarandon, Mandy Patinkin, Wallace Shawn, Billy Crystal, and Christopher Guest. Rob Reiner, who directed the film, performed the role of the grandfather/narrator (originally performed by the late Peter Falk). Josh Gad, Whoopi Goldberg, and Eric Idle filled in as other characters. The beneficiary was the Democratic Party of Wisconsin, one of half a dozen "swing states" where Biden needed to prevail if he was to win in 2020. A hundred and ten thousand people watched and contributed more than $4.2 million, the biggest grassroots fundraiser the Wisconsin Democratic Party ever had.

Since its original release in 1987, *The Princess Bride* had attained cult status for several generations who were happy to see it reenacted, but the film also had a weird political echo because right-wing Republican Senator Ted Cruz had often said it was his favorite movie. Cruz periodically inserted quotes from the script into his speeches, especially a phrase from Patinkin's character: "Hello. My name is Inigo Montoya. You killed my father. Prepare to die."

Patinkin had long been irritated by Cruz's out-of-context focus on the line, and he reminded the senator of the final words that Inigo Montoya said in the film: "You know, it's strange. I have been in the revenge business so long, now that it's over, I do not know what to do with the rest of my life." The outraged actor explained, "We in this country, Senator Cruz, have been living in a revenge mentality . . . restricting refugees when our country was based on welcome."

After the fundraiser was announced, Cruz tweeted that the film was "perfect" and he wished it would stay out of "Hollywood politics." Patinkin responded, "Senator Cruz, were you not politicizing it when you used this family favorite to win votes . . . and get applause?"

The following week, the Wisconsin Democrats were the beneficiary of another event, this time a *Veep* reunion that raised millions of dollars. Julia Louis-Dreyfus said of her character, "Selina began as somebody who was very self-centered and that focus on herself was completely reinforced by everyone around her. Nobody shut her down ever. Who does that sound like?"

Over the next few weeks, there were several more such fundraisers, including a virtual reunion of the cast of *This Is Spinal Tap* (which Rob Reiner had also directed). Tracee Ellis Ross, Regina King, Alfre Woodard, and Sanaa Lathan acted out scenes from a *Golden Girls* episode, with the organization Color of Change as the beneficiary. The table read of the 1993 cult comedy *Dazed and Confused* benefitted Voto Latino, the Texas Democratic Party, and the March for Science advocacy group. The event was promoted with the slogan, "A world without science leaves us all dazed and confused." (On October 11, 2020, the night of the event, Texas had the most new COVID-19 cases of any state in the nation.) Rosario

Dawson, one of the cofounders of Voto Latino, made introductory remarks at the reading. Patton Oswalt moderated a postreading discussion with original cast members Matthew McConaughey, Ben Affleck, Parker Posey, and the film's director Richard Linklater.

ABC announced two special episodes of *Black-ish* that would focus on the presidential and congressional elections. In the first episode, Andre Junior (played by Marcus Scribner) is excited to vote for the first time until he finds out that his name has been removed from the voting list. A few weeks earlier, Hulu aired a previously unseen *Black-ish* episode from early 2018; ABC had scrapped it because of its harsh criticisms of Trump.

Parallel to such election activism, politically charged entertainment continued to emerge. On September 12, HBO premiered the film *Coastal Elites*, which Paul Rudnick had originally written as a stage production for the Public Theater. Rudnick told *Rolling Stone*'s Jerry Portwood, "I started . . . over a year ago, when I realized everyone I knew was angry and heartbroken and concerned about the future of our country and I was trying to figure a way into that material. These were people who demanded to be heard."

One of the first dramas produced during the COVID quarantine, *Coastal Elites* consisted of segments in which characters spoke to their computer camera. Issa Rae played a philanthropist who had social encounters with Ivanka Trump. Rae's character pungently refers to the president's daughter's vapid smile: "It was like she was saying, 'I'm here . . . but I'm not.'"

Bette Midler portrayed a left-wing New York City public school teacher whose attitude about Trump was identical to the real-life Midler's. Her character lands in police custody after physically attacking a Trump supporter wearing a MAGA hat in the middle of Manhattan. Midler said, "It's like me going to Nebraska, wearing a yarmulke, waving a rainbow flag, while reading a book!" The *Daily Beast* called *Coastal Elites* "the most anti-Trump scripted programming to air on a major network."

EARLY CLOSING ARGUMENTS
Due to the sudden closeness of the election, and a pent-up desire

to more substantially express political thoughts beyond Twitter's character count cap, several stars made expanded comments on 2020 politics.

Jim Carrey had been largely apolitical until the Trump era. A native Canadian, Carrey first developed a following as a member of the ensemble comedy series *In Living Color*. His commercial breakthrough came in 1994 when he starred in *Ace Ventura: Pet Detective*. For the next decade, Carrey was one of Hollywood's top box office attractions.

After Trump secured the Republican presidential nomination in 2016, Carrey began posting devastating caricatures that depicted the future president as a grotesque villain. Following Trump's inauguration, Carrey portrayed the president clothed like the Wicked Witch of the West from *The Wizard of Oz*. Another drawing showed Trump with a swastika coming out of his head. In 2020, as the COVID-19 death count rose, Carrey depicted the president's head juxtaposed with a personified image of death. The caption for the cartoon read, "Grim Reaper officially jealous of Trump and GOP's ability to double the death toll."

One of Carrey's most memorable pictures showed Trump bloodied and sprawled out on a whale with a peg leg that had "GOP" scrawled across it. The caption read, "Like Captain Ahab, obsessed by a white whale of earthly dominance, Trump beckons all those who enable his madness to their doom. Will we awaken to the truth or ignore our own senses and blindly follow a maniac into the abyss?" The drawing also portrayed Trump spokesperson Sarah Huckabee Sanders and Fox News host Sean Hannity as demonic figures.

On the day before the 2018 midterms, Carrey had posted a caricature of a demented Trump raining terror on the US with the caption, "Shameless lies. Endless indictments. The rise of racist hate groups. Kidnapped children. Contempt for rule of law—and quite possibly TREASON. Let's end this ill-wind that's blowing America off-balance and turning us against each other. VOTE DEMOCRAT!"

As the 2020 election loomed, Carrey published an essay for the *Atlantic* where he explained his thoughts. He wrote that although he had spent most of his career trying to reach audiences through humor, "relying on jokes can sometimes cancel out the seriousness of what you're trying to say." At that moment, the actor felt, "the best anyone can offer is gallows humor. The truth is, we should all be seriously concerned."

He lamented that thousands of lives had been "ruined by the presidency of Donald Trump. The rule of law is imperiled, our unity has been shattered, the service sector has been obliterated, and major cities are suffering. Black Americans, who have endured half a millennium of wickedness and brutality, now face more injustice and death."

Carrey recalled that when he was a little boy growing up in Canada, he watched *Superman* reruns and had fallen in love with the United States. As a young adult he had moved to the US and became a citizen in 2004. But recently he felt that his adopted home had become almost unrecognizable and wondered what had happened to the slogan that Superman embraced, "Truth, Justice, and the American Way" He concluded: "That line was written when the Nazis were ravaging Europe and America was the hero of the world. It's more than a line in a TV show; it's a set of ideals we should always aspire to uphold. In November . . . we must vote for decency, humanity, and a way of life that once again captures the imagination of kids all over the world—kids like me."

After Trump attacked George Clooney for being a member of "the Hollywood elite," Clooney responded in an interview with the *Daily Beast*: "Hollywood elite? I don't have a star on Hollywood Boulevard, Donald Trump has a star on Hollywood Boulevard! Fuck you!" The actor recounted that he had grown up in Kentucky, and that his early jobs included working at an all-night liquor store and selling women's shoes. "I grew up understanding what it was like to not have health insurance for eight years. So this idea that I'm somehow the 'Hollywood elite' and this guy who takes a shit in a gold toilet is somehow the man of the people is laughable." Clooney explained that most people who worked in Hollywood came from the Midwest and moved there to have a career, and concluded, "This idea of 'coastal elites' living in a bubble is ridiculous. Who lives in a bigger bubble? He lives in a gold tower and has twelve people in his company. He doesn't run a corporation of hundreds of thousands of people he employs and takes care of. He ran a company of twelve people! When you direct a film you have seven different unions all wanting different things, you have to find consensus with all of them, and you have to get them moving in the same direction. He's never had to do any of that kind of stuff."

After Jane Fonda returned to the West Coast to film the seventh season of *Grace and Frankie*, she began taping a series of virtual Fire Drill Fridays for the Greenpeace YouTube channel, which, by the end of summer, had attracted more than four million views. In September, Fonda released an episode with Candice Bergen and Mary Steenburgen, costars of the 2018 film *Book Club*, which coincided with the publication of Fonda's new book, *What Can I Do?: My Path from Climate Despair to Action*. Steenburgen told Fonda how much her husband, Ted Danson, was inspired after getting arrested at a Fire Drill Friday protest earlier in the year.

The following week, the series featured a conversation between the actress and Representative Alexandria Ocasio-Cortez, who Fonda introduced as a "woman who will never be sucked into some neoliberal scheme—plus she has a great sense of humor." Asked why she recently played a video game while talking about voting on Twitch, a platform for gamers, AOC explained, "I can't tell you how often I'll be talking to my colleagues in Congress . . . and I'm talking about policy that young people care about and the answer is, 'Young people don't vote so why should we do anything for an electorate that is unreliable and doesn't turn out?' . . . We registered thousands of people to vote in the three hours that we were streaming." AOC added that she thought it was important that a young person's first encounter with an elected official be "a positive one and not lame."

Though they were of different generations and backgrounds, the two women had both found that activism gave purpose to their lives. AOC said, "I relate a lot to your story, Jane, when you talked about the despair that you felt before getting involved in activism work . . . I felt very powerless . . . I went to Standing Rock and that's when I engaged in activism and that's when I supported our Black brothers and sisters in the movement for Black lives. I felt like my life had a greater purpose than just buying stuff and working a low-wage job that people didn't respect." In the past, both Fonda and AOC had dealt with attacks from the establishment. AOC recalled, "The power of grassroots movements has really made me feel like I am being part of something that's bigger than myself. That feeling is what helps me keep going." Fonda nodded and said, "That's exactly what I feel too. I was always part of a movement . . . and that puts starch in your spine and hope in your gut."

Fonda asked AOC how she responded to those on the left who were hesitant to vote for Biden. The congresswoman carefully replied, "It's . . . important that we respect individuals who are choosing to be vulnerable when sharing their concerns. I think it's also quite ironic about how some Democrats will bend over backward and coddle Trump voters to try to get them to vote for them, but when it comes to nonvoters, some of those same Democrats . . . become very abusive." Nevertheless, AOC was clear about the stakes of the upcoming election: "I am casting this vote out of solidarity with our most marginalized and vulnerable communities . . . I don't think anyone can really look at me in the eye and genuinely tell me that immigrants, who are having forced hysterectomies, who are being put in cages in camps, who are being separated from their children . . . that they won't be . . . more protected under a Biden administration."

Fonda later gave an extended interview to Maureen Dowd for the *New York Times*, in which she explained how she saw the role of performers in politics, comparing them to electronic devices that spread information: "Repeaters are the antennae that you see on top of mountains. They don't originate the signals, but the bottom-of-the-valley signals get picked up and then the repeaters take them from the valley and spread them to a much wider audience. That's what celebrities are." She mused: "I am of the belief that evil deeds, which Trump is committing, are the language of the traumatized. And you can hate the deeds. Don't hate the person . . . I have empathy for him. I look at this person and I see a frightened child who is very, very dangerous because he's got his hands on all the buttons."

Although Fonda originally supported Elizabeth Warren for president, she and Lily Tomlin organized a virtual fundraiser for Biden. "My attitude is, look, I'd rather push a moderate than fight a fascist . . . We have to cut fossil-fuel emissions in half by 2030 . . . and I will be one of the people in the streets as soon as *Grace and Frankie* is over."

THE TWEETS GO ON

In Bob Woodward's book *Rage,* he quoted an interview he conducted with Trump in March, when the president privately acknowledged that the virus was much more lethal than the flu, even though he was voicing the opposite perspective to the public so that Americans "wouldn't panic."

Trevor Noah was incredulous: "Causing panic is literally his favorite thing." He rhetorically asked Trump, "You didn't want to create a panic? So what did you want, for people to very calmly be dying in the streets?" With a gleam in his eye, Noah said, "At first, I thought Trump was too stupid to understand what was going on with the virus. But it turns out that he was actually smart about it in private. But he's also stupid enough to tell Bob Woodward on tape." Noah also criticized Woodward: "Am I the only one who thinks it is crazy that people keep releasing books where they reveal that they have known the most incriminating things about Trump, but they only tell us about it now? I mean, imagine if Paul Revere had this attitude: 'Are the British coming? Find out by pre-ordering my book on Amazon.'"

On September 23, 2020, the Kentucky attorney general announced that no police officers would be directly charged in the death of Breonna Taylor in Louisville in March. Actress Viola Davis tweeted, "Bulls--- decision!!! BLACK LIVES MATTER!!! Cannot be said enough times." Sarah Silverman wrote, "I would like to know how this judge/jury would feel if their daughter was shot and killed in her home while she slept. Would this look like justice to them?" Snoop Dogg posted, "Breonna, I'm so sorry." Wanda Sykes tweeted, "Yeah, I'm pissed! And I'm sick and tired of feeling like this. VOTE! VOTE! VOTE! VOTE!!!!"

Alyssa Milano used the hashtag #BLM alongside a GIF that read: "White silence costs Black lives. Speak out . . . Sleeping while Black shouldn't get you killed . . . Fuel campaigns to end state-sanctioned violence, liberate Black people, and end white supremacy forever."

At the Emmy Awards, Regina King—who won the award for outstanding lead actress for her role in *Watchmen*—wore a shirt featuring Taylor's face. Uzo Aduba, who won outstanding supporting actress in a limited series for her role in *Mrs. America*, wore a shirt embroidered with Taylor's name.

September 29 was the night of the first Biden–Trump debate. The president repeatedly interrupted his challenger and refused to condemn white supremacy. Asked what he had to say to one white supremacist group, the Proud Boys, he replied, "Stand back and stand by." Alyssa Milano tweeted, "This debate is about good vs. evil."

Late-night comedians went nuts. Trevor Noah said, "Wow, there you have it, folks. Trump had an opportunity to be like, 'White supremacists, I don't fuck with you.' Instead he's like 'Stand by, guys, I never know when I'm going to need you.'" After the debate, "Weird Al" Yankovic released "America Is Doomed, the Musical," a music video in which the singer posed as the debate's moderator. Set to a dance pop melody, Trump and Biden's answers were auto-tuned and remixed into the song in which Yankovic sang, "We're livin' in the apocalypse / I'm beggin' you to put a stop to this."

Trump refused to promise that he would peacefully leave office should he lose the 2020 presidential election on November 3, merely speculating, "We'll see what happens." Jimmy Kimmel somberly told his audience, "We make a lot of jokes about this guy, but what he just said is terrifying. If he doesn't win, he wants to burn this country down."

In a lame attempt to smear Biden, Trump retweeted a video of Joe Biden dancing to N.W.A's "Fuck tha Police." The clip was doctored. Biden had actually been dancing to Luis Fonsi and Daddy

Yankee's "Despacito" at an event for Hispanic Heritage Month.

The death of Ruth Bader Ginsburg on September 18 sent shock waves through non-Trump America. Barbra Streisand posted, "Just heard the worst news . . . so sad! Ruth Bader Ginsburg you will live in history forever. May you rest in peace." Bette Midler concurred: "There are no words." Carole King called RBG "the epitome of a strong woman." Wanda Sykes tweeted, "2020 is a real muthafucka."

After Trump announced he was fast-tracking the nomination of Amy Coney Barrett to the Supreme Court despite the impending election, Barbra Streisand tweeted, "A spiteful Donald Trump picked a woman who is the polar opposite of RBG. Barrett opposes the ACA and a woman's right to choose her reproductive decisions. She will set the country back decades." Ione Skye wrote, "I am going to be calling these senators every day until enough of them have refused to approve any supreme court nominees until after the next presidential inauguration."

John Oliver devoted most of his next show to the Supreme Court. He said, "When Barrett is confirmed, a president who lost the popular vote will have picked a quarter of the federal judiciary and a third of the Supreme Court, and his choices will have been rubber-stamped by a Senate Republican majority representing fifteen million fewer people than the Democratic minority . . . The unavoidable truth is that the system is already rigged. And it's rigged in a way that has allowed a party without popular support to drastically reshape an entire branch of government for the foreseeable future by appealing almost exclusively to white voters in some of the least populous regions of the country. That is not a mandate or democracy. It's a fucking travesty. We're at the end of a generational battle and the heartbreaking thing is we lost."

The comedian then said what many Democrats were keeping to themselves—that if Democrats managed to sweep the upcoming election, they should abolish the Electoral College, establish statehood for Washington, DC, and Puerto Rico, and eliminate the filibuster in the Senate.

Oliver also took a shot at Jared Kushner, who had belittled the NBA's cancellation of playoff games after players protested another police shooting of a Black man in Kenosha, Wisconsin. In a CNBC interview, the president's son-in-law said, "I think the NBA players are very fortunate that they have the financial position where they're able to take a night off from work without having to have the consequences for themselves financially. So they have that luxury, which is great." An outraged Oliver asked, "Who exactly is in the right tax bracket to have their protest approved by Kushner?"

On *Full Frontal*, Samantha Bee referenced Kenosha, where seventeen-year-old Kyle Rittenhouse had just been arrested for killing two unarmed Black Lives Matter protesters: "We've known for, I don't know, *all* the years that the police treat Black people far different than white people. Federal agencies, after a decade of prodding, are finally publicly confirming that white supremacist violence is as great a threat as international terrorism. But what is most terrifying is that white supremacists and antigovernment militia groups have active links to law enforcement across the US . . . In cities all over the country, police are giving armed white jackasses a free pass to intimidate and attack protesters."

COVID-19 conspiracy theories had become an international phenomenon. In Ireland, Van Morrison released three songs that attacked government regulation designed to reduce the spread of the virus. In the song "No More Lockdown," Morrison sang, "No more taking of our freedom / And our God-given rights / Pretending it's for our safety / When it's really to enslave." On his website, Morrison wrote, "I call on my fellow singers, musicians, writers, producers, promoters, and others in the industry to fight with me on this. Come forward, stand up, fight the pseudoscience, and speak up." Mike Scott of the Waterboys called it "gold standard stupidity" and tweeted to Morrison, "Are you saying that everyone who wears a mask is a crook? Or just stupid? And what do you say to the families of people who've died from covid?"

Back in America, a handful of performers still aggressively supported Trump. Jon Voight, who the president had presented with the National Medal of Arts the previous November, periodically posted pro-Trump videos on YouTube. On September 14, Kid Rock headlined a Trump rally in Harrison Township, Michigan, along with Donald Trump Jr. and his girlfriend Kimberly Guilfoyle.

However, the drumbeat of opposition to Trump intensified in most of the creative community. In addition to her podcast and online activism, Alyssa Milano launched a six-episode web series called *Own the Vote 2020* to "educate and empower" the voting public. As she told the *Hollywood Reporter,* "I feel like the election is being threatened—everything from insecure voting machines to information warfare to our ability to vote safely. So we decided to get some people together to educate and empower the American people on not only election security but also voter rules and regulations for every state."

Dwayne "The Rock" Johnson had over 224 million Instagram followers, the fourth most in the world. When he and his family tested positive for COVID-19 in early September, the wrestler-turned–movie star posted a message to his fans: "Stay disciplined. Boost your immune system. Commit to wellness. Wear your mask. Protect your family. Be strict about having people over to your house or gatherings. Stay positive. And care for your fellow human beings."

For most of his career, The Rock had offered few political opinions, but in the summer of 2019, when the HBO series *Ballers* began its fifth season, the character he played was shown reading Elizabeth Warren's book *This Fight Is Our Fight*. On September 27, 2020, The Rock posted a video in which he said that he was a registered independent "with centrist ideologies." Although up until that moment he had never publicly endorsed a candidate for office, he said he was supporting Biden and Harris in 2020.

Around the same time, Chuck D wrote a viral social media post addressed to lefties who were still uninspired by Biden and Harris: "I'm gonna rock with Biden/Harris despite their pasts just like I rock with some of y'all despite your pasts."

CHAPTER 13
BACK TO THE FUTURE
SEPTEMBER 24–OCTOBER 14, 2020

GLORIA REDUX

I never loved William Faulkner's oft-repeated quote from his novel *Requiem for a Nun*, "The past is never dead. It's not even past." It implies an absence of free will, a lack of human control over destiny. Yet it was impossible to ignore the power of the past during 2020. The ghosts of right-wing villains like Roy Cohn, George Wallace, Richard Nixon, and Ronald Reagan, and progressive heroes such as the Kennedys, the Roosevelts, and Martin Luther King Jr., were everywhere. Two months before Ruth Bader Ginsburg passed away, John Lewis had left his mortal coil, but as Election Day 2020 loomed, many who had worked side by side with them were still on the planet and remained deeply engaged in American culture, including Norman Lear, Harry Belafonte, Joan Baez, David Amram . . . and Gloria Steinem.

Julie Taymor's impressionist biopic *The Glorias*, based on Steinem's 2015 memoir *My Life on the Road*, directly embraced the intersection between past, present, and future. Taymor cast four actresses to play Steinem at various ages: Ryan Kiera Armstrong, Lulu Wilson, Alicia Vikander, and Julianne Moore.

When Taymor first conceived of the film, she and Steinem hoped that it would climax with the election of Hillary Clinton in 2016. However, their disappointment at Trump's election helped fuel the film's development. As the director told *Vanity Fair*'s Julie Miller, "We were going to try to inspire voter registration and activism . . . to have an open, giant talking circle and really cross over the lines. Not just go to people who are already Democrats, but to really talk to people who don't know what women want or what women have been fighting for, or what's on the line." That plan went out the window when the pandemic hit, but Amazon still premiered *The Glorias* on September 30, five weeks before the 2020 election. Steinem hoped the film would "reenergize people in this depressing, dark moment of America . . . Racism, sexism, the ERA, abortions are on the line. All the issues in our film are out there right now. Isn't that crazy?"

Washington Post film critic Ann Hornaday, who was Steinem's administrative assistant at *Ms.* magazine in the eighties, told me that she felt that the time-shifting style and magical realism of the production captured Steinem's essence far better than previous depictions. (In addition to Rose Byrne's portrayal in *Mrs. America*, Christine Lahti had played Steinem in the off-Broadway play *Gloria: A Life*.)

Taymor's version of Steinem retained the vulnerability of other versions but also displayed her steely toughness. Early in the film, the older Steinem (Julianne Moore) tells a Ukrainian cab driver who subjects her to a racist rant, "If you don't like living in New York, you can move to fucking Norway," before jumping out of the taxi.

In a stylized sequence set decades earlier, younger Steinem (Alicia Vikander) wears a Playboy bunny uniform (she was undercover for the magazine article that propelled her to journalistic stardom early in her career). Steinem sarcastically suggests to a lecherous customer, "Grab my tail. That's what it's there for."

Hornaday spoke to her eighty-six-year-old former boss the day after Ruth Bader Ginsburg died. "It's very hard, because somehow I had persuaded myself that she would always be there." Steinem lamented. "We were only a year apart. Perhaps it's because we like to think we are immortal, so I thought she was immortal." Yet the indefatigable feminist still managed to see a silver lining: "People can all have a Zoom meeting with their friends [and] plot the kind of activism that they have access to, think is important and can be effective in . . . If we say to ourselves, 'What would Ruth do?' and do it, then she will still be with us."

SORKIN WEIGHS IN

In the years since producing *The West Wing*, Aaron Sorkin continued to chronicle American culture, most memorably in his screenplay for *The Social Network* and the theatrical adaptation of *To Kill a Mockingbird*. It seemed inevitable that Sorkin's version of the American political center would reemerge as the 2020 election approached, and it did so in the last weeks of the presidential campaign.

On October 15, 2020, HBO Max streamed a special *West Wing* reunion in which most of the original cast, including Martin Sheen, Richard Schiff, Bradley Whitford, Janel Moloney, Rob Lowe, and Dulé Hill, reunited to do a staged performance of the episode "Hartsfield's Landing," which was originally broadcast in February 2002 during the third season of the series. John Spencer, who played White House chief of staff Leo McGarry, died in 2005, so Sterling K. Brown filled in.

Filmed on a minimalist set at LA's Orpheum Theatre, the production was cosponsored by When We All Vote, an ostensibly bipartisan organization. Yet the exhortations encouraging voter turnout during the broadcast were dominated by Democrats, including Bill Clinton and Michelle Obama. The program also included vérité shots of the film crew wearing masks before the cameras zoomed in on the nostalgic restaging.

The get-out-the-vote messages aimed at young people seemed a bit delusional since it was hard to imagine that many under the age of forty were tuning in. Longtime *West Wing* skeptic David Sirota mocked the effort on Twitter: "While Trump stages a coup, every day in Democratic Washington is still just a *West Wing* episode. I don't know who needs to hear this, but Jed Bartlet and Josh Lyman won't stop Emperor Palpatine and Darth Vader." Nevertheless, the recreation was a gift to *West Wing* aficionados who loved the show and devoured Joshua Malina's popular podcast *The West Wing Weekly*.

Sorkin further entered the preelection conversation through his new feature film, *The Trial of the Chicago 7*, which he wrote and directed, about the infamous 1969 trial of Vietnam War protest leaders who allegedly conspired to foment riots outside of the Democratic National Convention.

The trial had been previously dramatized several times: in a 1987 HBO film directed by Jeremy Kagan that included inserts of the actual defendants interspersed with a dramatic rendering of the trial; in *Steal This Movie!* (2000), Robert Greenwald's biopic of Abbie Hoffman; in Brett Morgen's *Chicago 10* (2010), a hybrid of drama, archival footage, and animation; and in Pinchas Perry's *The Chicago 8* (2012). None of these films, however, attracted a mass audience.

In 2006, Steven Spielberg approached Sorkin to write a more commercial screenplay about the trial, but for various reasons the idea was scuttled. A decade later, after Trump was elected, Sorkin revisited the idea, this time as a writer and director. Spielberg produced *The Trial of the Chicago 7* and the film was released in a few theaters before a Netflix premiere on October 16, sixteen days before the 2020 election. The cast included Sacha Baron Cohen as Abbie Hoffman, Eddie Redmayne as Tom Hayden, Jeremy Strong as Jerry Rubin, John Carroll Lynch as pacifist David Dellinger, Alex Sharp as Rennie Davis, and Yahya Abdul-Mateen II as Black Panther leader Bobby Seale. Michael Keaton played Ramsey Clark, the attorney general for the Johnson administration who determined that the violence outside of the convention was caused by the Chicago police and not the demonstrators. (It was Nixon's attorney general, John Mitchell, who decided to prosecute the Chicago 7.) In a nod to 2020, Clark proclaims, "The president isn't the client of the attorney general."

In the introduction to an edited transcript of the trial published in conjunction with the film's release, Sorkin observed, "Although my screenplay is very different from the trial transcript, the country's mood in 2020 is eerily similar to what it was in 1968."

The Trial of the Chicago 7 became the subject of significant media attention. Some critics lauded it as an Oscar contender, while others were anguished by the film's inaccuracies. Troy Garity, son of Tom Hayden and Jane Fonda, expressed mixed feelings in a webinar that streamed on the fourth anniversary of his father's death shortly after the film was released: "I know how long Sorkin struggled to get it made. On the other hand, [it was] very disappointing. Defendants [were] criminalized and trivialized. Protesters didn't attack the police. Very irresponsible."

In an article for the *American Prospect*, historian Todd Gitlin, who worked closely with Hayden in the sixties, lamented, "Along the yellow brick road of good intentions, *Trial* is cluttered with misinformation, some gratuitous, some grotesque, some pandering." Heyday Books publisher Steve Wasserman, a friend of several of the defendants, concurred: "Even allowing for Aaron Sorkin's good intentions . . . [the film] is an exercise in neoliberal conceits, is at pains to flatter the media addiction of our aging cohort who prefer to countenance even a distorted reflection of themselves in the mirror of mainstream media rather than continue to be consigned to the invisibility of remaining off stage in the wings of history."

Among the criticisms was a sense that Sorkin minimized the extent of the police violence outside the convention and downplayed the shackling and gagging of Bobby Seale in the courtroom because of his demands to represent himself after Judge Hoffman refused to delay the trial so that Seale's lawyer could recover from a hospital stay. In the movie version, Seale is physically restrained for a single day. Rennie Davis, one of the surviving defendants, recalled in a Facebook post that "Bobby was chained and gagged for four days during the actual trial . . . Each day, the pressure bandages around his head got tighter and more and more intense. When I sat next to him I could see blood out of the side of his mouth."

Sorkin's script portrays Hayden as a tightly wound, tie-wearing, antiwar leader unhappy with theatrical Yippie tactics. As *Slate's* Matthew Dessem noted, "Hayden serves as a stand-in for liberals who are sympathetic to social causes but think prankish protesters like the Yippies went too far." In the movie, Hayden tells Hoffman, "For the next fifty years, when people think of progressive politics, they're gonna think of you and your idiot followers passing out daisies to soldiers and trying to levitate the Pentagon. They're not going to think of equality or justice. They're not going to think of education or poverty or progress. They're gonna think of a bunch of stoned, lost, disrespectful, foulmouthed, lawless losers, and so we'll lose elections." Dessem astutely pointed out how "that does not seem to be how Tom Hayden viewed the Yippies during the trial, but it might be how a screenwriter who came of age in the late 1970s and early 1980s would justify not taking the counterculture seriously."

The most serious political distortion was an invented scene in which Dellinger punches a marshal who manhandles him in the courtroom. This subtext seems to suggest that nonviolent activists are hypocrites when personally confronted. In a webinar, Dellinger's daughter Natasha stated that "my father was a lifelong pacifist, a follower of Gandhi."

In *The Trial of the Chicago 7*'s final scene, Hayden uses his opportunity to address the court prior to his sentencing to read the names of Americans killed in the Vietnam War. The defendants *did* attempt to observe the Moratorium to End the War in Vietnam by reading deceased names, but they included both American and Vietnamese fatalities. On the one hand, Sorkin's dramatized scene is an emotionally satisfying way to reinforce the initial purpose of the protests. Yet on the other hand, the scene reinforces the odious notion that American deaths are the only ones worth remembering.

As a friend of Hayden's during the last several decades of his life, I agree that his character was unrecognizable. But I also share Judy Gumbo's sympathetic take on the film. As the former partner of unindicted Yippie leader Stew Albert, Gumbo had attended the trial and worked in the Yippie office. She told a webinar audience, "Sorkin plays fast and loose with facts. But it's not a documentary. It is the major motion picture Abbie always lusted after. And it addresses racism. Despite its flaws . . . it's a blockbuster Hollywood movie in which the Yippies and the antiwar movement come off as heroes." Gumbo also argued that the film was particularly significant as the 2020 election loomed: "It shows we can win."

BACK TO THE TRUMP ERA

When making the two-part miniseries *The Comey Rule* for Showtime, Billy Ray kept the 2020 election in mind. It was based on the former FBI director's memoir, *Saving Justice: Truth, Transparency, and Trust*, and Comey occupied a prominent space in Trump's legacy. Trump's firing of the director in the spring of 2017 directly precipitated the Mueller investigation.

In addition to the *Hunger Games* script, Ray had written several films with political themes including *Shattered Glass*, *State of Play*, and *Captain Phillips*. Ray was another contemporary auteur deeply affected by *All the President's Men*. He cheerfully acknowledged that he'd "been stealing from it for my whole career." For *The Comey Rule*, Ray was the producer and director, as well as the screenwriter. The film provided the first fully developed dramatic version of Donald Trump; Brendan Gleeson played the president with the flair of a Shakespearean villain.

Ray told me that he, Jeff Daniels (who played Comey), and others cast members were motivated to make the film "because we wanted to affect the attitude of viewers about Trump. Everybody on the set saw it as a civic duty. We wanted to do something that in some small way could impact the election." In a guest appearance on *Morning Joe*, Daniels said that the Trump-era Republican Party was "no longer [the one] my dad belonged to," and opined that Trump was "lying about the pandemic to stay out of jail."

Ray spent a lot of time with Comey and his family while he produced the film, and came to see him as a "public servant whose heart was broken" by Trump. Comey was reviled by most Democrats because of the way he handled the "investigation" into the e-mails Hillary Clinton sent on her personal server when she was secretary of state. The FBI director deviated from Justice Department norms by publicly criticizing her twice during the 2016 campaign.

Although the script ascribes good intentions to Comey, Ray wrote a scene in which the FBI chief's wife prevails upon him not to make a public statement about Clinton: "You went [to the FBI] to put bad guys away, not to help one of them become president." The second episode opens with a video that first appeared on You-Tube, which Ray licensed for the film. The clip shows a young man playing an acoustic guitar and singing, "Fuck you, James Comey." The song goes on to blame the FBI director for Trump's election, a view widely shared among Clinton supporters.

The Comey Rule perpetuated the notion that the Russian government interfered in the 2016 election to help Trump get elected. There is a brief scene that appears to support the idea that the future president consorted with Russian prostitutes on a trip to Moscow, another that recreates Donald Trump Jr.'s meeting with a Russian attorney, and an imagined scene right after Trump was declared the winner in 2016 in which an unnamed Russian toasts a colleague and exults, "This was a moon shot and it landed."

In the first episode, Trump is but a minor character, yet he comes to dominate the second episode. Ray recalled, "It was like the shark in *Jaws*. I wanted to build up anticipation." It worked. As James Poniewozik wrote in the *New York Times*, Brendan Gleeson's "Trump is not the orange-haired clown prince of *SNL* and late-night talk shows. He's a crass, heavy-breathing mobster . . . driven by spite and vanity. A heavy-handed musical score portends menace whenever he turns up."

On network television, *The Simpsons* broadcast its annual "Tree-house of Horror" Halloween special, which opened on Election Day. Marge Simpson reminds Homer to vote. Lisa Simpson freaks out when Homer appears undecided about whom to cast his ballot for, and a scroll appears on the screen listing things that Trump has done that makes him an unacceptable choice in her eyes, including:

Made it okay to shoot hibernating bears
Put children in cages
Called Mexicans rapists
Imitated disabled reporter . . .
Said Jewish people who vote Democrat are disloyal . . .
Called white supremacists "fine people" . . .

Refused to release tax returns
Gutted the EPA . . .
Called Baltimore a "disgusting, rat- and rodent-infested mess" . . .
Brought Ivanka to the G7 summit . . .
Pulled the US out of climate agreement . . .
Invaded Portland . . .
Said to swallow bleach . . .
Destroyed post office . . .
Wanted to be on Mount Rushmore . . .

It was an extraordinarily explicit political statement from television's longest-running entertainment show. Almost as remarkable was *South Park's* "Pandemic Special," where Mr. Garrison—who had served as a stand-in for Trump on *South Park* for the past several years—refused to take an urgent call from Dr. Fauci. In a rare nonsarcastic moment for the series, the episode ended with an exhortation for viewers to vote.

Leading up to the election, weekly political comedy staples like *Real Time with Bill Maher* and John Oliver's *Last Week Tonight* continued to combine comedy and commentary. But *SNL* created the largest mainstream political impact, because clips from each episode were often shown on cable news and attracted millions of additional views on YouTube.

On October 3, 2020, one month before the election, NBC broadcast the first episode of *SNL* from their studio since March with a socially distanced live audience of frontline workers. The cold opening was a reenactment of the first presidential debate, with Jim Carrey making his debut as Joe Biden, and Maya Rudolph and Alec Baldwin reprising their impersonations of Kamala Harris and Trump. After Baldwin's Trump demurred on the topic of white supremacy, Carrey's Biden produced a remote control and "paused" the president midsentence: "Sorry, but I think we all needed a break. Isn't that satisfying?" He then added, "You can trust me. Because I believe in science and karma. Now, just *imagine* if science and karma could somehow team up to send us all a message about how dangerous this virus can be." Carrey glanced over his shoulder at the "paused" Trump and gave the audience a look that seemed to say, *If only this was possible in real life.*

Guest host Chris Rock's opening monologue began: "President Trump is in the hospital with COVID, and I just want to say my heart goes out to COVID." Rock continued in a more serious vein: "We need to renegotiate our relationship with the government . . . We need a whole new system . . . What job do you have for four years, no matter what? . . . If you hired a cook and he was making people vomit every day, do you sit there and go, 'Well, he's got a four-year deal; we've just got to vomit for four more years'?" He concluded with a quote from James Baldwin: "'Not everything that is faced can be changed, but nothing can be changed until it is faced.'"

SNL's musical guest, Megan Thee Stallion, gave a dramatic performance of her hit song "Savage," beginning with the sounds of gunshots followed by a recording of Malcolm X's voice saying, "The most disrespected, unprotected, neglected person in America is the Black woman . . . Who taught you to hate the texture of your hair, the color of your skin, the shape of your nose?" Megan Thee Stallion then declared, "We need to protect our Black women and love our Black women because, at the end of the day, we *need* our Black women. We need to protect our Black men and stand up for our Black men because at the end of the day, we're tired of seeing hashtags of our Black men."

The episode ended with a shot of Kate McKinnon in the audience, dressed as Ruth Bader Ginsburg, who she had frequently impersonated. The actress bowed her head as the screen displayed an image of the familiar neck collar Ginsburg wore over her judicial robe, a pair of glasses, and the words "Rest in Power."

Two weeks later, *SNL* opened with a parody of the competing town hall broadcasts, which were aired instead of the previously scheduled second presidential debate. Mikey Day played ABC moderator George Stephanopoulos and announced, "The folks asking questions are half pro-Biden and half anti-Trump." He then asked Carrey's Biden if he was ready to receive "softball questions from folks who are already voting for you." At the end of the sequence, Carrey put on a sweater and sang the Mr. Rogers theme song, "Won't You Be My Neighbor?" For those few minutes, there was no indication that Carrey was being ironic.

On the Trump side of the parody, Kate McKinnon introduced herself as "surprise badass" Savannah Guthrie and said, "We have lots of voters waiting to ask questions but I'd like to start by tearing you a new one." Baldwin's manic version of the president answered questions about white supremacy ("I've always more or less condemned it"), QAnon ("If anyone's against pedophiles, it's me, the man who was close personal friends with one of the most famous pedophiles on earth—rest in power, Jeffrey"), the Aryan Brotherhood ("They're very pro-family, that's all I know"), and the Ku Klux Klan ("Your car breaks down, you call Triple-K").

Beyond *SNL*, other performers accelerated their political activity in the weeks leading up to election. Taylor Swift formally announced that she would be voting for Biden, writing, "The change we need most is to elect a president who recognizes that people of color deserve to feel safe and represented, that women deserve the right to choose what happens to their bodies, and that the LGBTQIA+ community deserves to be acknowledged and included . . . America has a chance to start the healing process it so desperately needs."

Judd Apatow recorded a video with Adam Schiff in which the congressman said, "Register to vote. Make a plan to vote. And then vote." Schiff then pretended to be funny: "We are able to deliver that message leveraging my personal brand of comedy—subversive, yet relatable." While Apatow played the straight man, Schiff did intentionally terrible impressions of Kellyanne Conway and Rudy Giuliani, banged tunelessly on a keyboard, and offered to do a dance on TikTok.

Several *Avengers* cast members, including Don Cheadle, Chris Evans, Scarlett Johansson, and Mark Ruffalo, participated in a virtual fundraiser with Kamala Harris. The Biden campaign also hosted a virtual South Asian Block Party fundraiser with Mindy Kaling, Kumail Nanjiani, and Lilly Singh. Joan Jett performed an online concert for Congressman Eric Swalwell and other House Democrats.

The singer explained, "It's impossible to separate music from politics. Rock and roll is political. It's always been a meaningful way to express dissent, to stir up equality and fight for human rights. It's a subculture of integrity, rebellion, frustration, alienation—and the power that set generations free of suppression."

Samuel L. Jackson cut a campaign commercial in which he said, "Voter suppression has taken many forms. First, they used the poll tax to keep Black folks from voting. Then it was the literacy test, racial terrorism, and violence. New day, same old dirty tricks."

Lin-Manuel Miranda shot a Spanish-language commercial for the Biden campaign, specifically targeting Puerto Ricans living in Florida: "We need to vote for Joe Biden as president so he can help unify the country, take our small businesses forward, and respect and help the Puerto Ricans on the island."

Director M. Night Shyamalan held a contest for the Biden–Harris campaign in which he agreed to meet with three winners who had the best ideas about political storytelling. *Rolling Stone* produced a get-out-the-vote series in which performers like Selena Gomez, Paul Rudd, the Lumineers, and Arcade Fire's Win Butler spoke to politicians like Bernie Sanders, Elizabeth Warren, and Stacey Abrams.

Sarah Silverman, Tiffany Haddish, Chris Rock, Sacha Baron Cohen, and Chelsea Handler appeared naked in a video to bring attention to the issue of "naked ballots," which could be disqualified when voting by mail. Several members of Pearl Jam did a virtual fundraiser with Dr. Jill Biden and Douglas Emhoff, the spouses on the Democratic ticket. The Biden campaign produced *Team Joe Sings*, a weekly series of virtual performances to support the Democrat that featured artists like Los Lobos, Death Cab for Cutie's Ben Gibbard, and Kesha, the latter of whom said, "Our current president has proven over and over that he lacks basic empathy and honesty."

While giving her acceptance speech after winning the top song sales artist award at the *Billboard* Music Awards, Lizzo rhetorically asked, "Would I be standing here right now if it weren't for the big Black women who refuse to have their voices be suppressed? . . . When people try to suppress something, it's normally because that thing holds power. They're afraid of your power. There's power in who you are, there's power in your voice. So whether it's through music, protest, or your right to vote, use your power, use your voice, and refuse to be suppressed."

On the same broadcast, Demi Lovato performed her new song "Commander in Chief," which included the lyrics, "We're in a state of crisis, people are dying, while you line your pockets deep / Commander in chief, how does it feel to still be able to breathe?" The next day, after receiving criticism from Trump-supporting fans, Lovato defiantly told her ninety-three million Instagram followers: "You do understand as a celebrity, I have a right to political views as well? Or did you forget that we aren't just around to entertain people for our entire lives . . . that we are citizens of the same country and we are humans with opinions as well? I literally don't care if this ruins my career . . . I made a piece of art that stands for something I believe in . . . I take integrity in my work over sales any day. As much as I would like to be sad that I disappointed you, I'm too busy being bummed that you expect me, a queer Hispanic woman, to silence my views/beliefs in order to please my audience."

Older rock icons also weighed in during October. When Don Henley performed his track "Too Much Pride" on Stephen Colbert's show, he changed the lyrics to "Now listen, Mr. Trump / Empires rise and empires fall / You stick around here long enough, you'll see it all."

On October 9, Stevie Nicks released a new song, "Show Them the Way." The lyrics did not explicitly mention Trump or the 2020 election, but her description of a dream included references to President Kennedy and Martin Luther King Jr. A music video for the song, directed by Cameron Crowe, featured photos of King, Kennedy, Harry Belafonte, and, in a nod to bipartisanship, a brief shot of George W. Bush. Nicks told *Rolling Stone*, "Racism in the last four years is so much worse than it was. I'm seventy-two years old. I lived through the sixties. I've seen all this. I fought for *Roe vs. Wade*; that was my generation's fight. And I don't want to live in a country that is so divisive . . . If there's another four years of this . . . where can I go?"

CHAPTER 14
THE FINAL COUNTDOWN
OCTOBER 15-NOVEMBER 7, 2020

In the weeks prior to the election, several well-timed politically inclined pieces of entertainment were released. One such project was *The Good Lord Bird*, a miniseries adaption of a James McBride novel, starring Ethan Hawke as the mystical nineteenth-century abolitionist John Brown. Hawke, who also produced the seven-episode miniseries, had worked on the project for years, but a story that revolved around the evils of slavery inevitably resonated in the final stages of the 2020 campaign, when systemic racism was on the minds of many Americans.

The intentionality of the timing of Sarah Cooper's Netflix special *Everything's Fine* was unmistakable. Despite a conceptual, comic plot and a supporting cast of Fred Armisen, Whoopi Goldberg, John Hamm, Ben Stiller, Jane Lynch, Connie Chung, Maya Rudolph, Winona Ryder, and Marisa Tomei, the most memorable section featured Cooper doing the shtick that made her famous: imitating Trump. The climactic scene was filmed on a bus similar to the one where Trump made his notorious *Access Hollywood* comments about grabbing women "by the pussy" with impunity. Cooper lip-synched Trump's macho boasting while Helen Mirren did the same to Billy Bush's sycophantic response, a powerful reminder of the heart of darkness residing in the White House.

The most politically impactful film released in the months leading up the election was Sacha Baron Cohen's follow-up to his 2006 film *Borat*. The sequel was released on October 23, with the absurdly long title *Borat Subsequent Moviefilm: Delivery of Prodigious Bribe to American Regime for Make Benefit Once Glorious Nation of Kazakhstan.*

As in the original, Cohen was the bumbling Kazakh journalist Borat Sagdiyev. While the first film was played strictly for laughs, the sequel was a fierce satire of Trumpism. As in the original *Borat*, Cohen and director Jason Woliner integrated documentary footage into a fictional story, and some of the participants in the documentary sections were not in on the joke when their scenes were shot.

Like Charlie Chaplin and John Lennon, Cohen saw American culture through British eyes. As an undergraduate at Cambridge, he wrote a thesis examining Jewish involvement in the Civil Rights Movement of the sixties. In November 2019, Cohen made a widely circulated speech at an Anti-Defamation League event, in which he accused Facebook of complicity in the growth of populist fascism proliferating on the platform. Cohen asserted that if Facebook had existed in the 1930s, the social network "would have let Hitler buy ads."

Although some critics felt that the new *Borat* film dehumanized Trump supporters, the *New Yorker's* Masha Gessen, a scholar of totalitarianism who rarely wrote about entertainment, praised it as "a brilliant and layered exploration of the banality of evil . . . The movie layers conspiracies and conspiracy theories deliciously. The perfect totalitarian subject, Borat is ever ready to believe anything and nothing. Did a monkey, shipped from Kazakhstan, eat itself? Did the Holocaust ever happen? . . . Does coronavirus exist?"

As the film begins, Borat is in a Kazakhstani jail doing hard labor because of the embarrassment his first film caused the nation. He is released for a mission: return to America and bribe Vice President Mike Pence with a gift, so that the country's leader can join "the strongman club." Cohen's caricature of Kazakhstan depicts the most misogynist society this side of *The Handmaid's Tale*. Women are treated as chattel and have no rights whatsoever.

When Borat arrives in America, he meets two Southerners who parrot QAnon theories. He agrees with them that "Democrats are worse than the virus," and composes a ditty with the lyrics, "Obama was a traitor / America, he hate her," which he later sings at what appears to be an actual Republican rally.

Under the misconception that Trump's vice president is "America's most famous ladies' man," Borat decides to give his fifteen-year-old daughter, Tutar, as a gift to Pence. Tutar (played by twenty-four-year-old Maria Bakalova) has been living in a cage in Kazakhstan. The mission initially excites her because she aspires to be "like Queen Melania." Once in America, she gets a makeover and goes to a debutante ball to prepare for her big moment with Pence.

As an additional offering to Pence, Borat buys a cake made with icing that reads, "Jews will not replace us," hoping it will "put him in a good mood." Cohen shot footage of the actual vice president at a conservative dinner that Borat crashed in a silly Trump costume before being ejected. Realizing that Pence is not interested in his gift, Borat decides to give Tutar instead to Trump's "best friend," Rudy Giuliani.

At one point, Tutar meets Jeanise Jones, a nonactor who initially believed the fictional story and who provided the film with a moral center. Jones is appalled by the notion that Tutar is being presented as a "gift," and encourages Tutar to stand up for herself. (After the film came out, Jones complained about being deceived and underpaid; Cohen gave her an additional $100,000.)

Despite Jones's misgivings, Tutar goes along with Borat's plan for her to pose as a youth reporter for the nonexistent *Patriots Report* and interview the real-life Rudy Giuliani at a New York City hotel. Tutar feigns nervousness over meeting "one of my greatest heroes." They toast each other with what appears to be whiskey.

After the interview, Tutar leads Giuliani into an adjacent bedroom. Although she has indicated that she is fifteen years old, Giuliani asks for her phone number and address. As they remove each other's microphones, Giuliani pats Tutar on the waist. Then, lying back on the bed, the former mayor of New York City lowers his hand into his pants as Tutar stands nearby, before Borat bursts in and says to him, "She's too old for you."

Tabloids speculated that Giuliani was beginning to masturbate, though Giuliani attempted an alternative explanation: "When the electronic equipment came off, some of it was in the back and my shirt came a little out, although my clothes were entirely on. I leaned back, and I tucked my shirt in, and at that point . . . they have this picture they take which looks doctored . . . I'm tucking my shirt in. I assure you that's all I was doing." Giuliani, however, had no comment on the moment in the "interview" when he confidently repeated one of Trump's discredited conspiracy theories: "China manufactured the virus and let it out, and they deliberately spread it around the world."

A few days after the film premiered, Trump called Cohen a "phony guy" and "a creep." The auteur gleefully tweeted, "Donald—I appreciate the free publicity for Borat! I admit, I don't find you funny either. But yet the whole world laughs at you. I'm always looking for people to play racist buffoons, and you'll need a job after Jan. 20. Let's talk!"

RAPPERS FOR TRUMP

Kanye West was not the only rapper who had a soft spot for Trump. A few others supported his reelection efforts for the same reason that many white businessmen supported Republicans: lower taxes on the wealthy. On October 26, Lil Pump posted the following endorsement on his Instagram story: "All I gotta say is Trump 2020, bitch. Fuck I look like paying an extra 33 in tax for Biden . . . ? Fuck sleepy Joe . . . Trump 2020."

That same day, 50 Cent retracted a similar endorsement he had made the week before in which he complained about higher taxes, joking that he didn't want to become "20 Cent." His ex-girlfriend Chelsea Handler did not approve of the notion of a millionaire putting his anxiety about higher taxes above the specter of four more years of a racist president. In an interview with Jimmy Fallon, Handler explained, "I had to remind him that he was a Black person, so he can't vote for Donald Trump, and that he shouldn't be influencing an entire swath of people who may listen to him because he's worried about his own personal pocketbook." The next day 50 Cent tweeted a link to the YG song "Fuck Donald Trump," adding, "I never liked him."

Ice Cube's apparent support of Trump was more complicated. He had created a serious proposal for a $500 million Contract with Black America (CWBA). In early September he had a Zoom meeting with several members of Biden's campaign team, including Atlanta mayor Keisha Lance Bottoms and Congressman Cedric Richmond. That same week he met with Jared Kushner for three hours.

Ice Cube explained, "Both parties contacted me. Dems said we'll address the CWBA after the election . . . What I didn't hear is . . . what's in it for the Black community besides the same old thing we've been getting from these parties? . . . I don't really see them pushing their policies in any particular direction. It's still . . . 'people of color' shit . . . that don't necessarily include Black Americans." The rapper-turned-actor felt better about the Trump campaign, which "made some adjustments to *their* plan after talking to us about the CWBA."

Though this was not an explicit endorsement of the president's reelection, Trump advisor Katrina Pierson tweeted, "Leaders gonna lead, haters gonna hate. Thank you for leading!" This triggered an immediate backlash from several African American public figures. Touré said that Ice Cube was "being used" and Roxane Gay tweeted, "How . . . does the guy from N.W.A become MAGA?" One Twitter user accused Ice Cube of "working with the Darkside," to which the rapper responded: "Every side is the Darkside for us here in America. Our justice is bipartisan."

Chuck D, who had supported Bernie Sanders before endorsing Biden, tweeted a nuanced response to Ice Cube: "IF you're mad at my bro @icecube YOU have a reason to be very ACTIVE this year. VOTE & THINK about WORKing hardass as HELL after Nov 3 especially IF you Black. I KNOW who I'm trying to VOTE out. Last I guessed my bro pays a ton of taxes here BUT especially more than this 45potus . . . Ponder the fact that Cube is POST election thinking."

I spoke to Chuck D the week of these exchanges and he explained, "Ice Cube is skeptical about all the promises that he's seen the Democratic Party make. He speaks for a community that feels they have no power. The Ice Cube sentiment is mistrust of both parties." But Chuck D had no such ambivalence himself: "I like to narrow it down to what it is—a side that includes your own versus a side that hates you, that says your lives don't matter. Trump is twenty-first-century fascism with a different face. I've been around the world enough to recognize gun-to-the-head governments. You've got people who love fascism and you've got some people who won't admit it but they love racism." He hoped that the outrage at some of Trump's behavior would translate into a more long-term political strategy so that "people followed local politics as well as they followed [their] local sports team, hold them responsible from the bottom up, not just the beauty pageants of presidential and governor elections."

Chuck had turned sixty over the summer as he finished work on a new Public Enemy album, *What You Gonna Do When the Grid Goes Down?*, which was released September 25, 2020. He reiterated his feelings about Trump in an interview with the *Guardian:* "This guy has the governing power over three hundred million people and also a presence in the world. The dude has been a running joke. You know, he was just a half-baked celebrity real estate hypocrite from New York City that I kind of had known a large part of my adult life. To see this guy end up in the seat of responsibility was a call to arms the minute he got in there."

Ava DuVernay stressed the need for long-term thinking in an interview with Ari Melber: "Police are the most visible part of a system that has many tentacles . . . It's really a diseased—a disease that can't be solved with reform, that can't be solved with even one election. This is a generations-old, deeply ingrained system and atmosphere that we're within that we don't even understand. It's part of the air that we breathe, that we all play a part in it—it's not going to be solved in our lifetimes. But we can hopefully be the generation that starts on a road to some consistent transformation." She told Melber's audience, "Don't regurgitate what Ari just told you. Don't quote [James] Baldwin to me, right? Like, read

Baldwin, learn, and then act on it . . . What will you do? How will you contribute? How will you take the ideas and act on them, and put them into practice? How will you demand that they're put into practice?"

On October 22, DuVernay announced screenings of *Selma* and *Get Out* at a California drive-in theater that would also facilitate voter registration and the collection of mail-in ballots.

Rolling Stone published a dialogue between Princess Nokia and Alexandria Ocasio-Cortez. AOC told the rapper, "I really do believe that you and I do very similar work. We both take our experiences growing up and the communities that we love to really shape our worldview in a political way. Your music is political, but it's . . . also philosophical in who we are and how we deserve to exist in the world." AOC pointed out that they had both confronted condescension toward youth culture, "as if we aren't aware of the world or know what we're talking about." Princess Nokia said that she appreciated how the young congresswoman was "going toe-to-toe with a lot of scary people . . . and you're kicking butt."

For the final debate between the presidential candidates, it was announced that the producers would have a mute button to prevent the kind of interruptions that Trump made during the first one. Jimmy Kimmel quipped, "Muting the mics—it's the same strategy my daughter's teacher uses for Zoom kindergarten." Colbert, reflecting the exhaustion of the campaign, suggested, "While we're at it, how about a fast-forward button? Just zip straight to November 3."

The day after the debate, *Breitbart's* David Ng wrote an article headlined "Hollywood Celebs Rage at Trump, Gush Over Biden." The story complained, "Actress and Democratic operative Alyssa Milano led the parade by claiming that Trump is 'disgusting' for even bringing up the Biden family scandal. The Hollywood star also gave Americans an ultimatum, claiming that it is impossible for them to love both Trump and their country."

A *Forbes* magazine profile called Milano the "Democratic It-Influencer of 2020." She was arguably the first artist-activist since Al Franken for whom a political career was plausible if she chose to pursue one. Milano had more than three and a half million Twitter followers and almost three million Instagram followers. "I get annoyed when I look at a celebrity's platform and there's nothing—no human rights, no civil rights, it's such a waste of fame," Milano said. "If you're not going to use it for good, I don't see a point."

In the previous month Milano had joined Reverend William Barber's virtual Moral Monday march against poverty; attended a Zoom event with Michigan governor Gretchen Whitmer; phone-banked in Ohio, Nevada, and Florida; raised money for Illinois congresswoman Lauren Underwood; moderated conversations with Beto O'Rourke, Pennsylvania attorney general Josh Shapiro, and TIME'S UP CEO, Tina Tchen; and cohosted events with Women for Biden, Emerge Texas, and Annie's List. During this same period, Showtime premiered *Surge*, a documentary that Milano executive produced about female candidates who ran and won in the 2018 midterms.

THE RETURN OF MANDY AND KATHRYN

Mandy Patinkin told me that when he first started dating Kathryn Grody in the late 1970s, he was inspired by her passion for current events. "Her empathy moved me." Kathryn's father, Irving Grody, was a World War II veteran who had been part of the D-Day invasion. Although he never had great wealth or political influence, Irving regularly wrote letters about the issues of the day to California's US senator Alan Cranston. As Grody affectionately recalled, her father always got a response. Like many baby boomers, Grody's political consciousness was stimulated by opposition to the war in Vietnam. The Public Theater's Joseph Papp influenced her political thinking as well, accompanying her on the 1971 May Day protests to express dissent against Nixon's escalation of the war. Another one of her political mentors was Martin Sheen, whose oft-repeated maxim made an impact on her: "Our actions are the ground we walk on." Early in her relationship with Mandy, Grody introduced him to Sheen.

Mandy recalled, "We went to a coffee shop on Amsterdam Avenue and I mentioned to him that I was not as political as Kathryn was, that I liked to focus on art." Sheen asked him, "Do you breathe?" When he nodded Sheen said, "Then you are political." Mandy told me that Kathryn and Sheen "gently and patiently illuminated for me how every decision we make, every privilege we hold, every hardship we encounter, every service we partake in, every person we meet—literally everything we do is political."

I first met Mandy in 1986 when we were part of a delegation to El Salvador and Nicaragua organized by Margery Tabankin, who ran the Arca Foundation and wanted to broaden the opposition to Reagan's administration into the entertainment sphere. When they first met, Tabankin told Mandy "we need sparklers" to draw attention to issues. Mandy replied, "I want to be more than that. I want to learn about what I'm talking about." Tabankin took him up on it, including him on a visit to Central America to meet with a variety of leaders. He recalled, "That trip and the lobbying we did afterward changed my life." In the intervening decades he and Kathryn supported numerous human rights groups, including the International Refugee Committee.

Following the George Floyd killing, Mandy and Kathryn stopped posting family videos on their social media platforms. But after the Republican convention in August, their son Gideon asked them, "Is our empathy limited? Do we need a close family member to die of COVID or police violence?" Gideon insisted that election-related activism "is our job." As Mandy later reflected, "The holocaust was a big motivator. I always wanted to think that if we'd been alive there we would have tried to stop it. Every Jew I know is asking, 'Is this election potentially Kristallnacht?'"

Gideon reached out to his college friend Ewen Wright, an LA-based writer and director. Together, they collaborated via computer on informal advocacy videos featuring Mandy and Kathryn that focused on electoral messages. Gideon continued in his role as an interviewer to prevent the pieces from becoming too generic. He told me, "Most activist videos come across as content by committee. What brings people in is fun stuff . . . if you let people into your life a little." He realized that the power of "the vulnerable family vibe is very different than reality TV." They connected with the

Biden campaign, several Democratic Senate campaigns, and sympathetic organizations such as Swing Left, Indivisible, MoveOn, and the Lincoln Project.

I asked Mandy why he thought so many artists were progressive and he replied, "Some of us have heightened sensitivity to the human condition," and then paused before adding, "It's the same quality that leads a lot of artists to kill themselves. Others survive and fight on to face the horror of inhumanity and find ways to act."

In the two months leading up to the election, Mandy and Kathryn uploaded eighteen videos to Twitter and Instagram. In one of them, amid the now familiar banter and bickering, was a scene in which they physically addressed and mailed hundreds of handwritten letters to likely Biden supporters in swing states, urging them to vote. There were fundraising appeals for several Democratic Senate candidates in which Mandy offered to send a personalized "thank you" song to randomly selected donors.

In one clip, Patinkin sang a goofy song written for the election called "Three People," which urged everyone to get at least that many friends to vote. A few days later, Stephen Colbert sang "Three People" on his show. The *New Yorker*, CNN, *Rolling Stone*, and various network morning shows covered the family's political activity. On MSNBC, Jonathan Capehart asked the couple about Trump's latest White House balcony speech. On live TV, Mandy blurted out, "I don't give a shit." Immediately after the broadcast, Gideon shot his parents discussing the use of profanity on television. Kathryn said she was relieved that Mandy hadn't said "fuck."

In a video for the Jewish Democratic Council of America that targeted Jews in swing states, Mandy held the sword he had used in *The Princess Bride* and said, "Now I polish off my most powerful weapon once again." Yet instead of using the weapon, he pulled a pen out of his shirt pocket and, in an homage to his famous "prepare to die" line, Mandy looked into the camera and said, "Prepare to vote."

The Biden campaign asked the couple to participate in a series where celebrities meet with leading Democrats. They obliged and chose to sit down with Elizabeth Warren. But Warren didn't want to film a regular conversation; she wanted to do a "Mandy and

Kathryn style" video. In the resulting piece, Kathryn was shown freaking out about a comment from Republican senator Mike Lee in which he legalistically pointed out that the United States was not a democracy. She lamented, "I don't want to be a refugee in my own country." Mandy got agitated and they decided that the only person who could calm them down was Senator Warren. They connected with her via Zoom and she told them to breathe deeply and to "stay patient . . . It's a long game," and then listed specific things people could do to help. Warren brought her dog Bailey to the screen and Mandy and Kathryn dragged their new Labrador, Becky, to their laptop to see the senator's dog. The video got more than six million views. The following week, Mandy and Kathryn performed some silly dances on TikTok juxtaposed with appeals to vote, which were watched more than a million times.

On October 17, Laura Ingraham's show on Fox News featured a conversation with her colleague Raymond Arroyo about "unhinged lunatics" from the entertainment world who were weighing in on the election. Arroyo breathlessly explained that "even Mandy Patinkin, the *Homeland* actor . . . has gotten very political of late . . . and Mrs. Patinkin is now even doing her own hateful anti-Trump dances." The Fox program then showed a montage edited in a way that made scenes that were created humorously appear as if Mandy and Kathryn were actually hysterical. Gideon recalled, "We had some hateful trolling for the next twelve hours but it died away." Kathryn laughed off the attack. "It's a badge of honor."

THE LAST LAP

Two weeks before the election, Rosanne Cash and her husband and collaborator John Leventhal released a new song, "Crawl into the Promised Land." Cash wrote the lyrics shortly after George Floyd was killed. "I was so deeply affected by the Black Lives Matter protests, " she told me, "and I was continually outraged by Trump and obsessing about the election. I think it's a parent's responsibility to be optimistic. I didn't think I could steal my kid's future by saying we're so fucked and will never recover, so I wanted to say that even if we have to crawl we're gonna get there."

In an essay included with the release, Cash wrote, "We can get back to our dream of America . . . We're exhausted. We're disoriented. But I know we have the strength and will to deliver ourselves." An accompanying music video includes images from the feminist and civil rights movements. As Cash explained, "I wanted to connect the past and the present. The Voting Rights Act and the Women's March of 2017, the Civil Rights Movement and the Black Lives Matter protesters, Harriet Tubman and Ruth Bader Ginsburg, the workers in the cotton fields and the lives of those of us who live in privilege because of them, and the necessary gratitude for the humanity we share."

That same week, Bruce Springsteen released a new album entitled *Letter to You.* In an accompanying documentary he said, "I dwell in a house of a thousand dreams . . . I try to speak in the voice of my better angels. We have been given tools and the property of the soul to be attended to and accountable for, and that takes work. Work that we might build on the principles of love, liberty, fraternity—ancient ideas that still form the basis for a good life and human society."

Lest his views on the election be unclear to any of his fans, Springsteen articulated them loud and clear on an episode of his radio show:

> *In just a few days, we'll be throwing the bums out . . . There's no art in this White House. There's no literature, no poetry, no music. There are no pets in this White House. No loyal man's best friend, no Socks the family cat . . . There are no images of the first family enjoying themselves together in a moment of relaxation. No Obamas-on-the-beach-in-Hawaii moments or Bushes fishing in Kennebunkport. No Reagans on horseback, no Kennedys playing touch football on the Cape. Where'd that country go? Where did all the fun, the joy, and the expression of love and happiness go? . . . We used to have a president who calmed and soothed the nation instead of dividing it . . . We are now rudderless and joyless. We have lost the cultural aspects of society that have always made America great. We have lost our mojo, our fun, our happiness, our cheering on of others—the shared experience of humanity that makes it all worth it . . . We need to reclaim that country once again.*

Springsteen also did a voiceover for a Biden advertisement in which he said, "Scranton, Pennsylvania. Here, success isn't handed down—its forged with sweat, grit, and determination. This is his hometown . . . He is running . . . to give working people the shot they deserve . . . This is more than where he's *from*. It's who he's *for*." The commercial ends with a few bars of Springsteen's song "My Hometown."

Brad Pitt narrated a Biden ad that was broadcast during the fourth game of the World Series: "America is a place for everyone. Those who chose this country, those who fought for it, some Republicans, some Democrats, and most just somewhere in-between." Pitt added that Americans were looking for "someone who understands their hopes, their dreams, their pain. To listen, to bring people together, to get up every day and work to make life better for families like yours. To look you in the eye, to treat you with respect and tell you the truth. To work just as hard for the people who voted for him as those who didn't. To be a president for all Americans."

Other Biden ads were narrated by Sam Elliott, Harrison Ford, and Martin Sheen. One commercial featured Eminem's song "Lose Yourself" with its haunting lyrics that ask if you had one shot to "seize everything you ever wanted . . . would you capture it or just let it slip?"

Taylor Swift's song "Only the Young" was used in an anti-Trump ad that featured scenes from Black Lives Matter and Me Too protests, as well a shot of president Donald Trump removing his mask set to the lyrics "the big bad man" whose hands "are stained with red."

The week before the election, Bette Midler tweeted, "Donald Trump is a parasite; a leech. He robs the poor & gives to the rich; he's a poison running through the veins of our nation, killing anything wholesome or clean, or anyone trying to do good . . . Anyone supporting him is covered in shame." The following day, Jack Black and Kyle Gass from Tenacious D appeared on Ari Melber's show wearing hats that said, "Make America Rage Again." Black complained that Trump supporter Kid Rock and other Republicans were "trying to seize the rock and roll mantle. Like all of a sudden it's part of their branding . . . I remember a time when rock and roll was almost exclusively Democratic . . . All the best rockers were Democrats, so we're taking it back."

Although the left was, for the most part, reconciled to the need to vote for Biden, there was still anxiety in some quarters about what he would do in office. Producer Adam McKay retweeted a piece by David Sirota and Andrew Perez which included a section titled, "The Perils of Brunch Liberalism," and argued that "Obama helmed a presidency bankrolled by Wall Street donors that refused to prosecute a single banker who engineered a financial crisis that destroyed millions of lives." McKay commented, "This piece is spot-on and very (dare I say?) important." On the other hand, long-time Sanders surrogate John Cusack reassured the left about voting for Biden: "Bernie lays out why pressure on Biden is gonna work. He sounds totally bullish on getting a lot of his agenda done quickly with Biden. Remember—Bernie don't lie."

Pennsylvania was a prominent swing state in the election and celebrities did their best to help Biden win it. Bradley Cooper said, "I grew up in Montgomery County and . . . that's why I need to share this extremely important message with you PA voters . . . Human decency is riding on this election." Michael Keaton also posted a video aimed at igniting Pennsylvania pride: "This is it. It has come down to us. We get the chance to be the hero right now, the buzzer-beater, the walk-off." A virtual event for Pennsylvania Democrats included the Black Eyed Peas, Questlove, the O'Jays, Kevin Bacon, Jason Alexander, Julius Erving, and Senator Bob Casey.

Lady Gaga, who had performed at Hillary Clinton's final campaign event in 2016, appeared with Biden in Pittsburgh the weekend before the election, wearing a white sweater with the word "Joe" written inside a heart. Sitting at a grand piano, she pleaded, "Vote like this country depends on it."

Trump was in Pennsylvania the following day and he ridiculed Biden's celebrity supporters. "Lady Gaga—it is not too good," he said. "I could tell you plenty of stories. I could tell you stories about

Lady Gaga. I know a lot of stories. And Jon Bon Jovi? Every time I see him he kisses my ass."

The day before the election, Chelsea Handler posted a topless photo with "I voted" stickers on each nipple. Common tweeted, "To all my people feeling like these times are heavy, I understand . . . Breathe in all that's good. Release any negative thoughts and energy and remember that God created us to do great things."

The day after the election, as the country waited for Pennsylvania's vote tally to put Biden over the top, the soon-to-be-president tweeted, "Keep the faith, guys. We're gonna win this." Mark Hamill evoked his *Star Wars* character in a response: "Will do, Joe Bi Wan."

On November 7, 2020, the TV networks finally called the election for Biden. Within hours, a photoshopped alteration of the final battle in *Avengers: Endgame* (2019) appeared on YouTube. The video superimposed Biden's face onto Captain America as he vanquished archvillain Thanos, whose face was replaced with Trump's. That evening, as Biden approached the microphone to formally claim victory, Springsteen's "We Take Care of Our Own" played in the background.

Later that night, Dave Chappelle guest hosted *SNL* and waxed serious in his monologue. "I would implore everybody who's celebrating a day to remember, it's good to be a humble winner," he said. "Remember when I was here four years ago? Remember how *bad* that felt? Remember that half the country right now still feels that way. Please remember that . . . All these white people out there that feel that anguish, that pain, they are mad because they think nobody cares, and maybe they don't. Let me tell you something. I know how that feels. I promise you, I know how that feels. If you're a police officer and every time you put your uniform on, you feel like you've got a target on your back, you're appalled by the ingratitude that people have when you would risk your life to save them. Oh man, believe me, I know how that feels."

Addressing the chasm between Trump supporters and their opponents, Chappelle concluded, "You guys hate each other . . . I don't hate anybody. I just hate *that feeling*. That's what I fight through.

That's what I suggest you fight through. You got to find a way to live your life. You got to find a way to forgive each other. You got to find a way to find joy in your existence in spite of that feeling."

CHAPTER 15
OVERTIME
NOVEMBER 8, 2020–FEBRUARY 13, 2021

AFTERMATH

What Dave Chappelle had referred to as *that feeling* did not entirely go away. Trump did not concede. He falsely claimed that the election had been stolen from him and his attorneys lost more than sixty lawsuits in swing states, and a few in the US Supreme Court, in vain attempts to overturn the results. On *The View*, Joy Behar expressed my view of such denialism: "Trump believes he won and [his die-hard supporters] believe he won because they only count white people. They want to eliminate Black people from the rolls. They would like it to have only white people vote forever in this country. Then they can say they won."

Days after the election result appeared final, the focus shifted to Georgia, which Biden had narrowly won and where two Senate races were close enough to require runoffs. If the Democrats won both of them, Chuck Schumer would replace Mitch McConnell as the Senate majority leader—a big deal.

Show business activism for those Georgia races was a miniature version of the presidential campaign. Another *Veep* reunion raised $600,000 for the Georgia Democratic Party. An online table read of the holiday movie *Elf*—in which Will Ferrell, Zooey Deschanel, Bob

Newhart, and Mary Steenburgen reprised their original roles—raised more than $400,000.

Atlanta was home to many prominent rappers who supported the Democrats including Jeezy, who had included Georgia organizer Stacey Abrams in a recent music video. Jeezy explained that "if the right people are not in the Senate, it's gonna make it hard for the Biden–Harris administration to do anything they need to do and that they promised to us . . . What we did see by Georgia turning blue [and] by us being able to sway the presidential election and get it the way we wanted to get it, it was about people mobilizing . . . and every little thing made a difference . . . People have to see progress so that they understand what they're doing is making a difference . . . With this runoff, we have to continue to do the same thing."

Georgia was a sprint that the Democrats ultimately won, but the underlying struggle to define American political morality would be a marathon.

Bob Dylan's 2020 album, *Rough and Rowdy Ways*, the one that had the song about JFK, also included "Mother of Muses," one verse of which went:

Sing of Sherman, Montgomery, and Scott
And of Zhukov, and Patton, and the battles they fought
Who cleared the path for Presley to sing
Who carved the path for Martin Luther King
Who did what they did and then went on their way
Man, I could tell their stories all day

It was usually a fool's errand to ascribe linear meaning to Dylan lyrics, but in this case it seemed clear. He celebrated generals who won the Civil War against the Confederacy, and those who beat Hitler in World War II. Fascism had to be defeated for democracy to have a chance to flourish. The post-Trump struggle against fascism, however, would not be fought with force but with persuasion.

The single-mindedness that had characterized the efforts to defeat Trump was replaced by a variety of postelection agendas. Many activists yearned for a way to find human connections with the seventy-four million Trump voters. Others remained preoccupied with the ongoing fight against racism and fascism and with efforts to defend and expand democracy. Some Democrats felt that it was a political priority to keep anti-Trump Republicans in the Biden-era Democratic tent, while progressives were determined to pressure the Biden administration on issues such as raising the minimum wage, reducing college debt, and climate change.

Among the most passionate in the reconciliation camp was Penn Jillette, best known for his work in the comedy and magic duo Penn & Teller. He explained in a piece on CNN's website that he had previously identified as a Libertarian and had thought he disagreed with Joe Biden "on most everything," but that he had nonetheless voted for him against Trump in the recent election. "I wanted the other guy fired and I wanted Joe hired and for me the job description is now very simple. I need Joe to love all the Trump supporters."

Jillette wrote that in the current environment he didn't even care if Biden raised taxes or if, as president, he added to "stupid, counterproductive regulations." He had a single subject on his mind: "I don't care about anything except love and kindness. We need a Nelson Mandela. We need MLK. And it needs to be Joe. We need someone who can love the people who hated him and lied about him. He must rise to the occasion." Nearly half of America had voted for Trump, and Jillette felt that although "it's appalling and horrifying . . . these people are not monsters. These people are our neighbors and our relatives. These people are us, and we need someone who can teach us to love them again."

Bruce Springsteen was thinking about what motivated some Republican voters and acknowledged that a lot of his fans and even some of his family members had voted for Trump. "A lot of people just vote for their pocketbook: 'If you're for lower taxes, you're the guy I'm voting for.' [Trump] had no compunction in completely lying about what he could do for the working part of his audience . . . going to your town where you were suffering from factories closing down and saying, 'They're coming back.' There were people who wanted to believe that version of America could return." After a pause, the Boss acknowledged another key element to Trump's appeal: "The big one is *race, race, race.* How changes in demographics are creating a different kind of America and how that's frightened a lot of people who feel the only thing they have is status based on race."

Singer-songwriter Jason Isbell tweeted, "It would be GREAT if everybody learned through kindness but that's pretty clearly not gonna work. Sometimes you have to make ignorance embarrassing. Gotta make it uncool to be an asshole."

Policy mattered too. As Martin Luther King Jr. pointed out, "They say you can't legislate morality, but you *can* regulate behavior." Ending voter suppression was critical to preventing a resurgence of Trumpism. Alyssa Milano tweeted, "Organizers of color and voters of color continue to save the republic. Bills Democrats need to pass ASAP: 1. John Lewis Voting Rights Advancement Act, 2. The Anti-Racism in Public Health Act, 3. The Breathe Act, 4. George Floyd Justice in Policing Act of 2020." She included a GIF of John Lewis dancing at a 2018 campaign event two years before he died.

The Comey Rules writer/director Billy Ray saw things through a different prism. He had developed dual citizenship in the creative and political worlds. In 2018, his friend, novelist Gregg Hurwitz, introduced him to the Myers–Briggs theory of the "Big Five Personality Traits." As Ray explained, "Personality traits are hugely predictive of voting behavior. Conservatives tend to score high in conscientiousness (which codes for orderliness and industriousness) and liberals tend to score high in empathy and openness." Advising thirty House candidates in 2018 and forty-five in 2020, Ray trained candidates "how to sound less like a Democrat [and] how to make the kinds of arguments that independent voters can actually hear."

Ray felt that "what unites conservatives, on a psychological level, is their fear of chaos. Given a choice between authoritarianism and what they perceive to be lawlessness, conservatives will choose authoritarianism every time."

When I showed him Milano's antiracism priorities, Ray wrote

an e-mail expressing his dissent: "I disagree 1000 percent. Biden can be a transformational president. He can redefine what the word Democrat means. He can reverse the demonization of the entire party . . . but only if he holds the far left at bay and pushes for things like COVID relief, jobs, infrastructure, lowering the cost of prescription drugs, and the environment as an extension of our economic recovery (green jobs). Everything else is secondary. If America sees him doing that, it won't matter how much they're lied to by Fox News; they'll know Joe Biden is fighting for them."

Matthew McConaughey opined after the election that "liberals absolutely condescend, patronize, and are arrogant toward the other 50 percent." McConaughey was toying with idea of running for governor of Texas as a Democrat and called himself "aggressively centrist," but there was no reason to believe that such a posture would motivate the massive increase in turnout among Latinx voters and young people that would be needed to turn Texas blue.

Despite Biden's victory, Democrats had lost seats in the House of Representatives. Two days after the election, the *Washington Post* reported a contentious conference call among House Democrats. Centrist Virginia Democrat Abigail Spanberger, who barely squeaked out reelection, said, "We need to not ever use the word 'socialist' or 'socialism' ever again . . . We lost good members because of that."

Conversely, Pramila Jayapal, cochairperson of the Congressional Progressive Caucus, argued that Democrats shouldn't turn on ideas that energize the party base. Representative Rashida Tlaib added, "To be real, it sounds like you are saying stop pushing for what Black folks want."

It wasn't clear what the frustrated moderates wanted. AOC and Maxine Waters were not going to calibrate their public statements based on the views of those in Spanberger's district; they had their own constituents to worry about. The idea that movement leaders or protesters would limit their rhetoric to phrases approved by Democratic campaign consultants was delusional.

In an interview with Trevor Noah, Barack Obama sounded a cautionary note about using "Defund the police" as a slogan: "I think the concern is there may be potential allies out there that you'd lose. The issue always is how do you get enough people to support your cause that you can actually institutionalize it and translate it into laws?" John Legend understood this political calculus but only up to a point: "Black people are only 12 percent of America, so, by definition, we're not enough to win anything except majority Black districts. The Democrats have been the party that has been most attracted to Black people because the left has fought for civil rights laws and a stronger social safety net, but they've always felt like they had to make sure they kept enough white people to put together a winning coalition. If you want a majority in the House, you're going to have some districts that look like Conor Lamb's [in mostly white western Pennsylvania] and you're going to have some districts that look like Alexandria Ocasio-Cortez's."

Nonetheless, Legend defended the concept of defunding the police. He told me, "They were quick to throw us under the bus when they felt like they lost a few seats. We won all three elections: Senate, House, and presidency. What are we complaining about? There are people that don't like that rhetoric because they don't like the actual policy. They don't like the idea that we would take money from policing and put it in other things."

Legend continued: "We have to deal with the fact that if you spend all this money on this thing, that means you can't spend it on other things. Doesn't mean you're going to get rid of the police or you're going to decimate policing, but it does mean [that we should] analyze our priorities. I think it's our job to just keep pushing. I think saying 'defund' was a necessary push because it was moving the conversation to new ground, which is, I think, the right ground to be on—which is, how does this institution serve the entire public?"

No one could make the reconciliation argument as well as Barack Obama. On November 17, 2020, *A Promised Land*, the first volume of his memoir, was published. While promoting the book, Obama did an extended interview with Charlamagne tha God and appeared on the Showtime series *Desus & Mero*, which is hosted by two Bronx natives whose previous guests included rappers, athletes, and entertainers, along with a handful of politicians (AOC was a guest on their first show).

Obama also made an appearance on the YouTube channel *Twins-thenewTrend*, hosted by twenty-two-year-old brothers Fred and Tim Williams. Their shtick was to listen to classic songs from previous generations and react with wide-eyed enthusiasm. The video where they listen to Phil Collins's "In the Air Tonight" had been watched over eight million times.

The ex-president joined them in listening to Bob Dylan's "The Times They Are A-Changin'," which was featured on a playlist Obama had just released. "I've been a Bob Dylan fan for a long time," Obama told his young interviewers, "partly because I'm just older. He was part of that kind of social conscience that was in rock music and later in hip-hop music . . . Whenever you can find some musicians that really have a message about how America might be, how the world might be, that always is something that I pay attention to, and he's one of the greatest examples of that."

Obama thanked the twins for their open-mindedness: "The country's so divided right now. On the Internet, a lot of times everybody's just mad. But what you guys are doing—which is being open to new ideas, new experiences, and reaching out to different traditions—that's America at its best. I think you guys sending that message is powerful."

POSTELECTION ENTERTAINMENT

Despite the pandemic, some producers figured out how to finish and release new movies and television shows that debuted at the end of the year, in time to qualify for awards. Most had strong ideological subtexts.

A month after the election, *Mank* premiered on Netflix. Directed by David Fincher, the film starred Gary Oldman as screenwriter Herman Mankiewicz during the period in his life when he wrote the first draft of *Citizen Kane*, whose protagonist, Charles Foster Kane, was based on newspaper mogul William Randolph Hearst. In the 1941 film, Kane was played by Orson Welles, who also directed *Citizen Kane*.

Like Sorkin's *The Trial of the Chicago 7*, Fincher's *Mank* distorted history to make a political statement. In real life, Mankiewicz befriended Hearst in the late 1930s, but *Mank* suggests that several years earlier, the screenwriter was offended by the publisher's role in defeating Upton Sinclair, the muckraking novelist and socialist who won the Democratic nomination for California governor in 1934. As Harold Meyerson explained in the *American Prospect*, "Having won the Democratic primary . . . on a platform to 'End Poverty in California' (known as the EPIC movement), Sinclair appeared to be leading his Republican opponent, a reactionary named Frank Merriam, as November's election drew near."

Hearst's California newspapers ran false stories that "reported" Sinclair's plans (which did not exist) to expropriate small shops and homes. At the same time, MGM's production chief, Irving Thalberg (played in *Mank* by Ferdinand Kingsley), ordered the studio's directors to fabricate interviews with "prospective voters" that depicted Merriam supporters as solid white Americans and Sinclair supporters as bums or foreign-accented communists. Meyerson wrote, "They even appropriated footage . . . of their extras jumping from freight cars, which the newsreel narrators said were shots of dangerous hobos arriving in California in anticipation of a Sinclair regime that would pay them to loll around and make trouble." Those scenes were used in newsreels that were then shown to the millions of Californians who went to the movies every week. Merriam defeated Sinclair in November's general election. (The definitive account of the race can be found in Greg Mitchell's *The Campaign of the Century*.)

Several other postelection Oscar contenders were also period pieces with themes that resonated in contemporary America. *Ma Rainey's Black Bottom* was a cinematic version of August Wilson's play of the same name, with Viola Davis as the title character, a legendary blues singer, and Chadwick Boseman as one of her musicians. (This was Boseman's final performance before his death from colon cancer, three months before the film premiered in late November.) The story revolves around a recording session in 1927 in which Ma Rainey asserts her artistic will in the face of commercial pressure from white record executives at a time when Black performers rarely had any power.

One Night in Miami was based on a theatrical play by Kemp Powers, who also wrote the screenplay. The film marked Regina King's directorial debut and examined the complex pressures placed upon Black artists and thought leaders. The story is an imagined conversation in 1964 between Malcom X (played by Kingsley Ben-Adir), football superstar Jim Brown (Aldis Hodge), pop and R&B genius Sam Cooke (Leslie Odom Jr.), and Cassius Clay, who would soon change his name to Muhammed Ali (Eli Goree). Most of the film takes place on the evening after Clay won the heavyweight boxing championship against Sonny Liston.

Judas and the Black Messiah dramatized Black Panther leader Fred Hampton's (played by Daniel Kaluuya) last several months alive. At the same time that the Chicago 7 trial was going on, the charismatic twenty-one-year-old Chicago leader was killed by law enforcement in his bed. The film depicts J. Edgar Hoover (Martin Sheen) determined to destroy the Black Panthers, and a Black FBI informer, Bill O'Neal (LaKeith Stanfield), tasked with taking Hampton down. The film was a stark reminder that Donald Trump and his minions were not the first racists to wield power in the federal government.

The United States vs. Billie Holiday was directed by Lee Daniels and starred Andra Day as the legendary jazz singer. It focused on a vendetta again Holiday by some in the government who were disturbed by the political implications of her performances of the anti-lynching song "Strange Fruit." She was targeted by the Federal Department of Narcotics with an undercover sting operation led by Black federal agent Jimmy Fletcher (Trevante Rhodes) at the same time that they were having an affair.

Nomadland was directed by Chloé Zhao and starred Frances McDormand as a widow who was forced to sell her house and live in a van after her husband's death. With a cast consisting of several real-life American nomads, the film reflected the travails of those on the economic margins of society with an emotional intensity similar to that of *The Grapes of Wrath* during the Great Depression.

(Zhao and McDormand would go on to win Oscars in their respective categories.)

Two weeks before Biden's inauguration, John Fogerty released "Weeping in the Promised Land," his first new song in eight years. His lyrics refer to Trump's attacks on Dr. Fauci, health care workers, and the murder of George Floyd. Fogerty told *Rolling Stone's* David Browne that although he despised Trump's regime, he empathized with his reluctance to admit defeat. "It's kind of like being a rock star in a band and then the band breaks up. I used to stand in front of 30,000 or 40,000 people and they were all cheering for *me*. I know what that is. I understand the emotion he's feeling."

The same week, NBC premiered *Mr. Mayor*, a new series produced by Tina Fey and starring Ted Danson as the mayor of Los Angeles. The writing combined some of the anarchic political satire of *Veep* with the gentler mainstream wit that Fey had used in her previous series, *30 Rock*. Its goofy humor was the first politically tinged mass entertainment to have a post-Trump feel to it.

Many progressives saw similarities between the crises Biden was facing and those that Franklin Roosevelt encountered in 1933. FDR's New Deal included support for the arts via the Works Progress Administration (WPA). At the height of the Great Depression, the WPA helped artists like novelist Ralph Ellison, photographers Walker Evans and Dorothea Lange, composer Aaron Copland, painter Jackson Pollock, and dozens of actors and directors, including Orson Welles. Jeremy O. Harris, whose *Slave Play* had recently received a dozen Tony nominations, urged Biden to emulate the WPA to help save America's live theater, which had been decimated by the pandemic.

The *New York Times*' Jason Farago wrote, "The effects of this cultural depression will be excruciating, and not only for the symphony not written, the dance not choreographed, the sculpture not cast, the musical not staged. Beyond value in its own right, culture is also an industry sector accounting for more than 4.5 percent of America's gross domestic product, according to the US Bureau of Economic Analysis."

The United States had long lagged behind other Western countries when it came to supporting the arts, and the pandemic further widened this divide. As Farago explained, "Emmanuel Macron singled out culture as a sector in economic peril, while Chancellor Angela Merkel of Germany said that 'freelancers and artists fear for their livelihood' . . . [The US] government had barely acknowledged the crisis that COVID-19 has posed to culture. Nor have private philanthropists filled the gap; while some large foundations have stepped up their disbursements, total giving to North American arts organizations has slackened by 14 percent on average."

If politicians wanted to live in a country with the cultural benefits of progressive entertainment, they needed to make sure that the artists and craftspeople who help animate it could make a living.

INSURRECTION

Back in Trump world, the Capitol insurrection on January 6, 2021, provided a microcosm of the MAGA/show-biz dynamic. After Rudy Giuliani's call for "trial by combat," a two-minute film was shown on a giant outdoor screen to thousands of MAGA devotees, many of whom were about to try to prevent Congress from certifying Biden's Electoral College victory.

As Just Security's Jason Stanley wrote, the film began "with Trump's eyes in the shadow, and its second frame focuses the audience on the Capitol building . . . The third frame of the video is the Hollywood sign in Los Angeles. This image immediately directs the attention of an audience attuned to an American fascist ideology to the supposedly elite class of Jews who, according to this ideology, control Hollywood. The appearance of the Hollywood sign makes no other sense in the context of a short video about an election."

The following day, a cell-phone video was posted of Donald Trump Jr.'s girlfriend, Kimberly Guilfoyle, gleefully dancing to Laura Branigan's 1982 hit "Gloria" at a pre-insurrection party. Kathy Golik, the legacy manager for Branigan (who had died in 2004) tweeted, "It's absolutely appalling to hear Gloria being played in the background of a widely circulating video of Pres. Trump from yesterday, given the tragic, unsettling, & shameful happenings that occurred at the US Capitol."

Ariel Pink, an alternative rock artist, attended the Trump rally that led to the insurrection. After photos of Pink standing amid the MAGA crowd appeared online, he was promptly dropped by his label, Mexican Summer. In keeping with the Trumpist penchant for victimization, Pink, instead of expressing contrition for his complicity in trying to subvert democracy, told Tucker Carlson, "I'm sort of overwhelmed right now and I don't know exactly what to do." Apparently, Pink was oblivious to the irony of complaining about being "canceled" while appearing on the most widely viewed Fox News show.

One of the most effective condemnations of the insurrection came in the form of a seven-and-a-half-minute monologue posted to YouTube by Arnold Schwarzenegger. A former champion body builder, Schwarzenegger reached international fame as the star of *The Terminator* and other Hollywood blockbusters. He pivoted to politics in the early 2000s and was elected governor of California in 2003. His 2006 reelection was the last time a Republican won a California statewide election. In recent years, Trump and his allies had been determined to kill off Schwarzenegger's brand of moderate Republicanism.

In early 2017, Schwarzenegger briefly served as Trump's replacement host on *The Celebrity Apprentice*. On Twitter, the president belittled the rebooted show's ratings (even though the show began a precipitous decline during Trump's last year hosting). When Schwarzenegger turned down the chance to host a second season, he explained that the show had "too much baggage." He tweeted, "Hey, Donald, I have a great idea: Why don't we switch jobs? You take over TV because you're such an expert in ratings, and I take over your job, so then people can finally sleep comfortably again."

The emotional impact of Schwarzenegger's postinsurrection video was rooted in memories from the early part of his life, long before he became famous. Born in 1947, two years after the end of World War II, he grew up in Austria, a country that had been allied with Nazi Germany in the war. He described his childhood in "a country that suffered the loss of its democracy . . . Growing up, I was surrounded by broken men drinking away the guilt over their participation in the most evil regime in history. Not all of them were rabid anti-Semites or Nazis. Many of them just went along, step by step, down the road. They were the people next door."

He compared the Capitol riot to Kristallnacht (the "Night of Broken Glass") when synagogues and Jewish-owned businesses across Nazi Germany were vandalized "by the Nazi equivalent of the Proud Boys. Wednesday was the day of Broken Glass right here in the United States. The broken glass was in the windows of the United States Capitol . . . President Trump sought to overturn the results of . . . a fair election. He sought a coup by misleading people with lies. My father and our neighbors were misled also with lies, and I know where such lies lead. President Trump is a failed leader. He will go down in history as the worst president ever. The good thing is that he soon will be as irrelevant as an old tweet."

The video was shot at his home, but Schwarzenegger was professionally lit and he provided a musical score for dramatic impact. Near the end of his monologue, he held up a sword, a prop from the 1982 fantasy epic *Conan the Barbarian*, the film that had made him a star. Despite the gravity of the subject at hand, the movie star–turned-governor could not restrain a smile as he suggested that the prop was a metaphor for American democracy: "The more you temper a sword, the stronger it becomes."

Within days the video received more than five million views and was shown on several national TV news shows. Mark Hamill tweeted, "Thank you for having a servant's heart, Arnold. This is now my favorite Schwarzenegger film . . . EVER."

For some Trumpists, Hollywood was to blame for the insurrection. Before casting his vote against impeachment, Republican congressman Ken Buck of Colorado said that some of the people who vandalized the Capitol and killed a policeman had been motivated by "the socialists in Hollywood . . . Robert De Niro said that he wanted to punch the president in the face. Madonna thought about blowing up the White House. Kathy Griffin held up a likeness of the president's beheaded head, and nothing was heard and nothing was said by my colleagues at that point in time."

INAUGURATION AT LAST

On January 12, 2021, minutes after he was impeached by the House of Representatives for the second time, Trump awarded the National Medal of Arts to country music singers Toby Keith and Ricky Skaggs. A week later, on the night before the inauguration, Trump announced that he had commuted the jail sentence of Death Row Records' cofounder Michael "Harry O" Harris for attempted murder and cocaine trafficking (Snoop Dogg was among those who had urged Trump to do this). He also pardoned rappers Lil Wayne and Kodak Black, both of whom had been convicted on weapons charges.

The next day, just before noon, as Biden and Harris were about to take their oaths, Lady Gaga performed the National Anthem and Jennifer Lopez sang a medley of "America the Beautiful" and "This Land Is Your Land," the anthem written in the 1940s by Woody Guthrie, whose guitars had displayed the handwritten message, "This machine kills fascists." (A few lefties churlishly pointed out that Lopez did not include Guthrie's frequently banned verse that questioned the primacy of "private property," lyrics which Pete Seeger and Bruce Springsteen included in their performance of the song at a televised celebration after Obama's 2008 inauguration.)

In response to a last-minute request by Jill Biden, Garth Brooks sang an a capella version of "Amazing Grace." The artist who ended up earning the most attention at Biden's inauguration, however, was not a longtime celebrity but twenty-two-year-old Amanda Gorman, who had recently been named the country's first National Youth Poet Laureate."

In John F. Kennedy's 1960 campaign, he often ended his stump speeches with lines from Robert Frost's poem "Stopping by Woods on a Snowy Evening": "But I have promises to keep, / And miles to go before I sleep." After JFK was elected, he asked Frost to be the first poet to ever read at an inauguration. The eighty-six-year-old Frost recited his patriotic poem "The Gift Outright," which he had written during World War II. He also obliged the new president's request to change the last lines of the poem from "Such as she was, such as she would become" to the more optimistic "such as she *will* become."

Sixty years later, at Biden's inauguration, Gorman read a new poem, "The Hill We Climb." She wore a bright yellow coat, a thick red headband, and a broach that Oprah Winfrey had given her depicting a caged bird, an homage to a poem by Maya Angelou, who had read a poem at Bill Clinton's inauguration in 1993. "The Hill We Climb" began:

When day comes we ask ourselves,
where can we find light in this never-ending shade?

That evening's inauguration TV special, *Celebrating America*, began with Springsteen and his acoustic guitar standing in the thirty-degree weather in front of the Lincoln Memorial. Shortly afterward, he tweeted lyrics from the song he sang, "Land of Hope and Dreams":

Well, tomorrow there'll be sunshine
And all this darkness past
Well, big wheels roll through fields where sunlight streams
Oh, meet me in a land of hope and dreams.

The program also included appearances by Tom Hanks, Demi Lovato, Kerry Washington, Eva Longoria Bastón, Lin-Manuel Miranda, the Foo Fighters, and Jon Bon Jovi, who performed George Harrison's "Here Comes the Sun."

John Legend sang that night as well. Later, he recalled the event to me: "Washington was a ghost town. It was just troops and no one else. We didn't defund the National Guard, I'll tell you that. They were intent on making sure whatever storm that QAnon thought was going to happen did not happen." With a smile, Legend acknowledged that "it felt good. I literally sang the song 'Feeling Good.' It felt like a release. Am I going to agree with 100 percent of what Biden does? No, but I know that he's going to do what he thinks is right and he's going to do it in a way that I think is genuinely concerned about the safety and welfare of the American people. And that's a big change."

WHAT'S NEXT?

The following day, Jane Fonda tweeted her approval of one of Biden's first actions. "It's happening! By Executive Order: No Keystone XL, no drilling in the Arctic Refuge and we're back in the Paris Climate Agreement! And it's still Day One!!"

Biden's new press secretary, Jen Psaki, gave her first postinaugural briefing with a warmth toward the media that had been absent in the Trump years. At one point, in a sly homage to *The West Wing*, she told the assembled reporters that after his inaugural speech, the new president had asked his staff, "What's next?" MSNBC's Lawrence O'Donnell, who earlier in his career had been a producer for *The West Wing*, tweeted to Psaki: "Great to hear [you] quote [Biden] in Oval today saying, 'What's next?' (Yes, that was Martin Sheen's last line in pilot of West Wing.)"

What was next for the artist-activists of the resistance? One priority was to help maintain the left–center coalition that defeated Trump. A significant factor in Biden's victory had been the reduction of that unusually high 5.7 percent of voters who had chosen third-party candidates in 2016, back down to 1.7 percent. If the left and center became bitterly divided, a right-wing minority could seize power again. Some morbidly minded historians pointed out that Hitler had come to power in Germany in 1932 with only 37 percent of the vote because antifascist opposition was divided among several parties.

Maintaining Biden's 2020 coalition would not be easy. Although Bernie Sanders had assumed the powerful role of chairman of the Senate Budget Committee, even if the Senate changed the filibuster rule that required sixty votes to pass legislation, any one of the fifty Democratic Senators could prevent a bill from becoming law unless Biden could get Republican support, a quest which in recent years had usually ended in heartbreak for Democrats.

The unsexy but rational message of mainstream Democrats was to not make "the perfect the enemy of the good," a morally valid homily that was also cause for concern among young voters who suspected this was simply a neoliberal rationalization for not raising the minimum wage, addressing climate change, enacting gun reform gun policy, or eradicating student loan debt.

If the Biden administration was hobbled in the 2022 midterms, a more virulent version of Trump (either the aging former reality show host himself or a younger model) could be elected in 2024.

On the final day of Trump's second impeachment trial, one of his lawyers, Michael van der Veen, repeated the "blame Madonna" bit that House Republicans had used a few weeks earlier. He showed the United States Senate a video of excerpts from Democratic leaders such as Elizabeth Warren using words like "fight," and then sandwiched in one of Madonna's remarks at the 2017 Women's March: "I have thought an awful lot about blowing up the White House."

Thirty-seven years after Madonna released her hit album *Like a Virgin*, white Republican men of a certain age were still obsessed with her. It should go without saying that the people who listened to her speech were not the same people who attacked the Capitol building or assaulted the police officers defending it. For the record, the day after the Women's March, Madonna apologized for her incendiary language: "I know that acting out of anger doesn't solve anything. And the only way to change things for the better is to do it with love."

Shortly after Biden's inauguration, the BBC released a six-part series created by Adam Curtis called *Can't Get You Out of My Head: An Emotional History of the Modern World*, his first major work since *HyperNormalisation* had suggested how the use of mass psychology had paved the way for Trump. Like the director's previous work it was impressionistic journalism. Curating BBC footage from various eras, Curtis connected modern human behavior to old beliefs. He highlighted a Ku Klux Klan march on Washington in 1925 and an anti-immigration protest in London in 1968 as antecedents to Trump's election in the US and Brexit in the UK. The director's kaleidoscopic vision focused on America, England, China, Russia, and Europe. Among the catalysts Curtis cited for contemporary chaos were behavioral psychology, pharmaceuticals, oil, the Internet, and immigration.

The cast of characters in *Can't Get You Out of My Head* included Tupac Shakur, his mother Afeni (who had been active in the Black Panthers), and Mao Zedong's wife, Jiang Qing, who had been an aspiring film actress in Shanghai in the 1930s and later was China's minister of arts, propaganda, and culture, as well as the leader of the "Red Guards," a student group that killed many of Mao's political opponents.

Although Curtis's vision was generally gloomy, he concluded the ten-hour series with a Hollywood ending: "Try to imagine genuinely new futures. To do that we will have to regain confidence we have lost in this frightened and uncertain time. We may be far stronger than we think. The world of the future will be different. If we regain confidence we can influence how that future turns out."

Regardless of whether they were hopeful or pessimistic, the progressive artists of the resistance to Trump would continue to face opposition from a right-wing culture that was threatened by entertainers' ability to trigger populist emotion. In 2006, before hosting a Fox News show, Laura Ingraham wrote a book attacking artist-activists called *Shut Up and Sing: How Elites from Hollywood, Politics, and the Media Are Subverting America*. In the ensuing years, the likes of *Breitbart* and QAnon demonized artists and identified "Hollywood" as an enemy. Following the 2020 election, a YouGov poll asked one thousand Trump voters to rank groups by "temperature." "Hollywood actors and actresses" were viewed more negatively (59 percent) than "illegal immigrants" (57 percent), "feminists" (43 percent), or "Muslims" (30 percent).

Many artist-activists looked at such data and remember FDR's 1936 convention speech, when he identified the forces of "organized money" who detested him and then defiantly declaimed, "I welcome their hatred!" But such pugnaciousness had its moral and political limits. When Springsteen said, "Nobody wins unless everybody wins," he was including political opponents.

Separate and apart from the content and tone of day-to-day talking points, what is the course of Norman Mailer's "subterranean river" in the post-Trump era? What new songs and jokes and dramas and poems would be inspired by the pandemic, the awful persistence of racism, the legacy of Trump, and the triumph of the resistance? What old myths would be resurrected and which new ones would gain traction? How would artists show their audiences how, in Judd Apatow's formulation, "not to be an asshole"?

Many performers activated by the resistance to Trump were likely to stay engaged. Sean Penn told MSNBC's Joe Scarborough: "Once you've been of service, it's part of your DNA for the rest of your life." There were many issues, particularly those related to race and climate change, that would require decades of tenacious work.

There were some artists for whom certain political issues took on an ethical significance that was intertwined with their deepest spiritual beliefs. This is where Charlie Chaplin had been coming from when he made *The Great Dictator* in the shadow of Hitler's growing power. In the final scene, Chaplin's character insists that "the Kingdom of God is within man, not one man, nor a group of men, but in all men, in you, the people."

Eighty years after *The Great Dictator's* release, Mandy Patinkin blew a shofar on an MSNBC show to honor the late Ruth Bader Ginsburg. A writer for a Jewish periodical asked Patinkin if blowing the shofar was sacrilegious, since some interpreters of Jewish tradition suggested that ceremonial use of the shofar should be limited to religious observance during the Jewish New Year's high holy days. Although the question was about religious practice, Patinkin's reply had a spirit that spoke for the whole panoply of progressive artists with activism in their "DNA," whether Jewish, Christian, Muslim, Buddhist, Hindu, spiritual but not religious, agnostic, or atheist, for all of those who agree with Robert De Niro's assertion that there is right and there is wrong.

Patinkin answered, "I'll blow the shofar any day. I want those prayers to be heard because I don't believe what some rabbi told me, that the gates of heaven close at the end of Yom Kippur and they don't open up until another time of the year. I believe those gates are open twenty-four hours a day, seven days a week, 365 days a year."

Acknowledgments

My wife Karen's love, insight, and emotional support nourished me during the writing of this book. I hope I was half as helpful to her as she was to me while we holed up in Pound Ridge during the pandemic, working on our manuscripts.

I cannot sufficiently thank Johnny Temple and his colleagues at Akashic Books—including Johanna Ingalls, Aaron Petrovich, Susannah Lawrence, Sohrab Habibion, and Brady Brickner-Wood—for their support and all-around excellence.

Thanks for the encouragement of my colleagues at Gold Village Entertainment, Jesse Bauer and Shelby McElrath.

Thanks also to Steve Earle for two decades of brilliance, professional connection, and friendship—and for being right about Biden.

To Mike Scott for his perspective and passion.

To Martha Wainwright, Ben Lee, and the Trews for providing continual inspiration.

To my business managers Warren Grant, Lori Ichimura, and Estelle Thrasher for their gracious help, year after year.

To Joe Serling, my music business lawyer and a mensch.

To my agent Laura Nolan and her colleagues at Aevitas.

To Eric Alterman for reminding me of the Walter Lippmann quote, for inadvertently suggesting the title, for encouragement over the course of two decades and five books, and for his friendship.

To David Silver, BFF.

To Amos Poe for being a beacon of intelligence.

To Anthony Arnove and Eric Alterman for essential early notes.

To Gary Greenberg, Sidney Blumenthal, Michael Simmons, and Mark Jacobson for essential later ones.

To Robert Greenwald for carrying the torch.

To Ronald Brownstein for *The Power and the Glitter*, which made writing the introduction and first chapter a lot easier.

To Adam Sticklor for his *Medium* essay, "How the Left Should View the Biden Presidency," which informed my thinking about the last chapter.

To Katie Roberts for rationality and encouragement.

To Julian Schlossberg for being the older brother I never had.

To Kay and Max for being in my life.

To Hilda Charlton, always.

To Don Guttenplan at the *Nation* for publishing three pieces that helped pave the road to this book.

For their help:
Barbara Carr
Sara Davidson
Danny Feingold
Rich Greenberg
Ann Hornaday
Howie Klein
Jon Landau
Mary Mac
Meegan Lee Ochs
Jeff Rosen
Mark Spector
Vivek Tiwary

For speaking to me for this book:
Kurt Andersen
Rosanna Arquette
Lara Bergholz
Julie Bergman
Jackie Blumenthal
Sidney Blumenthal
Scott Z. Burns
Bobby Cannavale
Rosanne Cash

David Corn
Chuck D
Laura Dawn
Richard Eskow
Shepard Fairey
Sharon Gelman
Kathy Griffin
Kathryn Grody
Joe Hagan
Barbara Hall
Mark Jacobson
Earl Katz
Billy Kimball
Brian Koppelman
Spencer Kornhaber
John Legend
Annie Leonard
Adam McKay
Ari Melber
Graham Nash
Michael O'Keefe
Mandy Patinkin
Gideon Grody Patinkin
Daniel Rachel
David Simon
Ali Soufan
Andy Spahn
Mark Spector
Bruce Springsteen
Steve Skrovan
Bill Stephney
Marge Tabankin
Antonio Villaraigosa
Paula Weinstein
Ewen Wright